WRITERS OF THE PRAIRIES

Canadian Literature Series

George Woodcock, general editor

The Sixties

Wyndham Lewis in Canada, with an Introduction by Julian Symons

Malcolm Lowry: The Man and His Work

Dramatists in Canada: Selected Essays

WRITERS
OF THE PRAIRIES

edited by

DONALD G. STEPHENS

University of British Columbia Press
Vancouver

WRITERS OF THE PRAIRIES

International Standard Book Number: 0-7748-0021-6

Library of Congress Catalogue Card Number: 73-80446

Printed in Canada by
The Morriss Printing Company Ltd.
Victoria, British Columbia

CONTENTS

NOTE ON THE TEXT

Most of the essays collected in this volume were published over the last thirteen years in *Canadian Literature*. In these cases the contributions have been left as they were originally published, but the date of publication has been added at the end of each so that the reader will be able to establish the perspective in time from which it was written.

In addition to the Introduction, four previously unpublished pieces have been specially commissioned for this volume in order to add greater comprehensiveness to the field of survey. They are "Martha Ostenso's Trial of Strength" by Clara Thomas, "Spiritual Ecology: Adele Wiseman's *The Sacrifice*" by Hélène Rosenthal, "Robert Kroetsch and his Novels" by Morton L. Ross, and "Gabrielle Roy et la prairie canadienne" by Marguerite Primeau.

We thank the authors of all these essays and new press as the publishers of W. H. New's two essays, which appeared in *Articulating West*, for permission to print them here.

G.W.

INTRODUCTION

Donald Stephens

THE LITERATURE OF THE PRAIRIES makes peculiar demands on the critic, forcing him to involve himself more directly than usual with the creative process of the artist at work. The reason for this can be directly traced to the environment which overwhelms the author writing about the prairies. It is a landscape that is never merely tolerated; it is loved and hated with equal intensities. People hate the bitter, piercing cold of the winter, but praise the clear blue skies and the dazzling sun on the purple-tinged banks of snow. They dislike the blowing dust and bleak landscape of August but luxuriate in the never-ending sunsets and the rippled seas of grain. The pure physicality of the landscape is always with the people on the prairies, and its writers consciously and unconsciously reflect this world.

The critic cannot help but be caught by the effect of this environment on the writers that he is examining; in fact, it is imperative that he steep himself in the landscape so that he is always aware of it, forever pressing him into an attitude already dominant in the work of the writer he is examining. Rather than remaining objective, the critic must become part of a landscape that is both fictional and real. He co-creates, with the writer, the experience of life that is presented through the artist's pen, so as to enrich it, to extend the experience into something far greater than the ordinary critic achieves who remains outside the art he attempts to evaluate and criticize. The writer and the critic together add another dimension to the role of the literary critic, but it is one that never replaces the experience of the art itself. This is undoubtedly true of most good critics, but prairie writing appears to ask more; fortunately, the critics who have chosen to write about the literature of the prairies seem to have the facility for this kind of co-creation. The critic's work becomes not a secondary, or tertiary, activity, but rather a primary activity which enlarges the whole experience of reaction to the work he chooses to discuss.

The combination of landscape and climatic environment determines the whole range of themes in the literature of the prairies. This is the never-ending flat land where mixed farm and wheat fields are etched out of the barren plains and the snake-like fissures of the wandering rivers. Through the cold of winter and the heat of summer, man is constantly at odds with his natural environment; it is "next year country", when the garden will flourish again, when the weather will be beneficent, when the flower will bloom in the desert. Perhaps more than in any other place in Canada, the cycle of the seasons is reflected in the people as they wait for something wonderful to happen. Each season plays the role of some kind of talisman for the season to come; though the spring brings floods and heartache as in April's wont, there is the association of a beginning again; the summer brings heat and wind storms, and the grain seed is loosed to the air, but the heat haze soothes, creating a mirage on the landscape and in the mind; the autumn is a time for working with the harvest, gathering in the product of labour, the ripeness which is on the verge of decay, yet also, through the smoke of burning stubble, it brings a vision of the winter of sleep, of quiet and cozy thoughts of other and future times by the fire on an evening when the outside world is breaking in a whorl of snow and frost; and then the real winter that never seems to end, that brings death by cold, when the ice never seems to be ready for a thaw; but always the people know that some day, suddenly, it will be spring. And it will start again. It is a land of optimism, of hope, for everyone knows that the cycle will go on, and that some year, sometime, it will be the best year yet. The "garrison mentality" so obvious in the writing of Eastern Canada (in the Maritimes, Quebec, and Ontario) is not prominent in that of Western Canada (the Prairies and British Columbia).

The range of writers examined in this collection reflect this reaching out, this desire to see the world as something larger than the immediate, but always in range of that immediacy. On first glance, it may appear that their world is limited, that the vision is restricted by the microcosm into which they place their ideas and their characters, for it is a world created mainly through the imagination. The setting may be real, or "authentic", but it is used merely as a touchstone. Immediately, comparisons are asked for: if people can survive in such a landscape, against such odds, what could they do if they lived elsewhere? They would probably do the same thing, but then again, they might not realize the potentiality they show in one landscape if transferred into another. The prairie is a landscape that makes them greater than life; it is an environment that brings out the best, and the worst, in man. It is a prairie syndrome, perhaps, that the

2

agony of the destruction and beauty of the seasons makes for a larger humanism. And always, the optimism prevails, not the optimism associated with the "some-where-a-bird-is singing" school of writing, but an optimism that states that things can be better; not that they always are, but that they can be.

This final product, prairie optimism, was not something that happened over-night; it grew gradually as the country grew, as the writers turned to the wind-swept plains for inspiration. Ralph Connor saw it all, and witnessed to it in the many novels he wrote. But his approach was that of the visitor, the person from another background, schooled in the traditions of the nineteenth century and spurred on by his great faith in God. His approach is full of accounts of the magnificence of the men who carved a civilization out of the wilderness. But he hesitates, and sometimes stands back, to ruminate in a pensive, almost senti-mental, mood about the survival of man on these plains. His motivation is clear and keen; his tradition is focussed on the pastoral ethic where in the garden of the west the new dew of morning will bring renewal of the spirit, where life will be better tomorrow because man is strong through his faith in God.

Connor's faith in God is reinforced by his love of the natural phenomena of the prairies, viewed, from Manitoba, as the end of the frontier rather than the place to go through before reaching the mountains and the West Coast. The wilderness his characters approach strengthens them; they become stronger human beings through survival against the elements of man and nature — and through defeat by these elements; Frederick Philip Grove, writing later than Connor, moves away from a kind of Puritan optimism into an early version of existentialism, as Frank Birbalsingh's article points out. Grove, working from a continental European educational background, came to Canada and approached the landscape with the eyes of a naturalist schooled in the Zola tradition. The environment was harsh; it produced pain and anguish. But the details of the landscape were there to be explained, to be described.

At times this description tends to become over-specific and scientific, particu-larly in *Over Prairie Trails* where the author concentrates on the changes that the seasons make in the landscape as he repeats a journey a number of times through the changing year. Though he approaches his natural environment with an objective eye for detail, he does not externalize himself from the people he creates. Instead, he moves inside the mind of his characters, reminiscent in this way of Dorothy Richardson. In their interior monologues he projects the chain of the seasons, their growth and decay, always in awe of nature and her mani-festations. He does not trace his faith in the eternal to God but rather to an

3

cyclical concept of the functioning of the natural world. At times, the cycle becomes a treadmill that tramps out little hope for mankind.

Margaret Laurence, too, works within the Manitoba landscape, but she moves
beyond the concern for nature into the consideration of the lasting effects of environment on people. It is not what happens to people, but how it affects them
that counts. Though she works within an ambience of religious myth — as the
titles of two of her novels signify, *The Jest of God* and *The Stone Angel* — she
does not suggest that reliance on God will produce a happy world. Rather, it is
what people do because of their own belief, and especially because of their faith
in themselves as individual human beings, that is important. Hagar can be kind
to her son at the end of her life so as to make her death more easy for him; yet,
for her this has no meaning: it does not even give her satisfaction. Margaret
Laurence's characters learn to like themselves for their faults, but they do not
go on ego-trips to gain this insight. Instead, they learn to cope with the emotions
of others on their own terms. Men are islands, and the separation is essential in
order to survive.

Though Margaret Laurence concentrates on people, the prairie emerges as an
essential background to her portraits of them. The sensual appeal in the landscape is always felt; one can sense the wind and the dry heat; one can taste the
snow flakes and the Saskatoon berries; one can smell the dust, and the over-
stuffed and well-polished furniture; one can hear the Canada goose and the
meadowlark.

The appeal to the senses is often, indeed, intensified by writers on the prairies.
The meadowlark, for instance, is an essential symbol in W. O. Mitchell; it
heralds spring, and death, and love, and communion not only with nature but
also with man. Mitchell moved on to larger themes with *Who Has Seen the
Wind*, which deals with innocence and experience in a full Blakean sense, though
ironically his novel was at first thought to be intended primarily for younger
readers. Merging with the innocence/experience theme is the intransigent prairie
landscape with its circle of seasons, seasons that never end, merging into the wider
concept of space. The vastness of the prairie begins to invade the writers of the
plains as soon as they move away from Manitoba as the focus of their environment. The prairie stretches over many miles, and the tautness of the setting is
reproduced within its inhabitants; their energies are stretched beyond the point
of endurance, and they wait for something wonderful to happen to them. Such
writers can combine the quality of endurance and the quality of dream.

The sense of durability pervades Sinclair Ross's *As For Me and My House,* probably the most remarkable novel written within the prairie setting. The descriptions of the landscape are overpowering, but they seem never to intrude or stand out from the basic story of Mrs. Bentley and her husband. Ross has the capacity to integrate the descriptions with the psychological action so that it becomes whole. The tension of the Bentleys is reflected in the seasons on the prairie, and in the wind which sweeps across it, bringing blizzards and dust storms. But though the garden Mrs. Bentley plants flourishes only for a short time, then withers and dies, the novel ends on an optimistic note, a new "vacancy of beginning". And that, after all, is better than nothing at all.

This kind of silent optimism is present in many writers of the prairies, such as Laura Salverson, Martha Ostenso, Robert Stead. It is a harsh existence, this carving out of the broad plains a home for a family and the community, but it is worth the struggle, for only time makes one appreciate the space which soars over the drab prairie. Its beauty is for those who live there for a while, not often seen because the harsh realities of the weather tend to obscure its presence. In such a world it seems that when one is almost at the end of existence, something happens that re-emphasizes what is often forgotten: the glimpse of a sunset, the quiet impressiveness of the northern lights, the bud of a crocus beside the railway track that leads away but also leads back.

Though most prairie writers deal with small towns, or with life on a farm or ranch, a few deal with the city, but even then it is a small city on the fringes of that wide landscape of the plains. One of these is Adele Wiseman, who in *The Sacrifice* speaks of a small, immigrant-settled town, obviously Winnipeg. The setting plays an important role, for it is the new land, the new city, for those wandering Jews who travel to find a home. The city is there, and it isn't there; the neighbourhood, the Jewish custom, is so "Winnipeg" that it cannot be forgotten, yet it merely serves as a setting for the people Miss Wiseman wishes to examine. Only at the end of the novel, when Abraham goes to Mad Mountain on the edge of the city, does the landscape play an important symbolic role in the development of the novel's theme — the natural development of a man whose philosophy is to "discover, grow, and build".

As I was collecting these articles on prairie writing, it became apparent that there were few critics who dealt with the poetry of the prairies. And as I thought further, I realized that very few poets have sought the prairies as their landscape, and those few often write of the dry snow and cold that exists in almost any part of Canada and is part of the general Canadian myth about the environment. What is it about the prairie landscape that seems to produce writers who choose

5

prose instead of poetry? It is probably the complete orientation of a prairie dweller to the variations of climate, to the unpredictably dramatic incidents of life that demand the prose form rather than the poem. Why is there not even the narrative poem, in the style of Pratt or Birney? Yet as I read prairie novels, and the criticism of them, I notice that often the prose is described justly as "poetic". Who can forget those moments of Biblical prose in *Who Has Seen the Wind* or the descriptions of the prairie night and the dust storms in *As For Me and My House?* It is as though the landscape is so overwhelming that it cannot accept the confined form of a poem. The writer needs the prose form to draw the complete picture, to fill the page to its edges with description. Listen to prairie people describing a snow storm or a tornado, or the year the crops failed, or a hail-and-thunderstorm, or for that matter, a sunset. They have to talk on, to underline it with repetition, to describe it in many ways in order to transmit the whole magnificence of what they are trying to describe. Prairie people are never lost for words, probably because they have sounds around them all the time, sounds with which they have to compete. Wander alone on an apparently bleak prairie road bed, or down into a gulley where the spring freshets once swept; it is a lonely landscape to the eye, dour and unkempt. But stop, and listen. There are many sounds — of birds, of grasshoppers, of rustling wheat stems, of a wind that never stops. Go then to a quiet Maritime river or an Ontario lake, away from civilization. There, save for the occasional cry of a loon, or call of a crow, one can listen to the quiet. But not on the prairie. It forever speaks; it forever talks. And prairie people do the same thing. There, silence never is. And often, it is poetry they speak in their prose, an elemental voice that shouts to the rest of the world that survival is better than no life at all. This is the voice of the prairie.

WESTERN MYTH

The World of Ralph Connor

F. W. Watt

"Ralph connor" is a name which is virtually lost in the mists of time. Apart from librarians and specialists in Canadian literature, the few who remember it must do so with the nostalgic smile reserved for childhood things only valued because of their associations. I imagine few browsers in our libraries today let their eyes rest on the long shelf that contains his two dozen or more novels, and fewer still will have chanced upon *The Life of James Robertson, Missionary Superintendent in the Northwest Territories* (1908) and *Postscript to Adventure, The Autobiography of Ralph Connor* (1938) which carry his real name, the Rev. Charles W. Gordon. Half a century ago the situation was very different. For years the presses whirled frantically to keep up with the demand for *Black Rock* (1898), *The Sky Pilot* (1899), and *The Man from Glengarry* (1901), his first (and best) three novels. We are told that one publisher, George H. Doran, built his house on a foundation of Connor novels, and by 1937 when Connor died, his fame well on the decline, the total of copies sold was over five millions. Those books were read in Canada and abroad, by Scottish crofters and presidents of the United States, by businessmen, socialist thinkers, cabinet ministers, and ordinary people everywhere. When Connor travelled he was welcomed by high and low as a distinguished author. George Doran, in his lively autobiography, *Chronicles of Barabbas* (1935), records a typical incident: "The last time I saw him [Connor] was in London. I was to send him a letter. 'Where shall I send it?' 'To Number 10 Downing Street. I am stopping with the Prime Minister,' was his quiet rejoinder."

How are we to account for Connor's extraordinary popularity, and his equally extraordinary fall from favour? By way of answer it is necessary to consider for a moment the literary and historical situation in which he appeared.

7

The history of the Canadian novel is a more dismal story than that of Canadian poetry, and where the nineteenth-century novel is weakest — almost nonexistent in fact — is in the mode which depicts contemporary reality. We can understand this best if we remember that the novel in the realistic tradition depends heavily on a social context, and Canadian life, even where it had risen beyond the struggle for physical survival, was a rapidly growing, changing, evolving flux for most of the nineteenth century. Naturally, writers turned away from this confusing immediate scene to the more stable, clear-cut, traditional patterns of past communities for their matter, particularly to the colourful simplicities of early French Canada. Moreover the prevailing conventions of piety, decorum, and gentility in fiction discouraged any robust approaches to the contemporary scene — Goldwin Smith's "Seven Lamps of Fiction" are a good summary of accepted critical criteria — and so the serious problematical approach was ruled out or made very difficult. Contemporary reality, then, entered — if at all — in its most trivial and innocuous forms.

In 1898 into the quiet sheepfold of genteel society novels and historical romances Ralph Connor burst with his portrait of the raw, turbulent, crude life of a Rocky mountain mining camp, *Black Rock, A Tale of the Selkirks.* Having in 1890 accepted a call to "the new Presbytery of Calgary, the largest presbytery in the world" (as Superintendent Robertson called it), Connor had seen that life at first hand, experienced its hardships and dangers, and had caught the fever of its excitements. Just as the physical horizons of Canada were suddenly pushed back to allow the flow of settlers and opportunities to pour into the plains and mountains of a new world, so the literary horizons were expanded by an outburst of what appeared at first glance to be a bold, uncompromising realism, unafraid of hard truths, vulgarity, violence, sardonic humour, cruelty, immorality, and all the other things Canadian Victorianism preferred to turn its back upon.

Not everyone, of course, rejoiced in this pushing back of horizons at the opening of "Canada's century". The crude, boisterous era of western expansion, which began abruptly in the 1890's and tapered off only after the disillusioning impact of the First World War and its domestic consequences, provoked the disgusted reaction of many intelligent Canadians. Understandably so, for few periods of Canadian history can have been less comfortable for the sensitive artist or the intellectual to live and work in. Unable or unwilling to share in the scramble for easy money which land speculation, mineral discoveries, industrial expansion and the swelling immigrant population promised, intellectuals fled to the artistic Bohemias of New York or Europe, men like Carman, Duncan, and Charles G. D.

8

Roberts, the Father of Canadian poetry, who chose to spend twenty-five years of his paternity abroad. Those who remained turned in revulsion from sordid materialism; "Beauty has taken refuge from our life. That grew too loud and wounding," opined the austere D. C. Scott. Or they sought out quiet corners of the land where nineteenth-century peace and stability could be imagined still — Drummond's French Canada, or the idyllic Prince Edward Island of Anne of Green Gables. A few bolder spirits were prepared to contend with the enemy. Stephen Leacock humorously drew attention to the plight of the "little man" drowning in a world of increasing "bigness"; shot his satiric darts at the folly of little towns that rushed eagerly to meet their fates as big cities; and laid the whip on the corrupt urban Arcadias of the new plutocracy. Peter McArthur returned to his paternal homestead to defend the dwindling agrarian paradise against the serpents of commercialism and urbanism with his eulogies of farming as a way of life and his war-cry, "Back to the Land."

These were the "inner-directed" men, aristocratic, austere, puritanical, cynically witty, romantic, incorrigibly nostalgic (or whatever form their independence took), but they were the minority. Far more numerous, setting the temper of the era, were the Services and the Steads, who did not flinch from coarseness, vulgarity and materialism. They might prefer the pen to the shovel or the placer pan, or to the glib tongue of the speculator, but they could find thereby their own way to share in the profits. These were primarily writers who welcomed and exploited the opening of the West. Ralph Connor took his stand, though as we shall see a rather different one, with them.

In Eastern Canada the boom era showed itself in rapid industrial development, in the growth of urbanism, and, consequently, in that vast increase in social interdependency which brought an end to the nineteenth-century era of economic individualism, in fact and in myth. A social revolution was carried out which was not immediately grasped. The units in economic relations were no longer individuals, the employer and his employee, but combinations — corporations, trusts, mergers, unions, associations. "Bigness" had inescapably arrived. How to conciliate the large, powerful forces contending within the body politic became the main problem of astute politicians like W. L. Mackenzie King, whose recognition of the corporate nature of social life constituted a major change in the philosophy of Liberalism. Late nineteenth-century Canadian Liberals, by clinging to simpler theories of individual liberty, had remained out of touch with the contemporary trend to collectivism. Ralph Connor was committed temperamentally and by religious faith to an individualistic view of human experience. He had

9

first-hand knowledge of the social changes in progress, for he was for years in the thick of Winnipeg's labour unrest, and he acted as arbitrator (of the Mackenzie King school) in innumerable disputes. But the two later novels which deal with such subject-matter, *To Him that Hath* (1921) and *The Arm of Gold* (1932), treat social issues mainly in terms of personalities and individual sins and folly. It was only the West that provided him with matter his individualistic approach could handle to advantage. Western life was still too fluid in the early 1900's to crystallize into an urban civilization of any complexity, and the ideal of individual initiative could with some justice hold sway.

THE WORLD of Ralph Connor, in so far as it existed at all, lasted for only a short period. It was already passing as he wrote about it. And indeed, he was well aware of this, for he set himself in part the task of recording it before it was entirely lost. Why, it might be asked, did he choose for his subject what nineteenth-century Canadian novelists preferred to ignore for that very reason, the changing immediate scene? The answer is, I believe, that he saw what other novelists failed to realize: that the present moment, with all its novelty and its fluidity, is significant only in so far as it reveals an old, stable, enduring subject, man's essential nature and condition, and he felt the transient life of the West to be especially illuminating in this respect. Like James Joyce, Connor saw himself as writing a chapter in the moral history of his country, and the fact that his best novels can still catch at our attention despite their radical faults suggests to me that he sometimes came close to succeeding.

In the opening pages of that first novel *Black Rock*, the narrator Ralph Connor is led far away from the familiar East, from the "cosmopolitan and kindly city" of Toronto, into a primitive lumber camp six miles from the mining village of Black Rock in the heart of the Selkirks. Connor is a photographic observer, and we get details of the camp which make the then original setting vivid. The loggers are a tough, colourful, uncouth bunch — Connor nicely catches their mixture of dialects and accents — but they meet their match on Christmas Eve when the hero of the tale appears, the Presbyterian minister Mr. Craig, and proceeds to Christianize, willy-nilly, their rollicking pagan festival. The key-note of the book, and indeed of much of the later Connor, is struck when Craig, by telling the meaning of the Christmas story in the most informal of sermons, captures his reluctant audience, and especially the oldest, hardest, fiercest sinner of them all: "Old man Nelson held his eye steadily on the minister," Connor says. "Only once before had I seen that look on a human face. A young fellow had broken through the ice on the river at home, and as the black water was dragging his fingers one by one from the slippery edges, there came over his face that same look. I used to wake up for many a night after in a sweat of horror, seeing the white face with its parting lips and its piteous, dumb appeal, and the black water slowly sucking it down." Connor narrates as at first hand the long, violent, brutal and not entirely successful struggle of the powers for good, lined up with Craig, to save souls like Nelson's from their black waters of damnation, against the powers for evil, the bootlegger and gambler Slavin and his gang of rough-necks. The tale is full of action, from the vivid knock-down-drag-out fight between the Drys and the Wets, to the colourful race of four-horse combinations, in which the loggers' team edges out the citizens' and the miners' in a wild finish; but the theme of conversion and rebirth underlies it all.

The novels that followed in the next decade largely develop and vary the *Black Rock* formula. It had proved a sudden and unexpected success. There were, aside from the large official issue, eleven pirated editions of the first book. The Rev. Charles W. Gordon had become the famous novelist Ralph Connor overnight, and he worked his vein thoroughly. Take a wild, barbaric setting away from the civilized gentility of the East; fill it with a crowd of virile, bold, lusty, profane, hard-fighting and hard-living men, often with pasts to live down, who are exploiting the unrestrained individuality of frontier life to the full; introduce morality and religion, usually in the form of a Presbyterian minister who fights bravely against great odds to save the souls of the indifferent and hostile sinners; add a touch of romance, a virtuous maiden, wife or mother to soften and uplift the harder hearts; mix up the moral and physical battles, letting the blood flow freely, bring off victory for the forces of good; cap it with conversion and salvation for the evil as well. All this Connor did with considerable technical fluency, and a clever manipulation of tensions and contrasts and the simpler dramatic devices that appeal immediately to our feelings. The mild, gentle, boyish Sky Pilot, humble, aware of his own inadequacies as a man of God, shatters the cynical, callous indifference of the Albertan cowboys by his enthusiasm and his innocence. The Glengarry war-horse Macdonald, recently converted, endures the cruellest goadings of his enemies rather than forget the Lord's message, "Vengeance is *Mine*."

Individual scenes of dramatic power and photographic vividness stand out in each novel, as for example the funeral procession in *The Man from Glengarry*: at night by the light of cedar bark torches the body of young Cameron is carried home to his waiting parents, and when the bearers arrive the father silences the mother's terrible scream of grief, recalling her to her duty — "Whisht, Janet, woman!... Your son is at the door." Every novel has its special locality to exploit (the Selkirks, the foothill country, the Ottawa River, the Crow's Nest Pass, and the boyhood home described so lovingly in *Glengarry Schooldays*); there are many special customs or colourful local activities to describe: maple-sugaring, a stump-pulling bee, a house-raising, a wake, a harvesting contest, and so on. The informative scope is panoramic (Connor's regions include almost the entire breadth of Canada), and sometimes we are shown striking scenes and experiences once common enough in this country but long since forgotten. *The Foreigner* (1909), for example, describes the sordid shack-life of Russian immigrants in Winnipeg in the early 1900's; to find any other writer who dares deal with such material we have to turn to the sociologists, or rather to their only equivalent at that time, men like J. S. Woodsworth whose *My Neighbour* and other books angrily drew attention to the same situation. Throughout Connor's novels we get a sense of teeming vitality and an endless reservoir of varied experiences and exciting adventure. It is not surprising that the rough-riding Teddy Roosevelt and Ralph Connor were mutual admirers.

Through all the novels too runs a rich vein of humour. The vivid McGill-Toronto rugby match which is described at the beginning of *The Prospector* (1904) gains a dimension by the presence there of the pious little old Scots widow, Mrs. Macgregor, for whom the players' violence is nothing compared to the clan-wars she has known in the Old Country; who turns out to be an expert in the subtleties of the game; and who sends her giant of a son "Shock" into the scrimmage with the admonition, "Run away Hamish, and be careful of the laddies." The sentimentality of the Sky Pilot's funeral is cut astringently by the description of another funeral procession which ends in an unseemly race between the sleigh bearing the corpse and the two carrying the mourners and the pall-bearers respectively. Afterwards, the corpse-driver, having won the race to the burial-ground, "fairly distributed the blame", as Connor tells us: " 'For his part,' he said, 'he knew he hadn't ought to make no corp get any such move on, but he wasn't goin' to see that there corp take second place at his own funeral. Not if he could help it. And as for the others, he thought that the pall-bearers had a blanked sight more to do with the plantin' than them giddy mourners.' "

But humour is after all not an added feature, an occasional ornament or the sugar-coating to Connor's writing; it is an aspect of his essential good-will, high-spirits, tolerance, or to choose the best word — charity. There is a love of action,

of experience, and of people of all kinds and classes running through much that
Connor has written that makes far better Canadian writers seem by comparison
a little cold, narrow, priggish, snobbish, or desiccated in their orientation to their
own lives and towards their fellows.

T HE CHIEF REASON for the large sale of Connor's earlier
books was no doubt their timeliness. By the late 1890's all eyes were on the West.
The flood of immigrants from the East and from abroad so long expected was at
last flowing strongly. What was the new land they were going to really like?
Was it as thrilling as the reports claimed? Connor provided answers, and exciting ones at that. The country west of the Great Lakes was vast, infinitely rich in
potential. If at times the latter part of *The Man from Glengarry* now reads to us
like propaganda for the Canadian Pacific Railway, it is more likely that many of
its first readers were deeply stirred by the vision of the "empire of the Canadian
West" that it tries to project before our eyes. And it was the existence of real
opportunities, not merely enthusiasm, that peopled Connor's novels with men on
the make, young Scots from Glengarry or immigrant Slavs, rising in spectacular
fashion from ignorance or poverty to power, importance and the life of wealth
and refinement. The West, indeed, was a world on the make.

Naturally there was less time for some of the subtleties, even religious subtleties,
of more settled communities, and human beings were likely to appear in their
simplest, clearest outlines. The God of Connor's West is of an appropriate nature,
generous minded, not too concerned with the letter (too little the theologian to
satisfy Calvin, surely), sympathetic to the spirit in unlikely places, ready to have
His work done by whoever will put a hand to it. Presbyterian ministers, saintly
widows, Catholic priests, rough-mannered miners or lumbermen may equally
enter into and even (at a pinch) conduct religious services. The people tend to
be a little larger than life as the Easterner knows it. The men are tall, broad-
shouldered, immensely strong, hardy, brave and tender-hearted. There are of
course cads as well as Christian gentlemen (a distinction in nature, not social
class), but the most vicious of villains are redeemable despite their terrible cruelty
and wickedness; they repent movingly. The women are pure and modest and
maidenly and beautiful. Nothing quite equals in the power for good "the sweet
uplift of a good woman's face" (in those days no other uplift would have crossed
a gentleman's mind). Their voices have such a sweet, thrilling tone that the sav-
age breast is soothed with a single song; their eyes plumb the depths of a man's

13

heart and see what really lies there, or glow luminously with a warmth of simple love, or fill with tender tears, or disappear modestly from the too frank gaze of admirers. What mothers they make, and what wives! Timid and gentle, but brave as lions in the cause of virtue.

As the novels proceed we become aware that we are in the presence of a full-blown myth of the West, not merely a feeling of jingoistic patriotism or a sense of vast resources just being realized. When one of the characters in *The Foreigner* exclaims, "It is a wonderful country, Canada," she has something else in mind, for she says: "How wonderful the power of this country of yours *to transform men!*" In *The Prospector* (1904) Connor may be giving us an account of his own evolving experience when he describes the impact of the West on Shock, the book's hero:

> He was making the discovery that climate changes the complexion, not only of men, but of habits of thought and action. As Shock was finding his way to new adjustments and new standards he was incidentally finding his way into a new feeling of brotherhood as well. The lines of cleavage which had hitherto determined his interests and affinities were being obliterated. The fictitious and accidental were fading out under this new atmosphere, and the great lines of sheer humanity were coming to stand out with startling clearness. Up to this time creed and class had largely determined both his interest and his responsibility, but now, apart from class and creed, men became interesting, and for men he began to feel responsibility. He realized as never before that a man was the great asset of the universe — not his clothes, material, social or religious.

This is a somewhat startling position for a budding young Presbyterian minister to have reached (such is Shock) and for Connor it is an expression of a genuine break-through from the excessive refinement and gentility which swaddled many Victorian Canadians. The West had become a mythical land, a place where such revelations were forced upon one. Men went there to escape the old life and in search of a new life, and there the faith in conversion and rebirth took on a new meaning. It was a place where biblical parables easily merged with actuality. The Rev. Craig telling the story of the Prodigal Son's home-coming to his congregation of western fugitives and exiles (who listen like so many distraught Dean Moriaritys) concludes: "There you are, men, every man of you, somewhere *on the road*. Some of you are too lazy, and some of you haven't enough yet of the far country to come back.... Men, you all want to go back home." This is a world seen through Christian eyes, where all endeavour, temptation, success, failure and hope is translatable into terms of heroic Christian struggle.

No ONE WOULD THINK of Connor's portrayal of the West as realistic any longer. Far from it. Too often he stepped from actuality into far-fetched success stories or melodramatic love fantasies. But many of his distortions are of another kind, the result of his endeavour to see religious meaning in the drama of western life. It is for this reason that Connor stands above his contemporary Canadian novelists, and because he dared to write about things that really mattered — the state of his characters' morals and of their souls, not merely the historical past or the surfaces of contemporary life. In this way he often escaped the incredible triviality of so many of the other western writers, Nellie McClung, Stringer and Stead, for example, and there is often a touch of grandeur in what he was trying to do. Moreover, it is not because Connor was a preacher first and an artist second that he failed. Distinctions of this sort are based on a modern notion with which many great writers would have little patience. In fact one could argue that Connor failed because he did not take his role of preacher earnestly and profoundly enough, but gave it up at times for a feeble and debased notion of "novelist". For not being a good or a passionate enough preacher we must blame him; for his conception of the novelist we must blame his readers, his critics, his society as well. They wanted and expected romantic nonsense, and too often he willingly provided it. It is interesting to notice in this respect that the later novels, in which Connor is very rarely the preacher, are his most unconvincing and trivial.

For the writer of realistic fiction the chief challenge is to project an image of life which is both consistent and deeply problematical. Connor came within a hairsbreadth of a solution in his conception of the West. Here was an arena where the ancient battle was actually being fought out daily (or so it seemed to him) between good and evil, Christian and Hopeful and Mr. Valiant-for-truth against the forces of Appolyon and the temptations of Vanity Fair. Connor only regretted that his palette did not contain sharp enough whites and blacks to show the intensity of that conflict, in which the costs at stake were (to him the only ones that really mattered) the salvation or damnation of human souls. He tried to see life everywhere in the same thrilling terms. But, as I have said, Connor could never sustain a level of consistency for long. His realism had a disconcerting way of shifting abruptly into romantic fantasy and back again, like those incongruous mixtures of photography and cartooning perpetrated by Walt Disney. No doubt the life of the West failed Connor as much as Connor failed the West: it could scarcely avoid the descent to the ordinary and humdrum, losing its angels and its devils.

The Canadian novel since Connor has been tamed and trained. Flamboyance and grand (or grandiose) ambition has faded away. There is more artistic integrity, and the iron laws of probability are not so casually flouted. Though one cannot honestly lament the passing of Connor's world, there has truly been a loss of élan and an increased danger of that desert of exact likeness to ordinary reality in which Eliot feared realism would perish. However, the best recent writers have continued, mainly in the realistic tradition, to try to project deeply problematical patterns of experience, and with increasing success. F. P. Grove's flawed works are nearly redeemed by the greatness of his theme, the tragedy of the pioneer whose heroic conquest of nature brings to birth a new generation and a civilization in which he finds himself superfluous. Hugh MacLennan's earlier secular gropings for significance in the issues of Canadian nationality (Connor would have appreciated that vision of Canada as the future arch of the civilized world!) have happily given way to artistic exploration of more fundamental moral and religious issues. Morley Callaghan's whole *oeuvre* now takes on its full force when seen as a developing dialectic in which all the contemporary appeals to man's faith — naturalistic atheism or agnosticism, Marxism, and traditional Catholicism — compete for the souls of his characters. And to come closer to home, that latest addition to the novels of the West, Sheila Watson's *The Double Hook*, achieves what Connor might have valued most — a radically simplified but powerful image of human life freeing itself from the chains of its own sinfulness, a parable of rebirth. None of these earnest artists could ever share in the popularity and other rewards of this world that Connor enjoyed, though any one of them is a far more faithful servant of the Muses. But then art which is both fine and immediately or ever popular is too rare a thing for any writer to expect, least of all in Canada.

(1959)

GLENGARRY REVISITED

Roy Daniells

Ralph connor's works fill a whole shelf in any Canadian library, and though worn bindings on multiple copies show that someone has pulled them down pretty often, we should not be much tempted to do so now were it not for *The Man from Glengarry*, published in 1901. It has slowly assumed the status of a minor classic, after a period of immense popularity followed by total neglect. Reprinted for the New Canadian Library in 1960, with a brief but enlightening introduction by Ross Beharriell, it can stand alone as Connor's testimony, but is usefully thrown into relief if flanked by his autobiographical *Glengarry Schooldays* (1902) and *Postscripts to Adventure* (1938) and illuminated by an occasional dip into the other novels. Readers pursuing the Glengarry theme should, however, disregard *The Girl from Glengarry* (1933); it is a story of the stock market in the 1920's and demonstrates how bald and superficial Connor could be when his daemon deserted him.

"All that is set down in *Glengarry Schooldays* is true." This avowal answers for the author's entire work. There is in fact no change of persons between the Reverend Charles Gordon and the pseudonymous writer of stories. For most Canadians, the minister of St. Stephen's Church in Winnipeg, chaplain on the Western Front during the First World War and afterwards Moderator of the Presbyterian General Assembly, is quite simply Ralph Connor. Born in Ontario's eastern county of Glengarry in 1860, he looked out into the Glengarry farms and forests from the vantage point of his father's manse during the first ten years of his life. It is to this decade that we must turn for the primary pattern from which all his works unfolded. Familiar outlines are here superimposed: the Canadian bush, the Scottish clan, the doctrines of Calvin and the archetypes of a child's dream. Connor's perception of greatness, in this life and beyond, is directed down immemorial vistas.

His Glengarry lies at the heart of the most primeval of all forests, a Schwarz-wald antedating even the stories Grimm preserved. "It lines up close and thick along the road, and here and there quite overshadows it. It crowds in upon the little farms and shuts them off from one another and from the world outside, and peers in through the little windows of the log houses looking so small and lonely, but so beautiful in their forest frames." At the end of a perspective of time past, Connor sees this landscape of his childhood, simplified, stylized and lighted by a glow of warm affection. It is a fairyland, more solid and real than actuality. "A dim light fell over the forest from the half-moon and the stars, and seemed to fill up the little clearing in which the manse stood, with a weird and mysterious radiance. Far away in the forest the long-drawn howl of a wolf rose and fell. . . ." Or Spring is breaking: "The bare woods were filled with the tangled rays of light from the setting sun. Here and there a hillside facing the east lay in shadow that grew black where the balsams and cedars stood in clumps. But everywhere else the light fell sweet and silent about the bare trunks, filling the long avenues under the arching maple limbs with a yellow haze." This luminous veil belongs to *le temps perdu*, living only in memory: "The solid forests of Glengarry have vanished, and with the forests the men who conquered them."

Instinctively Connor brings his great Highlanders on stage as woodsmen rather than farmers. Salient ceremonies of this self-contained world in the heart of the forest are the sugaring-off, an annual tribute from the maple groves, and the logging-bee, a mass assault upon the brulé. The forest, moreover, is a main source of livelihood. Each winter the shanties are filled with Glengarry men who will fell the huge pines and with broad-axe square the timber ready for rafting down river to Quebec. When the scene shifts to that city or to the far West, there is a marked loss of intensity and loosening of texture. It is only in the forest world, where custom makes life sweet, that Connor is fully at home and his daemon fully functioning.

In Canada the Scottish unicorn retains his crown; compare the English coat of arms with that of Nova Scotia. Immigrants from Scotland have, from the earliest days of settlement and in all parts of the country, found Canada con-genial. Connor's Glengarry takes its name from a region in north Perthshire, on the southern edge of the Highlands. The confluence of the Garry and Tummel rivers lies just above Pitlochry, from whose streets the Canadian visitor looks northward into familiar landscapes. Glen Garry is part of the Atholl basin where a floor level of about fifteen hundred feet is ringed by mountains more than twice as high, pierced by the opposed passes of Drumochter and Killiecrankie. From this species of environment the transition to eastern Canada was an easy one. The Scottish inhabitants of Connor's Glengarry are "mostly from the Highlands and Islands" and their cohesiveness is strengthened by pressure from Irish and French-Canadian settlements bordering their territory. In Glengarry Macdonalds can comfortably coexist with Campbells although the latter have perpetrated "the vilest act of treachery recorded in any history, the massacre of the Macdonalds of Glencoe". It is as though a new Canadian clan with Glengarry as its patronymic had been, by agreement, created. Connor, as chaplain of the 43rd Cameron Highlanders of Canada, wore appropriately enough the "Glengarry" cap.

A strong family likeness marks the forest people, the Canadian clan. The hero, Ranald Macdonald, remains "the man from Glengarry", individualized only by the intensity with which the common flame burns in him. Connor's life and works in general abound with evidence that he shares with his hero this incandescence. In *The Doctor*, we see the Southern belle Iola Lane, "possessed of a fatal, maddening beauty" which works destruction among her lovers, closing her brief life by Loch Fyne in the West Highlands, where the sacredness of the soil and the scene are conducive to an edifying end. Connor's own feeling of rapture when first he visited Scotland is brilliantly captured in *Postscripts to Adventure*. The loyalty, strength and seriousness of Connor's heroes; their pride, élan and willingness to stand on a point of honour; their instinctive implementation of the Scottish regimental motto "Nemo me impune lacessit!": everything shows them to be Highlanders at one remove, their clan feeling intensified rather than diminished by the migration.

Other matters such as the virility and patriarchal authority of the men, the purity and noble compassion of the women, are perhaps best considered in the context of Glengarry religion, for it is hard to know where the clansman ends and the Calvanist begins. Connor's own degrees of emphasis should be taken note of: "The men are worth remembering. They carried the marks of their blood in their fierce passions, their courage, their loyalty; and of the forest in their patience, their resourcefulness, their self-reliance. But deeper than all, the mark that reached down to their heart's core was that of their faith, for in them dwelt the fear of God." Gradually we come to agree that it is the third strand, of religion, which twisted against the other two produces the magic thread, fastened to some archetypal bole in the depth of Connor's dream forest and giving him in all subsequent times and remote places a sure tug of orientation toward his centre of reference.

REGION, RACE AND RELIGION: this is Connor's perpetual trilogy. We see Ranald (clearly Connor's alter ego) become a successful business man and sportsman, idol of the Albert Club in Quebec, encountering the minister's wife, Mrs. Murray, who is there on a visit. "Then they began talking about Glengarry, of the old familiar places, of the woods and the fields, of the boys and girls now growing into men and women, and of the old people, some of whom were passed away. Before long they were talking of the church and all the varied interests centering in it, but soon they went back to the theme that Glengarry people everywhere are never long together without discussing — the great revival."

As we enter and re-enter the closed world of the forest we become aware that the little clearings, hewed out by a physical labour not less than heroic, are ruled by heads of households, each a tower of strength in his own domain. We listen to old Donald Finch when he learns that his son has resisted the schoolmaster: "Woman, be silent! It is not for you to excuse his wickedness. . . . Your children have well learned their lesson of rebellion and deceit. But I vow unto the Lord I will put an end to it now, whatever. And I will give you to remember, sir," turning to Thomas, "to the end of your days this occasion. And now, hence from this table. Let me not see your face till the Sabbath is past, and then, if the Lord spares me, I shall deal with you." The close association of parental and divine authority is no accident. Calvinism and the clan were two concepts upon which rested the whole fabric of Glengarry society. They were naturally complementary.

"Religion in Glengarry in those days was a solemn and serious matter, a thing of life and death." Calvin's conception of God as beyond reason, inexplicable, omnipotent and requiring no justification of his ways to men, suited perfectly the Highlanders' psyche. But the individual's reaction to so overwhelming a presence is not simple or single. God was viewed, rather remotely, as ruler of the universe, author and disposer of every man's being; predestinating some to heaven, leaving others for damnation; all this for causes which no discussion of foreknowledge could ever render acceptable to human reason. More immediately, God appeared as a super-ego, demanding all but impossible physical and moral effort from the elect — primarily from the minister of each presbytery — "He must be a man to whom God is more real than his universe." And since we tend to ask of others what has been asked of us, the same demanding quality, the same intention to dominate, possessed all relationships. "The Glengarry folk were a fighting people. The whole spirit of the school was permeated by the fighting motif. Every recitation was a contest. The winners went joyously to the top, the failures remained ignominiously at the foot. . . . The gravest defect in our educational system was the emphasis laid upon feats of memory. . . . In all my Glengarry school days I never drew a map." What need of maps when purpose runs in linear progression from one point of decision to the next? Bunyan's Christian was given no map to show his way to heaven, only the directive, Keep to the straight and narrow path!

Counterbalancing the imperious paternal figure is the female ideal, whether virginal or maternal, filling the roles of Beatrice and Our Lady of Perpetual Help. Here Connor's very limitations become strengths. Sexuality rises into an immense romantic sublimation, completely convincing because it must have corresponded to Connor's deepest experience and firmest belief. Mrs. Murray, the minister's wife, and Kate, the girl whom the hero wins at the close, are essentially the same. Spirited, radiant, resourceful, devoted, they are without weakness or lapse, but true to the experience of the idealist. Watching the sun set behind lofty crests of the forest, which gleam like spires against the light, it is easy to believe that "the streets of the city are pure gold" and to know toward what city Mrs. Murray is directing the gaze of her son. Connor's intensity of vision makes his stereotypes convincing; they reveal themselves as embodiments of some Platonic or Christian reality of an ultimate kind.

His conception of excellence is single and closely focussed. For those who fall outside its narrow range there is little comprehension. English, Irish and American characters are not denigrated; they simply and visibly fail to measure up to Scottish standards. Methodists, Baptists and Roman Catholics are not evil; they are denied the Calvanistic virtues. But what he lacks in breadth is made up in his capacity to rise to an O altitudo! The schoolmaster, Craven, is telling of the death of old Mrs. Finch: " . . . but believe me, sir, that room was full of glory. . . . There were no farewells, no wailing, and at the very last, not even tears. Thomas, who has nursed her for more than a year, still supported her, the smile on his face to the end. . . . I had no need to fear. After a long silence she sat up straight, and in her Scotch tongue she said, with a kind of amazed joy in her tone, 'Ma fayther! Ma fayther! I am here.' Then she settled herself back in her son's arms, drew a deep breath, and was still. All through the night and the next day the glory lingered round me. I went about as in a strange world. I am afraid you will be thinking me foolish, sir."

For reasons hard to formulate but lying deep in his own experience, Connor's stories are shot through with the idea of violence. From past generations of wild Highlanders the Glengarry men inherit a fighting spirit. And their pride as clansmen is strengthened by their sense of being among the elect, predestined to victory. From strength of will, to intense individualism, to boastful competitiveness, to open violence is an easy progression. Connor's imaginative involvement is complete, though his attitude is necessarily ambiguous. He may be a minister of the gospel but his delight in violence is almost ineradicable. He relates, in *Postscript to Adventure,* how "the tales of the fierce old days survived down into my time, stirring my youthful heart with profound regret that deeds so heroically splendid should all be bad. For in spite of the Great Revival we were of the same race, with ancient lust of battle in our blood." He records with pride how his brother, "stripped to his shirt on a winter day", dared any man from the next settlement to step out. "He had the strength of a bull."

How does this pride in primeval strength, barely out of touch with primeval ferocity, square itself with Connor's vocation as a servant of Christ? One searches for answers on several levels and amid some confusion of ideas. Macdonald Dubh, crippled by a dastardly blow from the Frenchman LeNoir and slowly dying as a result, not only forgives his enemy but persuades Ranald to forego the idea of vengeance. Each renunciation is arrived at after long inward agonies of father and son. The moral glow which ensues leaves certain shadows undispelled. LeNoir repents, after being saved from death by Ranald, but can we assume all scoundrels will do the same? And, initially, are we to believe that a straightforward blow delivered by an aggressor does no harm, least of all to a Highlander? And how are we to reconcile the God of vengeance, inhabiting the recesses of Connor's creed, with forgiveness of enemies, when Connor's own sentiments of Christian mildness are neighboured by his delight as, after a hockey game, the foul player is knocked senseless by one splendid retributory blow? The fact is that violence and competitiveness are instinctive and therefore inexplicable: "Glengarry folk, being mostly of Highland stock, love a fight." Connor's autobiography records how he could not refrain from striving to beat his own brother as a binder at harvest time and how for ten years after his overstrained heart showed the effect. The competitiveness at all levels appears meaningless and even the violence has an air of unreality, like the combats of Milton's angels. Connor's effort to take the sting out of vengeance by Christian forgiveness succeeds only in one exemplary case, where vengeance would mean murder. His tacit assumption that the good, like Milton's Abdiel, are basically invulnerable fails to convince. His concept of muscular Christianity finds us wondering with De Lacy, the Englishman, "Ye gods! psalms and hymns; and how the fellow knocked those Frenchmen about." Or we remain poised like the dialogue between Kate and Mrs.

Murray: "But isn't it awful, Auntie? They might kill him." "Yes, dear, but it sounds worse to us perhaps than it is."

Connor's plot is a string on which to thread significant incidents. His characterization is of significant types, with some variation within a type. These combine within an intensely realized physical and ethical setting, a boyhood memory preserved with that shining intensity of which the Victorians alone seem to be capable. "We will always be thinking of you," says Macdonald to his nephew, "and more than all, at the Bible class and the meetings she will be asking for you and wondering how you are doing, and by night and by day the door will be on the latch for your coming." For all its quality of dream, this is also the realistic record of a particular period and locale of Canadian sensibility. The more one reads the Glengarry trilogy, the less separable do fact and fiction appear. "The tales of the lumbermen in *The Man from Glengarry* are from real life."

TहE ULTIMATE QUALITY of Connor's writing, which puts him almost in a class by himself among our novelists, is his capacity for transcendence. It absorbs his absurdities, renders innocuous his irresolution about violence, and lifts him above the ranks of regionalists and deployers of local colour. His vision of greatness is compelling because he was himself compelled. The immense dignity of the homeward coming of Big Mack Cameron, drowned while trying to save a Frenchman among the logs, is in danger of being dissipated by an anxious sway of opinion among the mourners keeping the wake, as to their dead friend's calling and election, when Macdonald Bhain, grown calm and looked intently into the darkness, has a vision — "And yonder is the lad, and with him a great company, and his face is shining, and oh! it is a good land, a good land!" Abrupt but authentic, this surge of insight dispels all doubts. For Connor there is a dynamic even in memories of the departed. Ranald finds in Mrs. Murray "a friend whose influence followed him, and steadied and lifted him up to greatness, long after the grave had hidden her from man's sight". These solutions are typical of Protestantism, in that enormous stress is laid on the salvation of the individual, on his integrity and moral effort; of Calvinism, in that all action on the part of the elect is ipso facto portentous and determining; and, supremely, of primitive Puritanism, in that insoluble problems are transposed into a higher stratum, an eternal world, an ultimate vision. It has been recalled that among hymns sung in St. Stephen's, in Winnipeg, "Fight the Good Fight", "There were Ninety and Nine" and "Onward Christian Soldiers" held pride of place. And with reason there was appended to Connor's autobiography the familiar envoi Bunyan wrote for Mr. Valiant-for-Truth: "So he passed over, and all the trumpets sounded for him on the other side."

Connor's story, whether presented as fiction or related as personal experience, finally opens out into the expanse of the Canadian West, a mundane equivalent of his drive toward transcendence. "Wherever there was lumbering to be done, sooner or later there Glengarry men were to be found, and Ranald had found them in the British Columbia forests." Connor's imagination gives them a role beyond that of felling timber on the Pacific slope. They are the visible link between East and West, which have been politically united in Confederation and now, through the building of the C.P.R., will become one society. They are the bearers of an ethos of truth and honour without which Confederation is meaningless, "a common loyalty that would become more vividly real when the provinces had been brought more closely together by the promised railway". Such is the theme of Ranald's speech to a mass meeting in New Westminster and the crowd hails him, "Glengarry! Glengarry!"

It is natural to ask whether Connor's conception of life is relevant to an understanding of Canada. Without question he interprets reliably the dynamic of the four or five decades following Confederation, with special reference to Ontario and the opening West. His own role was not inconsiderable; his concepts of Christian truth, personal loyalty and political responsibility were shared, in varying degrees, by unnumbered Canadians. He did more than provide a locus classicus of the forest image, a uniquely Canadian *recherche du temps perdu*, and a synoptic view of the Scottish-Calvinist ethos. He rose above the particulars of his creeds into a vision of Canadian domain and destiny. The little world of rural virtues and rural violence, of skills learned in forest and farm, of individualism strengthened by clan loyalty, was precisely — in historical fact — a microcosm which could expand to become the larger world of Western Canada society and enterprise, before the pattern was again modified by rising immigration. Physical strength and adeptness played an overwhelming role in a world of railway construction, homesteading on prairie quarter-sections, and felling of great trees on mountainsides. The drive toward violence was absorbed in labour, deflected into hunting and field sports, transposed into construction, and sometimes, as Connor hoped, channelled into an assault upon wickedness in low places. It is worth remembering that our westward expansion was, in historical fact, accomplished with incredibly little open violence. The record of territorial

acquisition, of Riel's suppression, of the Pacific gold rush and the opening of com-
munications, is one of confused moderation, a collective desire to remain innocent
of outrage and excess.

To the latent issues of French-speaking versus English-speaking cultures and
of Catholic versus Protestant Connor turns an unseeing eye. Readers of *The
Man from Glengarry* may make what they will of the opening scene where the
Irish-French gang is blocking the mouth of the river but gives way to the demands of the Glengarry gang for free passage of their logs. They can, if they
wish, read significance into LeNoir, the French-Canadians' leader, who moves
from murderous hostility to outright co-operation with Macdonald. Connor's own
emphasis is on western expansion as absorptive of all energies, a cure for all
enmities. The imperial theme of the dominion fills his imagination, transcendence
enters as his solution, and "Glengarry forever!" becomes more than a cry to rally
a clan: it is the talisman, all suggestive and all sufficient, of Connor's sense of
greatness.

(1967)

WESTERN PANORAMA

Settings and themes
in Robert J.C. Stead

A. T. Elder

THOUGH THE NOVELS of Robert J. C. Stead have received some notice from the historians of Canadian literature, especially in Edward Mc-Court's *The Canadian West in Fiction*, no study has yet examined the entire range of Stead's novels on Western themes. Yet the full import of these novels is best revealed by considering them as parts of a single body of writing on the West. Considered individually, they seem chiefly remarkable for their flaws; considered in toto, with special attention to their settings and themes, they reveal a breadth of achievement not obvious in the single novels and a seriousness of purpose often obscured by the too-favourable view of the prairie environment, the occasionally weak characterization of major figures, and the runaway plots of the individual novels.

Stead's difficulty with plots is nowhere more evident than in his first novel, *The Bail Jumper*. Ray Burton, a store clerk unjustly accused of robbing a safe to which only he and his employer, Mr. Gardiner, have keys, has to contend not only with Gardiner, who is secretly trying to ruin him, but also with an obvious villain, Hiram Riles, a miserly bad-tempered farmer, and with two private detectives — one a female — who are searching for the missing money. If this had been Stead's only novel, it would scarcely warrant a second look. As the first of seven, it merits some attention, especially since it takes place in Plainville, Manitoba, and the Alberta foothills, the principal settings of the later novels, and suggests most of Stead's major themes.

Plainville is not specifically located in *The Bail Jumper*, but in *The Homesteaders* is placed east of Turtle Mountain, the approximate location of Cartwright, Manitoba, to which Stead, at the age of two, travelled with his family in 1882, the year in which the settling of the Plainville area begins in *The Homesteaders*. In this second novel, published in 1916, two years after *The Bail*

26

Jumper, we find references to some of the characters who appear in the first, including John Burton, the father of the hero of *The Bail Jumper*, and meet again the two villains of the earlier novel, Hiram Riles and Mr. Gardiner, who are also the villains of the second. Stead's last two novels, *The Smoking Flax* (1924) and *Grain* (1926), are also laid in the Plainville area, largely during and following the first World War. There is much more overlapping of characters and plots in this second pair of novels, but little connection with the early books, though, as reference is made to Sempter and Burton's general store, there is a slight link with Ray Burton in *The Bail Jumper*, who, in that novel's conclusion, agrees to manage the store owned by Mr. Sempter. Stead's other favourite setting, the foothills of Alberta, appears in the latter part of *The Homesteaders* and in *The Cowpuncher* and *Dennison Grant*, as well as in *The Bail Jumper*.

One can only begin to suggest the detail with which Stead presents his history of Plainville. Its beginnings are seen in *The Homesteaders* in the account of Harris's trek northward by sleigh from Emerson in 1882, his selection of a quarter-section and building of a sod hut, and the early development of the area as more settlers appear. The account to this point emphasizes the co-operation of the new community in the face of hardships. The changed attitude of the farmers as they achieve prosperity is the main theme of *The Homesteaders*; to present it, Stead, having barely established his settlers, skips twenty-five years to 1907. And, since the desire for new land and greater wealth leads John Harris westward and away from Plainville, we must turn for a fuller account of the community in these years to the story of Gander's growing up in *Grain*. Gander is born and raised in the house of poplar logs built by his father, Jackson Stake. At the age of five he goes to the country school, "a room of four walls and a ceiling, with a door in the east, windows in the north, and blackboards above the wainscoting on the west and south", where he learns to play Pom, Pom, Pullaway and "Drowndin' Out Gophers", and absorbs as little as possible of learning. Gander's real interest is in farming, so that by the time he is ten he is driving a two-horse team on a mower, not long after, a four-horse team on a binder, and soon is aspiring to operate a steam thresher.

The coming of war to Plainville is described in *Grain*. In 1914, when Gander is eighteen, his father finally builds the house he has been promising his wife for so many years.

> First a carpet, which cost him eleven dollars...; then...a parlor suite with birch mahogany arms and brightly patterned upholstery and crimson furbelows that hung close to the carpet, and a rocking chair with springs that squeaked...;

then a polished oak centre table on legs as spindly as those of a young calf, on which to set photographs and Minnie's copy of "Songs of a Sourdough" ....

This year also brings the telephone and the automobile, "that cost two cents a mile for gasoline an' the rest o' your bank roll for incidentals". Stirring as these events are, they are soon accepted in the excitement of the approaching war. On the day of its outbreak Gander and Jackson Stake drive to Plainville, to find its streets "lined with buggies and motor cars; the livery stables full; every hitching post occupied". Even the Stakes, both unused to displaying emotion, are smitten with war-fever and cheer a gang of youths parading an effigy of the Kaiser into the Roseland Emporium to demand a sauerkraut cocktail. While the Germans are forcing their way across the Yser, Gander takes over the operation of Bill Powers's steam thresher, throttling the forces impelling him to war by working fourteen hours a day on the farm. Though touched occasionally by the war on his infrequent trips to Plainville, he is more interested in the new forms of power than in world events, hanging about the grain elevators, fascinated by their gasoline engines. That year Jackson Stake buys his first Ford car, which prosperity replaces with a Dodge. *Grain* concentrates on the effect of the first World War on Gander, but we see as well its impact on the whole community: the recruiting of men, the news of the first casualties, the rise in the price of wheat, the efforts — not for money — to grow more grain, the end of the war, and the return of the veterans.

Grain pays little attention to the rural life of Manitoba following the war, but this part of Plainville's history is filled out in *The Smoking Flax*. Some elements in the picture are unchanged: the school Cal Beach's adopted son Reed attends is that to which Gander went, and the upholstered chair in Jackson Stake's parlour is the same that added glory to the new house in *Grain*; but many changes are evident. Plainville itself, with its double row of cars on Main Street, has changed greatly from the settlement that Ray Burton knew. It is still a makeshift community, but one with a growing social sense: "To the first generation of pioneers the farm-hand is preferred above the bank clerk; to the second, the bank clerk is preferred, a little, above the farm-hand; in the third, collars and cuffs are in the saddle."

There Plainville is left at the pinnacle of its pre-World-War-II development. We see that no strict chronological sequence is followed in the novels; indeed, there is much leaping about in and overlapping of time. Obviously, then, Stead did not intend a connected history of more than forty years in the life of a Manitoba farming community or a saga of the people of that community. Rather, having created the setting in his first novel, he retained it as a convenience and provided only the slenderest links between the early and later pairs of novels. Nevertheless, though Stead's interest in the development of Plainville is only incidental to the telling of his stories, these four novels give a rather complete picture of the growth of a Manitoba farming community up to and following World War I.

T HAT STEAD could have dealt with Plainville in the stagnant thirties is doubtful, for he gloried in expansion. He had found another scene of rapid development in the foothill country of Alberta. Again we are introduced to this setting in *The Bail Jumper*, as Burton flees from Plainville to escape punishment for the crime he has not committed. He eventually reaches the open ranges of the foothills where, hired to raise grain in ranch country, he is conscious of and sympathetic to the cowboys' conviction of their superiority to him:

> He envied them their wild free life, their rides over the limitless plains, their "leave and liking to shout," while he sharpened the binder knives and tacked new slats on the canvases, and made fly-blankets for the horses out of twine sacks.

Attracted as Stead is by the free life of the range — its spell is acknowledged in the openings of *The Cowpuncher* and *Dennison Grant* as well as in *The Bail Jumper* — he is more thrilled by the prospect of a settled and developed country. That he would prefer an orderly development is obvious from his description of the western boom in *The Cowpuncher*:

> The thing grew upon itself. It was like a fire starting slowly in the still prairie grass, which by its own heat creates a breeze that in turn gives birth to a gale that whips it forth in uncontrollable fury. Houses went up, blocks of them, streets of them, miles of them, but they could not keep pace with the demand, for every builder of a house must have a roof to sleep under. And there were streets to build; streets to grade and fill and pave; ditches to dig and sidewalks to lay and wires to string. And more houses had to be built for the men who paved streets and dug ditches and laid sidewalks and strung wires. And more stores and more hotels and more churches and more schools and more places of amusement were needed. And the fire fed on its own fury and spread to lengths undreamed by those who first set the match to the dry grass.

Not content to present the mere physical evidence of the West's explosive growth, Stead is also interested in the psychological effects of the boom. John Harris, in *The Homesteaders*, is a conservative all his life, but in the heady at-

29

mosphere of Alberta, "where the successful man was the man who dared to throw discretion to the winds and take the chance", he eagerly surrenders to the gambling spirit of the new land. He is not alone in his consequent sufferings. Dave Elden, in *The Cowpuncher*, a man of some principles who has risen from cowboy to millionaire real estate promoter, finds himself involved in "the thing" and helpless to extricate himself or his victims. Yet, in these accounts of an empty land filling with settlers, of cow towns exploding into cities, Stead finds satisfaction in the many who are not mere speculators. Ray Burton, viewing an orderly crowd assembled to file on homesteads that will be open for entry in two days' time, finds men "gathered from the corners of the globe and waiting patiently through night and day, through heat and cold, through wind and rain, through any trial and any hazard for the God-sent privilege, born of a new country, of calling the land beneath their feet their own". These hopeful settlers, whose household goods and effects were piled in great heaps in the railroad yards, represented the real promise of the West to come.

A major interest in Stead's novels, then, is their account of the West's development in the years between 1882 and the middle twenties. The novels laid in the foothills cover a shorter interval than the four Plainville novels, but they concentrate on the exciting period of the boom preceding the first World War — the years, incidentally, when Stead was living in High River and Calgary. The remaining novel, *Neighbours* (1922), laid in Saskatchewan north of Regina just after the beginning of the century, describes the efforts of two Eastern couples to establish themselves on homesteads, and serves to amplify the account of the settlers in the opening chapters of *The Homesteaders*.

Although Stead has been praised by all his critics for his realism, a reading of his seven novels proves that it is a limited realism. The details are accurate, but carefully selected, and despite occasional references to the hardship of life on the prairies, the privations of the settlers are submerged in a generally buoyant tone:

> It was a life of hard, persistent work — of loneliness, privation, and hardship. But it was also a life of courage, of health, of resourcefulness, of a wild, exhilarating freedom found only in God's open spaces.

Neighbours, to take an extreme example, presents a Saskatchewan prairie almost devoid of wind, dust, drought, hail, grasshoppers, mosquitoes, blazing heat and freezing cold, yet this is the book in which the idyllic strain which runs throughout the novels finds its most lyrical expression.

My earliest recollection links back to a grey stone house by a road entering a little Ontario town. Across the road was a mill-pond, and across the mill-pond was a mill. . . . Beside the mill was a water-wheel, . . . which, on sunshiny days, sprayed a mist of jewels into the river beneath with the prodigality of a fairy prince.

My father['s] . . . days were full of the labor of the mill, but his evenings and the early, sun-bright summer mornings belonged to his tiny farm at the border of the town. We had two cows, a pig or two, some apple and cherry trees, and little fields of corn and clover.

These opening words of the narrator, Frank Hall, in *Neighbours*, set the tone maintained throughout the novel as Frank with his sister, Marjorie, and Jack Lane with his sister, Jean, locate their homesteads, sharing a treed coulee watered by a running stream; turn the first sod on the boundless prairie, and work out their obvious destinies under the equally boundless sky. Jean becomes a prairie Lucy, whose idealism contrasts with the practicality of Marjorie, who recognizes from the outset the necessity of marriage between the pairs of brother and sister. Stead achieves a triumph in his handling of the relations between the two couples in love living in isolation in neighbouring shacks on the Saskatchewan prairie; the reader is left convinced that the couples are as innocent in their thoughts as Keats's Madeline. The plot, chiefly concerned with the difficulties preventing the marriage of Frank and Jean, reaches its conclusion as Jean emerges from the prairie pool, clad in a bathing suit, to accept her lover. The level prairie, unrolling to the horizon on all sides of the lonely shacks, supplies the isolation necessary to the idyll.

The idyllic note so evident in *Neighbours* is associated in the other novels with characters either close to nature or living in the simple economy of the pioneer settler or rancher. It touches the description of ranch life in *The Cowpuncher* and *Dennison Grant* and appears also in the account of the early settling of the Harrises in the Plainville area and Beulah Harris's retreat to the Arthur's ranch in *The Homesteaders*. It appears, too, in the carefree, roving life of Cal Beach and his sister's son in *The Smoking Flax* and in the lakeside retreat to which Cal retires to write articles on sociology after his marriage to Minnie Stake. It is present as well in *The Bail Jumper* in Burton's flight to the McKay ranch.

Although Stead views with evident nostalgia the arduous but uncomplicated life of the pioneer, he is interested as well in the stresses that develop in the set-tler's life when his days are no longer filled by necessary labour and when he be-comes more dependent on the services of others. The appearance of these stresses accompanies a thread of social criticism which runs through Stead's novels. In

The Bail Jumper, it is limited to passing comment on the sharp practices of merchants and their equally resourceful customers, on the advantages taken of farmers by grain companies, on the weaknesses of the law, and on the timidity of churches faced with a question of conscience. It is more central to *The Homesteaders* and *The Cowpuncher* as Stead attacks man's greed in his treatment of the Western boom. It is very prominent in *Dennison Grant*, involving an exposition of unorthodox economic doctrine, but in the later novels the evils of society are seen from a sociological rather than an economic point of view.

Stead's concern about these evils is first clearly revealed in a minor theme of *The Homesteaders* that explores the discontent of women on the farm. Mary Harris, willing to labour long hours to establish the farm, finds that even after she and her husband have become prosperous life remains for her a wearing grind. She complains to her daughter, Beulah:

> Here I've slaved and saved until I'm an — an old woman, and what better are we for it? We've better things to eat and more things to wear and a bigger house to keep clean, and your father thinks we ought to be satisfied. But he isn't satisfied himself. . . . He knows our life isn't complete, and he thinks more money will complete it. All the experience of twenty years hasn't taught him any better.

Mrs. Stake, in *Grain*, does not get her long-promised new house until she is about forty-five — "and farmers' wives are sometimes old at forty-five" — and even then, after Minnie has left her to attend high school and business college, she carries on alone her multitudinous duties. Only an outsider, Cal Beach, a graduate in sociology, realizes her crushing burden and sets out to help her by using gasoline power to run the cream separator and the washing machine and to pump water.

Cal Beach becomes concerned as well about the problems of the farm labourer and of children leaving the farm. Earlier, in *The Homesteaders*, Stead lays the blame for the exodus from the farm in part on the farmer himself, who desires "something better" for his children.

> It is a peculiarity of the agriculturist that, among all professions, he holds his own in the worst repute. As a class he has educated himself to believe that everybody else makes an easy living off the farmer, and, much as he may revile the present generation for doing so, he is anxious that his children should join the good picking.

The problem of the farmer's son is treated both in *The Smoking Flax* and *Grain,* largely through Jackson Stake Jr., who leaves because his father refuses to agree that his son, as much as the hired man, is entitled to a wage. The problem of the farm labourer is faced by Cal Beach when he wishes to marry Minnie Stake and realizes that though he is working hard and earning what is called "good wages" he cannot afford to marry.

The problems of the farmer's son and the hired man are at least in part economic, but the farm wife faces a broader problem that concerns Stead in almost all his novels: the need in farm life for an expanded horizon.

As with most of Stead's themes, we first encounter this, somewhat crudely expressed, in *The Bail Jumper*. It appears in the opening chapter as Ray Burton, at the supper break in the square dance, recites "The Nautilus", to which only Myrtle Vane, a cultured Eastern visitor, responds. Myrtle Vane is an apostle of broader horizons; her text, the masterpieces of English literature; her principal convert, the Barnardo boy. To him, after exposure to her influence, "there were greater things in life than cows, and gardens, and fields of wheat; and in a dim way these things of which he had not so much as guessed were opening to his astonished vision."

Myrtle Vane is only the first of a number of cultured Easterners who help to raise the eyes of Westerners beyond the boundaries of their farms. However, the Western women are more conscious than the men of the need for something in life beyond acres and barns. Beulah Harris, in *The Homesteaders*, frequently feels a gap in her existence: "She was not unhappy, but a dull sense of loss oppressed her — a sense that the world was very rich and very beautiful, and that she was feasting neither on its richness nor its beauty." This sense of a defect in farm life is shared by Jean Lane in *Neighbours* and Minnie Stake in *The Smoking Flax*. Jean's need to have something beyond farm life is an integral part of the plot as her search leads her to imagine herself in love with Spoof, the remittance man, and to refuse to marry her lover from childhood, Frank Hall, until he remedies his defects. Not until Jean refuses him, however, does Frank turn to Byron, Gibbon, Shakespeare, Whitman, Burke, and Burns:

> At first I had to drive myself to it, but presently I began to be carried away in the spirit in the new world which was opening before me. With joy I noted, suddenly, that I had forced my boundaries far beyond the corner stakes of Fourteen, beyond even the prairies, the continent, the times in which we live. My mind, from sluggishly hibernating for the winter, became a dynamo of activity. . . . I was so filled with thoughts that I threatened to burst.

Though Jean is at first suspicious of Frank's demonstrations of his new breadth of outlook, as the reader may well be, she is finally satisfied. Minnie Stake, more fortunate than Jean, falls in love with Cal Beach who recognizes the farmers' lack of vision. Minnie does not, however, share his hope of bringing about a permanent change in the Western way of life: "They haven't a glimpse, and so they're content. I had a glimpse, and it drove me from the farm. You have a glimpse, and it's making you do wonderful things — . . . if only they'd last!" Beach's purpose is nothing less than to "bring order into the chaos of farm labor, . . . [to] touch with one glimpse of beauty the sordidness which was expressed by 'forty dollars a month and found', . . . [to] awaken to spiritual consciousness the physical life of which the Stake farmstead was typical. . . ."

Stead's belief in the farmer's need for an expanded horizon helps to account for the end of *Grain*, which Professor McCourt is unable to accept. Gander's decision to go East may not be consistent with his character as it is presented up to this point, but his awakening to the need for a broader life is something that Stead believes ought to come to every Western farmer. Indeed, the ending is not so inconsistent as it seems at first glance, since Gander's second love, next to farming, is machines. More difficult to explain, is the interest taken by Jerry Chansley, the Eastern girl, in making Gander's escape possible. Jerry, in fact, remains little more than a mouthpiece for Stead's ideas: "That is what you lack here, Gander. You don't see enough people. New people give you new ideas, and make life more worth living. . . . They draw you out." Her effect upon Gander, prior to this speech, has been precisely of the kind she has described, though not precisely in a way that she would welcome, since Gander has been busily imagining how he would rescue her if the car turned over.

The little we learn of Jerry Chansley suggests that if Stead had developed her character she would have turned out to hold unconventional, but by no means loose, opinions. It is Polly Lester, the girl detective in *The Bail Jumper*, who suggests the basic attitude of Stead's heroines: ". . . I am not a woman as other women are. I defy traditions; I defy conventions. I claim the right God gave me to live my life as I will, where I will, how I will, with whom I will." Though Stead's heroines usually observe the moral conventions, Zen Transley in *Dennison Grant* is willing to break with them to the extent of taking up her romance with Grant after she is married. The others do not go so far. Beulah Harris, the runaway daughter in *The Homesteaders*, quits her family to seek freedom with the Arthurs family in the foothills. Minnie Stake, in *The Smoking Flax* and *Grain*, insists on staying alone with Cal Beach on a Saskatchewan homestead while she nurses Reed Beach, who is ill with typhoid. Reenie Hardy, a refined Eastern girl in *The Cowpuncher*, finds on the Elden ranch a world where "conventions had been swept away, and it was correct to live, and to live!" On returning East, she disposes of her mother's choice of suitor in an unusual way. Having gone with him to the theatre, she returns with dishevelled hair and flushed cheeks to walk unsteadily across her mother's room. When her mother anxiously inquires if she is ill, Irene replies that she is drunk and angrily rejects the soothing suggestion that she has only had too much champagne:

> Mother! I have had too much champagne, but not as much as the precious Carlton of yours had planned for. I just wanted to see how despicable he was, and I floated down the stream with him as far as I dared. But just as the current got too swift I struck for shore. Oh, we made a scene, all right, but nobody knew me there, so the family name is safe, and you can rest in peace. I called a taxi and when he tried to follow me in I slapped him and kicked him. Kicked him, mother. Dreadfully undignified, wasn't it? . . . And that's what you want me to marry, in place of a man!

Though Stead's heroines often express themselves melodramatically, one ought not to ignore their "thrust for freedom".

It IS A PARADOX in Stead's novels that the Easterners who seek so earnestly to open the minds of Westerners are contemptuous of the conventions of the East that has produced them, and all find in the West a freedom that attracts them. Dennison Grant is foremost among these refugees from the staid East, and the book in which he appears provides the largest gallery of unconventional people. Zen Transley is only one of these, for Phyllis Bruce, Grant's secretary in the East, in her first conversation with her new employer, immediately wins his respect with a statement that marks her as the Stella to his Swift:

> The position I want to make clear is this: I don't admit that because I work for you I belong to a lower order of the human family. . . , and . . . that, aside from the giving of faithful service, I am under any obligation to you. I give you my labor, worth so much; you pay me; we're square. If we can accept that as an understanding I'm ready to begin work now; if not, I'm going out to look for another job.

Grant himself, upon his return to the West after the war, is "happy in his escape from the tragic routine of being decently civilized. . . ." His primary function in the novel is to expound his economic doctrines, which he does to Zen — as Professor McCourt complains — even under the blaze of a full moon on the open prairie after he has rescued her from death in a prairie fire. He then explains why he had left his father's prosperous firm, founded on the profits of a lucky investment in land, to come West:

> I told him that I didn't believe that any man had a right to money unless he earned it in return for service given to society, and I said that as society had to supply the money, society should determine the amount. I confessed that I was a little hazy about how that was to be carried out, but I insisted that the principle was right.

Notwithstanding his view of wealth, when his father and brother are killed in an accident, Grant accepts the duty of returning East to carry on the family business until with the outbreak of war he winds up the concern in order to fight. In spite of the emotional scene in which Grant informs his staff of his intentions, painful reading for one acquainted with the aftermath of the war, his actions and words are in keeping with his character and beliefs. Upon returning to find that his riches have increased in the interval, he determines to put the money to work in a utopian scheme for settling returned soldiers on the land. Grant summarizes his "Big Idea" in this way:

> I propose to form a company and buy a large block of land, cut it up into farms, build houses and community centres, and put returned men and their families on these farms, under the direction of specialists in agriculture. I shall break up the rectangular survey of the West for something with humanizing possibilities; I mean to supplant it with a system of survey which will permit of settlement in groups...where I shall instal all the modern conveniences of the city....Our statesmen are never done lamenting that population continues to flow from the country to the city, but the only way to stop that flow is to make the country the more attractive of the two.

Though Professor McCourt objects to the mixture of "social doctrine with romantic adventure" in *Dennison Grant*, it is the social doctrine, along with Grant's unconventionality, that makes the book something better than popular romance. The weakness lies less in the mixture than in Stead's failure to make Grant a convincing figure and to make the economic theme intrinsic to the plot. Grant's speeches are invariably stodgy, and he is at times merely eccentric, as when with rough lumber he converts the living room of his city apartment in the East into a replica of the interior of his ranchland shack. However, those who object to *Dennison Grant* may read a version called *Zen of the Y.D.*, published in England by Hodder and Stoughton, from which all economic theory and eccentricity have been cut. This version, by manipulation of the plot, makes

36

possible the marriage of Grant and Zen Transley. The changed ending provides a more satisfactory tying up of events in the novel, but I am convinced that anyone who reads the two versions will prefer the uncut, for the second is popular romance and nothing more.

The outcome of the plot of *Dennison Grant* is determined not by Grant's unorthodox economic theories but by a moral principle that could be basic to Grant's thinking in economics, though this connection is not made by the author. Towards the end of the novel, when Grant and Zen Transley are on the verge of destroying her marriage, Zen leaves her son with Grant for the night while she sees her husband off on a trip. When a tremendous thunderstorm sweeps out of the mountains and the boy wakes, Grant soothes him and, comforting the boy, recognizes the wrongness of his intention of destroying Zen's marriage and the necessity of renouncing her for the boy's sake. Soon after Grant has made this decision, Zen arrives, having driven through the storm from town, to announce that she had reached the same conclusion.

This theme of self-sacrifice receives its most elaborate development in the preceding novel, *The Cowpuncher*. Lack of space forbids a full explanation of its working out in the novel, but Elden, in the course of events, is persuaded that forgiveness and service should be part of his creed. His service takes the form of serving his country, and his dying words, uttered in Flanders, reflect both his earlier belief that the innocent always suffer and his later that one must be ready to sacrifice oneself:

> ...I said it was the innocent thing that got caught. Perhaps I was right. But perhaps it's best to get caught. Not for the getting caught, but for the — the compensations. It's the innocent men that are getting killed. And perhaps it's best. Perhaps there are compensations worth while.

Stead pursues the same theme in *The Smoking Flax* and *Grain*. In the first of these, it is once more associated with the need for forgiveness implicit in the text from which the title comes: "bruised reed shall he not break, and the smoking flax shall he not quench." In this novel Cal Beach gives up his chance for happiness married to Minnie Stake in order to protect Reed, illegitimate son of his sister and Minnie's elder brother. These events, which appear again in the later novel *Grain*, help to account for Gander's rather improbable decision to go East. When Minnie explains to Gander that Cal ran away to protect Reed, Gander, on the verge of winning the love of Jo Klaus, the wife of an invalid war veteran, perceives that to preserve the honour of the Stake family he too must run away.

37

Thus the working out of this theme in *Grain*, complicated somewhat by the inclusion of events from *The Smoking Flax* that help to lead to his decision, serves to explain in part the otherwise unlikely flight of Gander from the farm.

The reader of any single novel by Stead, with the possible exception of *Grain*, may not perceive through the multiplicity of incident the seriousness of the author's intention. Or, having learned that Stead was a publicity agent for colonization during the years in which his novels were being written, he may conclude that the author, in presenting so favourable a view of Western life, was merely fulfilling his other role in society. Yet such a judgment would be extremely unfair, for though the books were written by a publicity man and seem to have been directed at the popular taste, they are not invariably optimistic. Indeed, they frequently have rather unhappy endings: John Harris in *The Homesteaders* suffers a serious financial loss, Dave Elden dies in battle, Dennison Grant is not allowed to win romantic Zen, and Gander is forced to forego the pursuit of his childhood sweetheart. What is more, the major figures in the novels, whatever the weaknesses in their characterizations, are by no means the conventional heroes and heroines of popular fiction. In addition, though Stead may moderate the physical harshness of the prairie environment, he stresses in all his novels the intellectual dearth in and the aesthetic drabness of prairie life. And, in spite of the limitations already noted, the novels still succeed very well in imparting the atmosphere of the times about which they are written. Above all, however, Stead's themes are usually critical of society and consistently serious.

(1963)

MARTHA OSTENSO'S
TRIAL OF STRENGTH

Clara Thomas

IN 1925, MARTHA OSTENSO won the $13,500 Pictorial Review, Dodd Mead, Famous Players-Lasky prize for her first novel, *Wild Geese*. Her success pre-dated *Jalna*'s winning of the Atlantic Monthly award by two years, in cash terms her award was far larger than Mazo de la Roche's — and *Wild Geese*, in its setting, characters and story was far more authentically "Canadian" than the romance-saga of the Whiteoaks. And yet, neither then, nor in the course of a writing career that stretched through some dozen works over the next twenty-five years, was Miss Ostenso commonly recognized as a "Canadian" writer, nor were her obvious fictional strengths given particular critical consideration in this country. Even in as recent a work as *Butterfly on Rock*, Douglas Jones has not included a reading of *Wild Geese*, though its theme and characters are most strikingly apt to the thesis of his book.

In the United States, however, *Wild Geese* marked Martha Ostenso as a novelist to be treated with critical respect. Stuart Sherman praised her "genuine dramatic imagination", her "power to penetrate to the viscera of very diverse lives", and her "sense of form which has rarely been coupled in American writers of fiction with anything like Miss Ostenso's vital sense for substance".[1]

In 1928, after her third novel, Grant Overton wrote an essay on Martha Ostenso's progress in fiction-writing. He began by congratulating both the author and her publishers for her demonstrated "story-power and staying-power" — "a prize contest is the blindest of adventures. Therefore, it was a very special triumph to uncover Miss Ostenso by means of one — for here, as is now manifest, we have no one-book writer."[2] (Never, in fact, for Canadian work, have the awards of American publishing houses been so triumphantly vindicated as in the decade of the twenties which began the unfaltering Mazo's triumphant procession and the less dazzling, but steady course of Martha Ostenso.)

39

In the same article, Mr. Overton printed the only autobiographical sketch that Martha Ostenso ever wrote, its tone and content the blend of high romance and well-defined detail that characterizes her best fiction.

> Where the long arm of the Hardangerfjord penetrates farthest into the rugged mountains of the coast of Norway, the Ostenso family has lived, in the township that bears its name, since the days of the Vikings ... the land that borders the lonely fjord is still in the family's possession, handed down from eldest son to eldest son.

Martha was born in her mother's village, Haukeland, high up in the mountains of Norway, and soon after, her parents emigrated to America. Her father did not readily find his niche in the new land — or the wanderlust of the Viking ancestors was deep in him — for she calls the story of her childhood "a tale of seven little towns in Minnesota and South Dakota. . . . They should have a story written about them, those seven mean yet glorious little towns of my childhood."[3] In fact, she had begun very early to write stories herself, and at eleven she was a regular and sometimes even a paid contributor to the *Minneapolis Journal*.

The eighth town for Martha Ostenso was Brandon, Manitoba, where her family moved when she was fifteen. She went to high school there, then to the University of Manitoba and finally, in 1921, to Columbia for a one-year course in the technique of the novel. The climax of her autobiographical sketch is a paragraph on the experience of Northern Manitoba that stirred her to write *Wild Geese*.

> It was during a summer vacation from my university work that I went into the lake district of Manitoba, well toward the frontier of that northern civilization. My novel, *Wild Geese,* lay there, waiting to be put into words. Here was the raw material out of which Little Towns were made. Here was human nature, stark, unattired in the convention of a smoother, softer life. A thousand stories are there, still to be written.[4]

Wild Geese was not, however, the first of Martha Ostenso's works to move from that sombre northern vision to its issues in the lives of men and women. In 1924 she had published *The Far Land*, a book of poems, and several of its works pre-figure her strongest fictional themes, the death-in-life of the spirit of man and his terrible isolation.[5] "Wasteland", a description of the northern wilderness, is at first reminiscent of A. J. M. Smith's "The Lonely Land", "broken by strength but still strong".

40

> Here the lichens cling
> To the grey rocks
> Like the faltering
> Ragged locks
> Of an old she-fox. . . .

But Miss Ostenso's emphasis is quite different: there is no figure in Smith's land-scape, while the whole effect of "Wasteland" builds towards the final desolation of its last line — "But his soul is dead."

> Here's a wrinkled grape
> Like a blue knot
> On a thread — the shape
> Of life caught
> In the death rot.
> . . . .
>
> Here a man may own
> His bare soul instead
> Of a beauty-blown
> Rose, t'is said.
> But his soul is dead.

"Wasteland" could, of course, be an epigraph for *Wild Geese* whose Caleb Gare destroys his own humanity and enslaves all his family in service to the land. Martha Ostenso's vision comprehended the physical and psychological demands that a harsh land and a hard life make on men and women. Her imagination did not move toward the heroic, but rather toward the grotesque, an expression of her perception that a situation requiring an enormous effort of will and endurance would often lead, not to an almost super-human being, but to an inhuman one. So it is with Caleb Gare who is monstrous in the distortion of his spirit. He has none of the heroic stature of the early Abe Spalding, a mythic man behind his plough, or of the giant man against the western sky in Henry Kreisel's essay "The Prairie as a State of Mind." Caleb is, rather, diminished — less, not more than human.[6]

> Far out across the prairie a lantern was swinging along the earth, and dimly vis-ible was the squat, top-heavy form of a man. It was Caleb Gare. He walked like a man leaning forward against a strong wind. He frequently went out alone so, with a lantern; no one knew where, nor why; no one asked. Judith had once told Amelia scornfully that it was to assure himself that his land was still all there. . . .

41

Caleb is obsessed with holding and adding to his land, and his children are the means to his end. Amelia, their mother, is the instrument of their enslavement. She is in terror of Caleb and in total submission to his will through her fear of his power to harm Mark Jordan, her illegitimate son. Caleb's obsession pushes him farther and farther from his own humanity; he is a menacing, demonic and tortured figure, blighting all the lives around him and destroying his own. His children are crippled into a death-in-life, except for Judith, who alone has the strength of spirit to fight for her right to live her life. Amelia never loses the reader's sympathy and pity, and this is a tribute to Miss Ostenso's powers of strong and balanced characterization, for Amelia too, becomes grotesquely life-denying. She chooses to sacrifice the real lives of her children, who are all around her, and who, pathetically, bear Caleb's tyranny for her sake, in favour of the dream of the far-away son she does not know.

> Caleb's children could wither and fall like rotten plants after frost — everything could fall into dissolution. He was his father's son, Mark Jordan, the son of the only man she had ever loved. Ellen, Martin, Judith and Charley, they were only the offspring of Caleb Gare, they could be the sacrifice. She would bend and in-ure them to the land like implements, just as Caleb wished her to do. She would not intercede in their behalf hereafter. She would see them dry and fade into fruitlessness and grow old long before their time, but her heart would keep within herself and there would be no pity within her for the destruction of their youth. Amelia's face grew pale and hard as she knelt in the garden. A distinct change had come over her.

In this first novel Martha Ostenso combined her study of obsession and its soul-destroying outcome with the theme of man's loneliness and isolation that she had already set down in another of her early poems, "First Snow".

> Stand still in this strange glimmering
> Enclosure of whiteness.
> There is no living sight nor sound.
> A bodiless lightness
> Are we, without form or motion,
> Buoyant in the soft and slow
> Interlacing, mazing ghost-drift
> Of the frost-clusters of snow.
> . . . .
>
> How solitary each descends!
> Almost, two meet, then one
> With swift preen of crystal pinions
> Glides to faint death alone.

> Draw near to me lest we be two,
> I, alone, and alone, you.

Lind Archer and Mark Jordan, the onlookers to the Gare drama, are constant spokesmen for the theme, and it is present in the recurrent patterning of the wild geese imagery throughout the novel.

> Lind felt humble as she heard the wild geese go over. There was an infinite cold passion in their flight.... She knew in her heart that Mark Jordan was like them — that he stood inevitably alone....
>
> Far overhead in the night sky sounded the honking of the wild geese, going south now ... a remote, trailing shadow ... a magnificent seeking through solitude ... an endless quest....

The strength and validity of Martha Ostenso's perceptions and their imaginative translation into the lives of her characters is unquestionable. When *Wild Geese* fails to satisfy, it is because of the weaknesses of technique which Professor Carlyle King has long since outlined in his introduction to the work.[7] No character, not even Caleb, quite satisfies, because in this first novel, Miss Ostenso could not control all the elements she had introduced. However, in her fourth novel she worked again with the themes of isolation and obsession. She narrowed her focus and by this time, she had greatly strengthened her control over her work. The result is *The Young May Moon* (1929), a novel whose seriousness of theme is more satisfyingly matched by its tightness of structure and total artistic consistency.[8]

In *The Young May Moon*, Miss Ostenso moved to the "little towns" of her autobiographical sketch. The novel is again set in Manitoba.[9] It tells the story of Marcia Vorse (and would be far better titled, *The Ordeal of Marcia Vorse*), who married Rolf Gunther in passionate love, but also to escape her home town of Bethune and the shame of her father's responsibility for his own death and the death of two other men. Living in the smaller town of Amaranth, however, with Rolf's fanatically religious mother (and Dorcas is another Grotesque), and feeling a reserve in Rolf that she cannot understand or tolerate, Marcia rebels and runs away.

> I've lived all winter with ghosts, Rolf. I can't go on with it. Now you must listen to me. I want more and more of life, Rolf — not denial. I must tell you this, dear — I *must!* Can't you see it all for yourself — as I see it? I can't go on living with your mother. I loathe — I loathe her vicious denial of life. Oh, I know she

is a good woman, Rolf, and she *is* your mother — but I'm telling you that I shall loathe her unless you take me away from her. I can't stand her sense of sin any longer — I can't because I never understood it. I never shall understand it.

When she returns in the night, Rolf is not there and in the morning he is found drowned. Marcia stays with Dorcas, partly out of the need for a home for herself and the son she bears some months later. But largely she stays and continues to stay out of guilt, a sense that to stay is her atonement, and also through fear of her guilt being revealed to the town by Paul Brulé, the doctor who knows her secret. Her first move back from passive suffering to active living leads her to defy Dorcas and her gossiping friends.

I'm not surprised that little Hally's mother left. She left because she wasn't strong enough to stay and work while women like you, Laura Prouty — and your mother, here — flayed her with your tongues. She couldn't bear up under it. But I — I wouldn't go, I'll tell you. I'd stay — no matter what I had done — and no matter what you had to say about me. I'd stay until I starved to death rather than give you the satisfaction of thinking you had run me out of town.

She rejects Paul Brulé's efforts to bring her back into life.

I could understand you for despising me for what I did — Rolf was your friend before he knew me. I want you to despise me. I want you to hate me, if you like. But I don't want your pity. You may look after the health of Rolf Gunther's son, but I'll look after my own. If I go mad — well, I'll go mad! . . .

Marcia flung herself toward him, tempestuously. Why should you want to make me over? This is what you wanted me to become, isn't it? This is the atonement you wanted me to suffer, isn't it? Tell them the truth about me. Let's have no more secrets. I am sick of it. Tell the town that I — I killed Rolf Gunther! Tell them! Tell them, too, that I've died a thousand times, over and over — but that I have a life of my own, a precious thing, that none of you can touch. . . . Tell them that — but leave me alone — to myself. . . . I don't ask another thing from any of you.

She confesses to Dorcas her part in Rolf's death, and she goes out with her child, away from the town to a ruined house on a hillside where she engages in another and a different trial of strength. This time she must survive, both psychically and physically alone, and she must also support her child.

Marcia does develop both physical and psychic strength from her isolation, but she comes to know that her "castle on the hill" is also her self-made prison and that she is becoming distorted, a scarecrow-spectacle to the town children and, increasingly, frightening to herself. She is a strongly sensual woman, and what

44

she recognizes and acknowledges as physical desire for a passing gypsy youth both shames and shocks her. She is terrified of degenerating into an inhuman, witch-like woman.

> What had she become, what was she becoming? A rough woman of the land . . . on the outskirts of Bethune, when she was a little girl, there had been such a one. The woman had raised corn and turnips, acres of them, and her prize hogs had had a white band around their shoulders. She had been known for her temper and had lashed about her with a great black-snake whip when she was cross. There had been a story of a man who had stayed with her and had been found up the road in front of her farm, beaten and strangled until he was half dead. The woman had become a name, a legend — old Lottie Tibbets and her pigs!

Marcia's movement throughout the novel, of rejection and return to life, is anticipated and parallelled by Paul Brulé's. He is a doctor, an outsider to Amaranth who has become a wounded onlooker to life because of his obsession with the wife who deserted him. He involves himself in Marcia's problems, first for the sake of the child, Rolf, and then for her own sake. And as he is further along the path towards finding again some meaning in existence, he can and does act, uninvited and unwelcomed, as Marcia's mentor. Both his role and Marcia's are, in the superficial sense, stereotypes of romantic fiction; but Martha Ostenso is engaged in questioning human actions and their implications with unrelenting honesty and her seriousness gives her characters both dignity and depth.

Paul has faced his isolation — and man's — and he forces on Marcia both the bleakness of his view and its requisite acceptance of moral responsibility.

> "I can't tell you how I feel," she told Brulé. He suddenly lost his bantering manner. "That's it, that's it!" he said quickly. "None of us can, because we're alone. So damned alone. Just look at it will you: Here's our little preacher, this Reverend Neering — going about the country, always in a hurry, doing all he can after his own fashion to make this rotten world a decent place to live in. Think of the hours he must have by himself — for after all he isn't a fool — think of those hours when he has to fight like hell against despair — and do it alone — all by himself — on a lonely country road, perhaps, at night? . . . And old Dorcas, lying on her bed, seeing visions — talking to the God she believes in, and hearing him talk to her — talking to her son — think of the solitude of that shrivelled old woman going out alone!
>
> "We fill our lives with ideas — loves, hates, and visions — thinking to make companions of them, so to speak. But something in us always remains separate, nevertheless, unapproachable. You, now — you and your puny stubborn will — you've been deceiving yourself with the belief that all life hangs on this something you call atonement — nothing but an illusion — a companion in your own

peculiar aloneness. There is no such thing. . . . It's nothing but a device by which you shield yourself from the unbearable truth."

"And that is — " Marcia looked down at her hands, lying tightly folded on the table.

"That you have done something irrevocable. Atonement, remorse, repentance, all hokum."

Marcia's third flight, in panic and rejection, is the third and final point of decisive action in the book. Brulé has just told her of seeing his wife again, of testing his own strength and of finding that he had finally freed himself of his destructive obsession, that "it's possible for a man to find his way back — back to the tangle and unravel it." Then he asks Marcia to marry him "for love". This seems an utter incongruity to Marcia in a man who has insisted on her facing life without the veil of romance she used to give it, and also without the armour of pride that she has grown to endure it. She will not allow herself to give in simply to physical desire for Paul Brulé, so "tomorrow she would have to leave Amaranth."

The book could end there and it would be an honest treatment of Marcia's search for meaning in life, her gradual acknowledgment of choice and her acceptance of responsibility for choice. But its final chapter shows Marcia stumbling back along the railway track from Bethune to Amaranth as we saw her at the beginning. Now, however, she has strength in the knowledge and acceptance of her limitations and of life's. She has grown beyond her youthful expectations of romantic love and beyond a puritanical shame at the strength of her physical desire for Paul Brulé. She goes back to the house on the hill with a positive commitment to the acceptance of life's whole fabric.

And now — the void under the bridge was baying again, after six years of silence. No, not again. This was the first time. She was living, not again, but *still*. Time was not something that passed. All eternity was but a single fierce stroke of rapture. Existence was all a weaving to and fro upon the same dim loom. One never escaped that. . . .

In the morning she would go down to the Stormos', and bring little Rolf home to the castle. Before noon old Jonas would wander up to begin cutting the birch from the new hillside acre. Also, there were those new potatoes she had promised to take to Herb Lundy's; she would have to send Jonas down with them in the afternoon. In the evening, Paul Brulé would come once more up the pathway. He had said he would. . . .

She rested her head back against the tree trunk and closed her eyes. A slight wind moved through the thorn apple tree; it moved across darkness and sleep, on and on.

46

Structurally, *The Young May Moon* is very tight, framed by Marcia's first and final flights along the railway tracks between Bethune and Amaranth, and coming to another major climax in the centre of the story, when she flees to the ruined house on the hill above the town. Bethune, the slightly larger town, is no key to a wider world, but simply the only outer point of a constricting environment, within which Marcia must make her journey toward freedom. Miss Ostenso's justice, her artistic judgment, and her affection for the "little towns" of her childhood, all come into play in her depicting of Amaranth, the town in which the action takes place. It is no part of her purpose to shift Marcia's own responsibility for her maturing to the restrictions of the small town or the shoulders of its citizens. She does not romanticize Amaranth's shortcomings, but she does take care to give us a many-faceted view of it. In the beginning, we see it through Marcia's eyes at night and at peace.

> The town slept with the resigned and trustful sleep of the very young and the very old. From the edge of the meadowland that bordered it on one side, Marcia could look down and see the two rows of lights, like a thinly-studded cross, that marked the only two paved streets in Amaranth.
>
> There was the meadowland to traverse now, before she could reach the slim white Lutheran Church, with its six lean box-elder trees, standing there so serenely at the edge of the town. . . .
>
> It was ironical, she reflected, that she should have chosen a route home that would oblige her to pass two churches, the Lutheran, with its bleak little graveyard where the first pioneers, Germans and Scandinavians, slept; and the Baptist, Dorcas Gunther's church, with its grey stone tower. She had to pass the house of Hector Aldous, too, the town banker, who owned half of Amaranth — and every one of its few hundred souls. The dew-saturated blooms of lilacs leaned from the Aldous hedge and touched her face; if they had only known, she thought, they would have drawn back from her as she passed. On the Aldous lawn the spiraea bushes were white; the lawn itself, terraced and green, was smooth as the coil of a great wave.

And later, in the grip of fear and guilt, Marcia still can hear the church bells of Amaranth as a call of the spirit.

> In thin melancholy, its notes separate and pure as the beads of a rosary, as the words of an old song, as the tears of a familiar sorrow, came the angelus from the southern dwindling of the little town. As the last note failed and merged into the twilight sky of September that pierced the heart with it intimations, three chimes sounded from the northward, from the belfry of the Lutheran Church there. Three high and fragile echoes they were, faltering into the notes of the first bell like a frail hand laid within a dying.

47

Years ago, scrupulous Lutherans of Amaranth had protested against the introduction of this custom, scenting popery. But the two old men of God, fast friends
for years, never known to have discussed their doctrinal differences together, had
continued to ring out every evening upon the town their tranquil benediction,
and reassurance of each to the other that life was good.

In her "castle" on the hill, as she begins to recognize and fear the disturbing
effects of her self-exile, Marcia acknowledges Amaranth as, simply, a microcosm
of the social world she must learn to live in.

Running from Amaranth and Laura Prouty and Dorcas Gunther and Paul Brulé
— that was running from life. They *were* life. Another town, perhaps ... but
there would always be the Laura Proutys and the Dorcas Gunthers and the Paul
Brulés. There would always be the fight against hate and jealousy and mean-
ness — and love.

Finally, as she stumbles back to Amaranth the town is again absolved of blame.

Amaranth lay before her now, pathetic and small and helpless in its slumber in
this cradle of the earth. How fantastic it all was. A little, anxious, decorous town,
clinging like a cluster of barnacles on the surface of a globe in space.

The Young May Moon is far from flawless — its lushness of language fits well
enough the intensity of Marcia Vorse, but also diffuses the force of her recogni-
tions and of the reader's. However, Marcia's strength and her perceptions, honestly arrived at and convincing in their psychological truth, cannot be doubted.
In his introduction to *Wild Geese*, Professor King remarked upon the absence of
literary precedents for Martha Ostenso's particular strengths and insights in the
American or Canadian fiction of her time. It may well be that her imagination
was caught by Sherwood Anderson's "Book of the Grotesque", Chapter 1 of
Winesburg, Ohio (1919).

It was the truths that made the people grotesque. The old man had quite an
elaborate theory concerning the matter. It was his notion that the moment one
of the people took one of the truths to himself, called it his truth and tried to
live by it, he became a grotesque and the truth he embraced became a falsehood.

But it also seems highly likely that Miss Ostenso's true North American mentor
was Nathaniel Hawthorne. *Wild Geese* and *The Young May Moon* are built on
a foundation of intense moral consciousness and questioning that no technical
flaws can demolish, and both of them make a bond through time with *The
Scarlet Letter*. Roger Chillingworth is a great realization of the Grotesque in
North American literature, a death-in-life man, monstrously distorted in the grip

of his obsession — and Caleb Gare is recognizably of his tribe. And the ordeal of Marcia Vorse, her path away from life and back to acceptance of it, is at many points parallel to the ordeal of Hester Prynne.

The cumulative effect in each of these novels is a testimony to affirmative living that is essentially existentialism in its most positive form, though Miss Ostenso would certainly not have been aware of the term, nor of the corroboration her convictions would ultimately assemble in philosophy and literature. As Marcia Vorse sits by Dorcas Gunther's death-bed, the old lady "forgives" according to the conventions of her faith.

> "But I could not go — without telling you — that you have my forgiveness for what you did — to me — and mine. May God have mercy on you."
>
> The voice paused once more and in that moment of silence the heartless humor of life revealed itself in Marcia's mind. She struggled against the acceptance of it, fought against the stupid compromise that insulted both intelligence and emotion. All her sensibilities shrank from this picture of an old woman who had lived without charity and now, confronted with death, coddled about her still all the strange shibboleths of her literal creed.

In the year 1929 a writer on this continent who assaulted the trappings of orthodoxy as "the stupid compromise that insulted both intelligence and emotion" was unlikely to be encouraged to pursue her moral questionings; in fact, the seriousness of Martha Ostenso's themes was largely lost on reviewers and readers who only expected, and only found, decorously passionate love stories in her novels.

After 1929, Miss Ostenso never returned to the power or the honesty of vision she demonstrated in *Wild Geese* and *The Young May Moon*. She moved to the Hudson River Palisades in New Jersey, too far away from Northern Manitoba where she had seen material for "a thousand stories" to retain her stark vision of it. Besides, her reading public rewarded her for romances, stories like *The Mad Carews* (1928), vivid in characterization and fast in plot, but essentially dynastic westerns where the regenerative power of a strong, good woman always, finally, harnessed and mellowed the incorrigibly boyish anarchisms of the frontier male.

Ironically, Martha Ostenso had already recognized the trend of her talents before she had published any novels at all; the poem "So I Say" in the 1924 collection prefigures the choice that she eventually made.

> Down into the unrevealed lands
> Of my long-cherished sorrow

Shall I unfaltering go.
Well I know the way: On either hand
Unvoiced and still of wing,
Snared in nets of shade,
Birds of ecstasy complain and fade.

Down such caverns shall I go
That, returning, none will know
The witch-pale face, the lips of me
Sealed and cold as the frost-bound leaf
Of the wintery wormwood tree,
Sealed in a song of toneless grief.

So I say. And yet I sing
To a fairy harp, and faintly hear
The sunlit hoofs, a-dancing near,
And like the foam-thin seashell dare
Not tell the truer, darker thing,
Nor whisper of it anywhere.

(1973)

NOTES

[1] Grant Overton, *The Women Who Make Our Novels* (N.Y.: Essay Index Reprint Series, 1967), p. 252. First published 1928.

[2] Overton, pp. 245-6.

[3] Overton, pp. 246-7.

[4] Overton, p. 248.

[5] Martha Ostenso, *A Far Land* (N.Y.: Thomas Seltzer, 1924).

[6] Wolfgang Kayser, *The Grotesque in Art and Literature* (N.Y.: McGraw Hill, 1966). *cf* "The Grotesque in the Nineteenth Century," pp. 100-129.

[7] Carlyle King, Introduction to *Wild Geese*, New Canadian Library (Toronto: McClelland and Stewart, 1961).

[8] Martha Ostenso, *The Young May Moon* (New York: Dodd Mead, 1929).

[9] The town, Amaranth, in a small valley with a college, suggests Brandon. Its neighbour, Bethune, could be Portage La Prairie. However, Amaranth is set on the Vermilion River and this suggests Dauphin in Northern Manitoba, the area where *Wild Geese* was set. The setting is, then, a composite, but certainly Manitoban, the only novel after *Wild Geese* to be so.

FREDERICK PHILIP GROVE

An Impression

W. B. Holliday

ONE DAY IN THE FALL of 1939 I was wandering among the book stacks in Eaton's Toronto store. A novel, *Two Generations*, by Frederick Philip Grove, caught my eye. Grove's picture was on the dust cover with a brief account of his life. I noted that he owned a farm near Simcoe. The photograph was of a thoughtful man in his forties wearing a high, old-fashioned collar. He was looking away from the photographer with a detached expression. In his eyes a certain kindliness and modesty seemed to mingle with a suggestion of tragedy. He appeared to be somehow vulnerable, approachable. I decided to write to him and ask for work on his farm. I had literary ambitions.

He replied to my letter four days later. He acknowledged that he owned a farm, but a tenant worked it. "Still," he wrote, "if you were here, I might, in the long run, be able to do something for you. We have, for a year or so, had a young man in the house to act as a sort of janitor in return for his board; and we have not yet filled the position for this winter. We conduct a private school here...." He named a meeting-place in Brantford which he would be visiting a few days hence.

His tone was cordial but I had misgivings and I allowed the day of the suggested meeting to pass. The following week-end I took the bus to Simcoe and walked the mile from the town to Grove's house. He was in his garden kneeling among the vegetables. He looked up from his weeding. I identified myself. "Oh, yes," he said without surprise. "I thought you'd changed your mind." He pointed out that he would be unable to pay me. I expressed indifference to money. He said nothing.

I studied him closely. His head was massive and well-shaped; I noticed particularly the impressive distance from the top of his head to his ears. His sandy, cropped hair gave him a youthful appearance and I judged him to be in his fifties. (I learned later that he was sixty-seven.) The day was raw and a drop of moisture clung to the tip of his long nose. His eyes were pale and framed by heavy pouches. He was polite and receptive, but there was something in his manner which made me wonder if he was indifferent to my presence.

I watched his thick fingers expertly grasp the weeds and pull them from the black soil. But it was disillusioning to see the man whose picture I had observed on the jacket of a novel crouching thus upon the earth and performing such a lowly task. I began to question him about books and authors. He offered his views pleasantly but with authority, even with finality. When he expressed esteem for D. H. Lawrence I was reassured.

Presently we went to the house for tea. Mrs. Grove, a business-like person, questioned me discreetly about my intentions. She seemed faintly incredulous that I was prepared to leave a job in Toronto in order to live with them. Grove, smoking a cigarette in a holder, sat with his long legs crossed, occasionally interjecting a remark.

When the time came for me to catch the bus, Grove rose and shook my hand, looking down at me in a friendly way. "I'd like to come," I said. Both appeared to welcome my words yet plainly they wished the decision to be made solely by me. I returned to Toronto, resigned my office position and within three weeks I was living with the Groves.

Life in the household ran a simple, Spartan course. There were four of us, including Leonard the son. We rose early and by seven-thirty we were at breakfast. Everyone ate oatmeal porridge, soaked overnight. By eight o'clock Grove had sharpened his pencils in a school room and was on his way upstairs to his study. He was typing the final draft of *In Search of Myself* and the rattle of his typewriter was heard until noon. After lunch he returned to his study to read or he worked in the garden; on two afternoons a week he taught French to the dozen or so pupils attending the school. (Teaching the students bored him.) After supper he and I walked together or he spent some time with Leonard; frequently he went to his study and played solitaire while solving the problems his writing posed him; he rarely made social calls though occasionally friends visited the house; he never went to a motion picture. By ten o'clock the house was quiet.

Grove was essentially a European. He was, one critic has stated, the Canadian Thomas Hardy. To him life was complex, full of tortuous depths, hidden motives, inevitable suffering; a struggle against a blind, impersonal fate. One must have patience, endurance; these brought resignation and with resignation might come wisdom. His opposition to Magna Charta — it replaced the tyranny of the king with the tyranny of the masses — together with his admiration for Goethe, the enemy of the French Revolution, baffled me at first; his views seemed perverse, at war with the bland assumptions, the facile optimism of the North American. I concluded that he must have reflected with wonder during his years in Canada upon the strange twist of fortune which had placed him as a youth in an environment so alien to all that was congenial to him.

In 1941 he wrote to me: "You will probably see through the papers . . . that I have been elected a fellow of the Royal Society, the highest honour which can come to a Canadian man of letters; so be sure to put the 'FRSC' behind my name henceforth. It's as good as a title they tell me." Obviously, under the banter, he was deeply touched by the distinction. Nevertheless, apart from a few discerning critics and a small but growing audience, popular acclaim never came to him. He told me that the works of George Meredith met with indifference until the author's death; afterwards Meredith's heirs reaped the rewards of posthumous fame. In cheerfully dismissing the public he ascribed its inattention to distaste for his forthright message. "I am hard at work," he wrote to me in December, 1940, "on another of those novels which I shall never publish; I have half a dozen such on my shelves. If I published them the people of Canada would have *me* stoned or call *them* pornography. You see, publication means nothing. What matters is solely that the work be done, the book be written, the beauty created. The rest of my work counts for little. But I once published the least 'objectionable' of those novels which comprise my real work (*Settlers of the Marsh*) and the libraries barred me; and my friends cut me in the street. So why should I even try to publish. Quite apart from the fact that I can't. But that is no reason for not writing those books, to me." He declared his independence of the reader again in a letter of November, 1941. "Work on a long book makes the rest of life seem irrelevant. What difference does it make whether, from day to day, you are dissatisfied with what you are doing, whether, perhaps, you are almost starving; even whether your book progresses satisfactorily; so long as it either is alive or is coming to life; gestation is not a fast process; it demands time, and you can't hurry it. But when the book is born, it is a miracle to you, like every birth."

Grove's words betrayed a certain gnawing contrariness of which I was to see other examples. On the one hand, he is pleased with the few honours that have come his way — honours, though, which only the appearance of his books could bring him; on the other hand, publication means "nothing". He was contemptuous of politicians, inferring that, in the main, they act out of self interest; yet he showed me, with some satisfaction, a letter he had received from Mackenzie King thanking him for the copy of *Two Generations* Grove had sent him. To my

53

doubts that I was sufficiently independent of public opinion to write as my heart willed he encouraged me: "As far as that normality of which you speak, naturally we are anything but 'normal people'; and we hold those that are a bit in horror; at least I do; my wife certainly to a less extent." He affected to despise cities; they were monuments to a soulless materialism. Yet as an affluent youth astir with dreams of great accomplishments he had moved with ease in the great cities of Europe. I suspected that his professed dislike was based on the knowledge that when among the inhabitants of those places he was unknown, anonymous like themselves; their indifference to him was the measure of his failure as a writer. And he was ready to overturn my pride as a Torontonian in the Canadian National Exhibition by dismissing it briefly in 1941: "The exhibition was a disappointment to everyone of us. We went home about 3 p.m."

From a perspective of twenty years I believe Grove was disappointed that his pen had failed to earn him a decent livelihood. He was a patrician by nature as well as by birth, and wealth would have allowed him to live in style. During my stay he was earning a modest sum as a reader for Macmillan's. His own works were paying him little; he told me with amusement that once he received a royalty cheque amounting to sixty cents.

Yet Grove would have spurned the suggestion that he debase his talent for money although, on one occasion, when his wife needed a refrigerator, he wrote a pot boiler to get it. But this deliberate act must have been a rare perversion of his muse, for deep within him burned a constant flame that was his integrity. He knew what he had to say and he knew the only way in which he could in all honesty say it. As an impressionable youth I found this almost stubborn probity an impressive and exhilarating influence. Doubtless never very far from Grove's thoughts were his models, the great writers of the past, and I believe that their example was supported ultimately by a strong belief in his own worth as a novelist of importance.

I have listened with Grove to the Ninth Symphony, observing how Beethoven's hammer blows seemed to parallel his own searching views on the human condition. And watching him studying a folio of the frescoes in the Sistine Chapel, I have marked his love for the eternally beautiful. But it was Grove's opinions as a writer that I wished to know. And he gave his views willingly. *War and Peace* was the greatest novel ever written; *Anna Karenina* was next in importance. When I surmised that Galsworthy had little sympathy for Irene Forsyte, he said: "You must have read the book with little understanding; he pleads her cause on every page." He denied that Dickens was merely a caricaturist; he was a "great psychologist", a novelist with few peers; "he is underrated just now." Grove appeared to have little interest in American writers, though he admired Thoreau deeply, possibly because of Thoreau's rejection of the superfluous in life. Several times during my stay he repeated with thoughtful amusement Thoreau's dictum that it is wise to avoid the beginnings of evil. He said: "A novel is essentially the road pursued from an idea to an act that bears it out." He told me that once, during a short illness, he had read the complete works of Shakespeare. He referred to Stefan George, André Gide and Rainer Maria Rilke admiringly. He told me that one day, in his youth, he had brashly called upon Swinburne.

But I doubted, as I listened to him day after day, that he felt for the mass of human kind that high regard which he had for his intellectual peers. He was kind and magnanimous in his daily relationships, but he was inclined to scoff at the pretensions of little men and at the weaknesses of those in public life. I think that, to him, mankind on the whole made a poor showing; indeed, the life of many men was scarcely justifiable. In his novel *The Master of the Mill*, a copy of which he gave me, his preoccupation with the forces that impel mankind rather than a feeling for the individual is apparent; his characters are at the mercy of the novel's preconceived design; they lack an inner life of their own; they are shadowy pawns. Thus the book is curiously lacking in warmth. I readily identified the author as the man whose personality I was beginning to know.

When the war began Grove followed events closely. He listened regularly to the dry, factual reporting of Elmer Davis. Subsequently, when I left the household and had joined the service, he commended my action: "Were I younger, I should no longer hesitate. We live in a world of insanity. I recommend to you *Out of the Night* to allay any lingering scruples. I have no sympathy with the author; but essentially what he says is the truth."

From this time my life took a new direction. But I often thought of Grove; from a distance of two thousand miles the recollection of my stay with him became increasingly precious. In 1943 he sent a short note which proved to be his last letter to me. As usual it was typewritten and signed F. P. G. He was still writing "but it is next to impossible to publish my sort of thing." And he added gloomily: "Life runs its humdrum course; and only Leonard has so much before him that he still looks for great things." His words were dispiriting, but I was heartened to know that in spite of the distractions of a world conflict as well as the realization that he could not expect the acclaim which he may secretly have continued to expect, he was still at his desk. One day, while on leave, I journeyed to Simcoe. Grove had suffered from one of the strokes which ultimately killed him. His right side had been paralyzed and he had made an incomplete recovery. He spoke with difficulty. He had received an honorary doctorate from the University of Manitoba, but he seemed more amused than grateful; perhaps the recognition had come too late. His manner was remote, passive. Mrs. Grove told me that he wanted to die. I understood, for he could no longer write: his usefulness, he doubtless believed, was at an end. When I left Grove that day I knew I should never see him again.

No one who knew Grove could fail to be conscious of his profound integrity. It is this attribute to which I return again and again when I think of him. To the end he retained an admiration for that which is excellent; and excellence as a writer was ever his goal. As an interpreter of his adopted country, he never veered from his resolve to portray her with all the honesty of which he was capable. His death was marked with deep regret by a few; but one day Canadians will become aware that no man understood so well the forces shaping their character as the gentle European novelist who dwelt so long unnoticed in their midst.

(1960)

GROVE AND EXISTENTIALISM

Frank Birbalsingh

Born in 1871 of mixed parents (Swedish father and Scottish mother), Frederick Philip Grove spent some of his early, most impressionable years in Paris, Rome and Munich where he acquired interests and attitudes that influenced him throughout his life; but in 1892 he came to North America where, except for brief absences, he remained until his death in 1948. His published work, consisting of eight novels, three volumes of essays, sketches and addresses, some short stories and an autobiography, has been regarded as predominantly of Canadian interest. In spite of their author's long residence in North America, however, and their predominantly Canadian settings, Grove's writings suggest that his preoccupations are primarily European. The treatment of his principal themes, free-will and humanism, reveals insights that are similar in kind, though neither in cogency nor intensity, to those of well known European writers.

The theme of free-will is introduced in the first published novel, *Settlers of the Marsh*, which describes the everyday routine of pioneer Canadian prairie homesteaders during the early years of this century. The Swedish immigrant hero, Niels Lindstedt, is puzzled by the apparently ineffectual nature of his own wishes and desires, and is consequently drawn into frequent speculation about God. The sudden death of a fellow immigrant homesteader prompts Niels to question the significance of events around him:

> What was life anyway? A dumb shifting of forces. Grass grew and was trodden down; and it knew not why. He himself — this very afternoon there had been in him the joy of grass growing, twigs budding, blossoms opening to the air of spring. The grass had been stepped on; the twig had been broken; the blossoms nipped by frost . . .
> He, Niels, a workman in God's garden? Who was God anyway?

Such questions come instinctively and with special urgency to the lonely pioneers of Grove's four novels set in the Canadian West. So often is patient toil on the land made fruitless by natural disaster, or careful plans ruined by misfortune, that they feel an acute sense of mortality and show a morbid curiosity in the unseen agency which treats their most determined efforts with neutral indifference.

A similar curiosity is evinced by urban characters in *The Master of the Mill,* in which the mill owned by the Clark family makes persistent mechanical demands on its workers and is just as indifferent to their wishes as God is to the plans and labours of Niels Lindstedt and other homesteaders. Yet the exact nature of God or of the mill remains mysterious: all that the homesteaders or the mill workers can glean is the inexorable logic by which God, at least, functions; they are vouchsafed no really satisfactory explanation. Their common ignorance, with which all the author's characters perforce play the game of life, is expressed by Samuel Clark's son, Edmund:

> We are sitting at a table playing a game of chance the laws of which we don't understand and somewhere around the board sits an invisible player whom nobody knows and who takes all the tricks; that player is destiny, or God if you like, or the future.

But Grove's characters do not respond passively. Although they acknowledge domination by mysterious and hostile forces, they summon up all possible inner resources in a show of fierce resistance, even when they realize that resistance is futile. John Elliott of *Our Daily Bread*, Abe Spalding of *Fruits of the Earth* and Len Sterner of *The Yoke of Life* all succumb, or are likely to succumb to dominant extra-human influences; but not without, initially, waging valiant and resolute struggle. John Elliott's whole life is dedicated to settling his children on farms around him, each doggedly ploughing a successful living out of the reluctant soil; while Spalding, exercising enormous strength of will and body, strives unavailingly to dominate the land that can yield him sustenance, wealth even; and Len Sterner tries persistently to acquire education in circumstances that scarcely permit him to subsist, much less to read. Ralph Patterson of *Two Generations* (a novel set in Ontario), although more successful than his Western counterparts, is equally prepared to subdue the recalcitrance of either his land or his family. Not in one instance does the author counsel supine fatalism or facile optimism; for, while his characters acknowledge the ultimate futility of human aspirations, they nevertheless enjoin unremitting struggle, not instant submission.

Since they are capable of independent decision, these characters cannot be correctly regarded as mere pawns or as impersonal beings responding mechanically to external stimuli. Implicitly they exercise a certain measure of free-will even if its exact degree and moral implication remain vague. At the same time their actions lack adequate self-consciousness and appear automatic: defiance is so instinctive as to be almost reflex, which has led to the belief that Grove's characters are, in fact, mechanically determined by local factors.

Yet Grove was no naturalist. His characters are anything but impersonal beings reacting mechanically to outside influences, nor do they transmit inherited traits and behaviour patterns from one generation to the next like the Rougon-Macquarts in Zola's great twenty-novel sequence. More often than not younger characters are at loggerheads with their elders precisely because they wish to assert contrasting individual concerns and interests. If their rather quick, retaliatory actions lack sufficient premeditation and due self-consciousness, it is not because they represent a consciously naturalistic outlook, but because the author fails to provide his characters with a satisfactory intellectual framework to define the moral significance of their actions.

The stress on the distinctive individuality of each character is in fact incorporated in a separate theme — humanism. Humanism in Grove's novels is concerned with the sanctity of human personality and with respect for the homely virtues of a Wordsworthian life close to Nature; it emphasizes the pre-eminence of fundamental human values over artificial, technologically-inspired ones. In the prairie novels the simplicities of rural, family life are reverenced, and patient tilling of the soil for one's daily bread is regarded as sufficient for complete satisfaction. On the other hand, urban industrialism denies satisfaction by inducing servility, as in the following illustration given by Bruce Rogers, foreman of the Clark mill:

> Suppose a new hand starts work with us. He's an ordinary human being: he laughs and jokes as he goes to work. But within less than a year something comes over him. Whatever he does, he seems to do automatically; in reality, the pace forces him to be constantly on the watch; it isn't that he becomes a machine; that would be tolerable if undesirable. What he becomes is the slave of a machine which punishes him whenever he is at fault.

Rogers asserts a belief that the influence of machines can be evil, that their uncontrolled power can dehumanize, and what he implies is that true value resides in the farmer, the lone individual who makes life with his own heart and hands.

In stressing the pre-eminence of personal values, Grove's novels in fact counteract the naturalistic overtones which some have found in his writing. His characters stoutly defend their basic humanity from threatened domination either by

59

natural adversaries or by artificial ones present in industrial conurbations. Instinctively they reject the mechanical determination of their lives by any agency, and their motives are not narrowly social or political like those of the author's American contemporaries; for example, Sherwood Anderson and Theodore Dreiser, who also warn against the sacrifice of human rights and liberties to the God of industrial Mammon. The Americans speak mostly from Marxist or quasi-Marxist convictions, whereas Grove's view is certainly non-Marxist. As will be shown later, his chief characters may often be taken as spokesmen for the author himself, and it is the author's view that Edmund Clark expresses when he tells his father: "Let all men be equal in an economic sense and one incitement to live is gone." Grove's anti-industrialism is not narrowly political. Passionate support for individual integrity and unyielding belief in the sovereignty of fundamental spiritual values derive from a wider if not deeper philosophical outlook that is neither socialist nor naturalistic but existentialist.

Existentialism not only contradicts naturalism; it belies the fatalism and determinism which are sometimes attributed to Grove. Fatalism signifies weak-kneed acceptance, an abdication of human responsibility; determinism, likewise, implies that all our actions even those involving moral judgments, are wholly determined by previously existing causes. Existentialism, by stressing the value of independent, personal choice in defiant action, both acknowledges human responsibility and affirms man's ability to live without panic or hysteria in a world of growing uncertainty and seeming hopelessness. Grove's protagonists voluntarily oppose cosmic odds whether in the form of inexorable Fate or of suffocating industrial organization, and although they fail in the end, they never flinch from the struggle or give way to despair. Theirs is an enforced, sisyphean way of life that is resigned without being defeatist, combative but not aggressive. To them neither despair nor hope, pessimism nor optimism, are practical alternatives. Samuel Clark sums up their approach when he says with impassive finality: "Life is a concatenation of events beyond praise or blame."

However diffuse it may be as a systematic philosophy, existentialism usually advocates vigorous protest against policies of action in which human beings are regarded as helpless pawns or as wholly determined by the regular operation of natural process: as already shown, all Grove's heroes vividly demonstrate this type of protest. These heroes are caught in situations similar to those in the plays and novels of Jean-Paul Sartre and Albert Camus, who usually portray ostensibly helpless people trapped by ordinary and natural processes. Indeed, the characters of Sartre and Camus feel a more intense and pervasive awareness of human inadequacy than Grove's protagonists. Circumscribed by hostile forces which all but annihilate him, Roquentin, the hero of Sartre's *La Nausée*, faces a predicament familar to all Grove's heroes; only he experiences such an intense form of spiritual impotence that for much of the time he is incapable of either protest or defiance; certainly he does not react quickly or instinctively. Unlike Grove's heroes, whose sole interest is to get out of their predicament, Roquentin is as much concerned with investigating his as with getting out of it. He therefore gains a fuller understanding of his predicament; and so does the reader.

Camus also writes about people with a strong, almost hypnotic sense of crippling limitation and total helplessness; nor do they always achieve that defiant act of will that comes so readily to Grove's characters. Although he goes through distressing experiences, Meursault, hero of Camus's *L'Etranger*, manages no more positive emotional reaction than a sort of dazed bafflement: he commits murder and is condemned and his most visible reaction is listless detachment. Roquentin and Meursault desire "engagement" — the existentialist term for defiant act of will — more desperately than Grove's heroes, but they encounter greater difficulty in achieving it. Instead they transcend their pressing need for "engagement" by finding salvation in thorough analysis and understanding of their problems. Mathieu Delarue, hero of Sartre's three-volume *Les Chemins de la liberté*, fails to commit himself to any positive action until the end of the third volume, but during his lengthy period of indecision he searchingly probes the apparently absurd circumstances of his concrete situation, thus laying bare its precise moral characteristics. Since self-knowledge is gained during the time that he is perplexed and undecided, indecision itself proves as much a part of his salvation as the positive commitment he finally makes. In existentialist terms salvation is the fullness of being which he gains by self-conscious probing of his whole experience.

The basic assertion of Sartre and Camus, as well as Grove, is that in an absurd or irrationally organized world men have liberty of personal choice to make what they want of their lives. All three writers present characters in roughly the same predicament, and all three prescribe roughly the same remedy — the achievement of salvation by a self-conscious act of will (which may or may not be defiant in Camus). Where the comparison breaks down is in the process of achieving salvation: Roquentin, Meursault and Delarue take a long time investigating the moral imperatives open to them, and in so doing they clarify and illuminate their predicament, while Grove's heroes are instantly defiant and so achieve the required act of will almost automatically, thus avoiding the introspective probing and analysis which might have illuminated their actions and given them moral significance. The result is that the reader comes to see the existentialist situations in the French writers more clearly and to understand their perceptions and intuitions with greater intelligence, whereas Grove's situations remain largely obscure and his existentialist insights appear inchoate and stunted.

Parallels between Sartre and Camus on one hand and Grove on the other come from their common ideological background — the ferment in Europe at the end of the nineteenth century. Two major influences at this time were Kierkegaard and Nietzsche. Kierkegaardian futility within a Christian universe jostled with an insatiable Nietzschean will to live, and the intellectual flux thus produced contained the essential elements out of which existentialism was to emerge. Under the influence of Jaspers, Heidegger and others, existentialist ideas gradually took coherent shape in the early decades of the twentieth century until they were moulded into a more or less consistent system of thought principally by Sartre in the World War II era. One reason why the intellectual framework of Grove's novels is fragmented is that he was not open, in Canada, to the direct cultural associations of constructive comment, analysis and discussion available to Europeans like Sartre and Camus. The philosophical ideas which he brought from Europe in 1892 and which remained largely stagnant in his mind more accurately represent an earlier nascent existentialism out of which the coherent theories of Sartre and Camus later evolved.

The influence of this earlier, unstable existentialism is to be found in the work of Europeans such as Ibsen, Strindberg, and even — earlier — Dostoevsky. Like Grove, these writers portray tormented and strong-willed protagonists opposed to either a moral or a social order which is contradictory if not incomprehensible. Yet the struggles of Ibsen's heroes and heroines against a stifling bourgeois social order are carefully analysed, the sexual conflicts in Strindberg's characters are brilliantly illuminated, and the crises encountered by Dostoevsky's heroes are searchingly investigated so as to bring out and clarify the moral problems involved. Ibsen, Strindberg and Dostoevsky may offer different solutions to their underlying problem of reconciling harsh human reality with the dominion of a supposedly loving Christian God, but they explore the problem comprehensively and their reputation rests on this inspired exploration rather than on the solutions they offer. Ibsen and Strindberg lean towards Nietzsche in asserting a powerful will to survive, while Dostoevsky tends towards Kierkegaard in stressing human fulfilment by deeds of love and compassion; together these three writers may be said to anticipate twentieth-century existentialism. Their philosophical sources were also volatile and unstable, but they were able to marshal them into sustained, whole and original perceptions.

Grove's work suffers by comparison either with his successors, the mature existentialists, or with his immediate European predecessors whose plays and novels anticipate existentialism. The immature or stunted quality of his thought cannot therefore be wholly attributed to deficient historical or cultural influences. Since they do not enlarge the reader's perceptions, the arbitrary constraints and harassments visited upon his protagonists appear gratuitous, and the gratuitous presentation of a whole series of characters who are physically persecuted and spiritually tortured only to be destroyed conveys a strong flavour of sadomasochism. When the unmistakably masochistic overtones of his novels are set against the author's own extremely harsh experiences in North America, it becomes clear that his art does not serve simply as a vehicle of objective views and judgments, but also vicariously as a means of projecting subjective dissatisfactions that are exclusively of personal interest. The ragged intellectual framework of his novels comes out of the unstable contact between his mixed European inheritance and his unhappy life in Canada. This contact engendered irrepressible tensions in Grove, and fiction provided him with a convenient means of release. This explains why he re-states identical themes in seven novels without ever probing them, for constant re-statement satisfies urgent psychological need; that it ignores purely aesthetic criteria was apparently of less moment.

From his arrival in North America, Grove endured poverty, illness, bereavement and what he, at any rate, thought was shameful neglect. In his treatment of free-will, the dogged but vain resistance of his heroes partly registers self-pitying disappointment with his own untiring but largely unsuccessful literary efforts. His attitude to failure is clearly stated in his autobiography *In Search of Myself*:

Perhaps, very likely even, I was foredoomed to failure in my [literary] endeavour; in fact, I seemed to see even then, that I was bound to fail; but the attempt had to be made.

63

Unwavering dedication to literature sublimates what really is an intolerable disappointment in himself as a writer, and it is partly to stabilize himself psychologically for renewed efforts that he wishfully projects a dedicated but assumed fighting spirit in all his chief characters.

Similarly limiting personal motives enter into his representation of humanism as well. Concern for the mill workers in *The Master of the Mill* is not closely integrated into the novel's unwieldy plot; it is prompted, it would seem, by strong prejudice rather than by artistic considerations. The suspicion of prejudice is reinforced when we discover the author's expressed animus against American industrial social organization. In *In Search of Myself* he deplores the ascendancy of purely acquisitive instincts over more genuinely creative ones in America, and American subservience to a morality based on credit elicits contempt:

> It is the peculiarly American philosophy of life that to have is more important than to be or to do; in fact, that to be is dependent on to have. America's chief contribution to the so-called civilization of mankind, so far, consists in the instalment plan; and that plan imposes a slavery vastly more galling, vastly more wasteful than any autocracy, any tyranny has ever imposed. A free life is impossible under its rule except for the rich who can dispense with it.

These obviously exaggerated feelings become especially significant when we realize that it was principally his anti-Americanism that drove the author to a miserable existence on a bleak and inhospitable Canadian prairie. Like dogged resistance in his treatment of free-will, Grove's humanistic belief in individual integrity largely expresses a narrowly idiosyncratic resentment. In the former case resentment is directed against the failure of his writing, while in the latter it is pointed at American social values.

The sexual attitudes revealed in Grove's novels also underline the undue subjectivity of his art. In *The Yoke of Life* Len Sterner plainly states his expectations of Lydia Hausmann:

> He saw Lydia etherealised, de-carnalised.... She stood before his mental vision, untouched, all the more desirable for having been tempted, white in immaculate innocence. In order to justify his condemnation of the world, he needed to idealise her; and he did so with the facility of youth.

When Lydia, without convincing psychological pretext, suddenly turns from virgin innocence to besmirching promiscuity, Sterner's ethereal illusions are shattered and he "cursed the world and all the facts of life". He then endures prolonged self-torture which is finally relieved only by suicide. Grove's own sexual attitudes are not much different; he writes in his autobiography:

Woman as such remained a mystery to me. Even the prostitute whom I had seen through the open door of the brothel seemed a superior being to me, something almost divine because it was different from myself.

Although we may not know for certain that Grove experienced consequent frustration similar to Sterner's, we can be reasonably certain that his rather innocent idealization of women was contradicted by actual experience, and if the passion he shows in his reaction to literary failure and American society is genuine, he is likely to have responded to sexual frustration with the same intensity as he shows in his main themes. This would explain why there are scarcely any happy sexual relationships in the novels or why his women are drawn without subtlety, either as wicked and promiscuous like Clara Vogel and Lydia Hausmann, or as saintly and virginal like Ellen Amundsen and Alice Patterson; for, as in his main themes, Grove is not so much giving an objective portrait of credible human relations as expressing unbalanced, unstable and probably uncontrollable retaliatory feelings born of his own frustrations.

Sterner's reaction when disillusioned by Lydia is revealing, because it clearly illustrates the masochistic, self-pitying spirit of grievance common to all Grove's heroes. Their pathological outlook makes them retaliate blindly and irrationally against life itself, not simply against specific sources of irritation or dissatisfaction. In psychological terms Grove's themes are undeveloped because his heroes are too overcome by emotion to keep the bare minimum of moral equipoise necessary to any successful character in fiction. Sterner and his spiritual kindred in the other novels are not ultimately convincing as human beings in whom both emotional and cerebral impulses co-operate to maintain some form of equilibrium as in normal experience. All that they do is either to inflict or to endure punishment, and in the end their sadomasochistic activities are too non-cerebral and therefore too unbalanced to sustain moral examination. Their real value is not artistic but psychological — in providing the author with a means of airing strong grievances or prejudices and thus relieving powerful inner tensions.

No assessment of Grove's novels that ignores either his existentialism or his psychological dependence on his writing can arrive at a fair estimate of his achievement as a novelist, for these two are essential factors of his art. The evidence already presented suggests that his purely artistic intention, namely to represent a view of life that is basically existentialist, is corrupted by an extra-literary motive, that of fulfilling wholly personal psychological needs and expectations. The aesthetic content of his work is thus undermined and his novels are of inconsiderable value as art; their most successful feature is patient documentation of pioneer homestead routine which is both solid and authentic. The best of Grove's writings are, in fact, not the novels, but the autobiography, the sketches and essays, in which compelling, idiosyncratic dissatisfactions can be freely expressed without much regard for aesthetic form or objectivity. On the whole we do not much admire the man's writing, but we do not fail to admire the man himself — his astonishing singlemindedness, his tenacity and his courage in the face of great adversity.

(1970)

GROVE AND THE
PROMISED LAND

Stanley E. McMullin

SINCE FREDERICK PHILIP GROVE had been writing for thirty years before he sold a book, the chronology of his novels is hard to establish. *A Search For America*, the first book conceived, was the fourth book published. In the thirty-five years between its birth and its publication the book was revised at least seven times. Many of his other books underwent extensive revision. *Settlers of the Marsh* was cut by a third from its original form as a trilogy called "Pioneers". That trilogy began to take shape in Grove's mind in 1917 and by 1923 he had completed the final version. Upon being informed that "no book of that kind stood a chance in Canada", he reduced the three volumes to one, which was published in 1925. In 1920, Grove tells us that he "simultaneously . . . re-sketched and largely rewrote . . . four other books".[1] These books were *The Turn of the Year*, "Adolescence" (later published as *The Yoke of Life*), *Our Daily Bread* and "Pioneers". *Fruits of the Earth* took forty years to take its final shape, going back to 1894 when Grove met a man who became a prototype for Abe Spalding. *The Master of the Mill* was conceived much earlier than its publication date. In 1928 Grove made an exhaustive examination of the flour-milling industry. In 1934 he accepted advance royalties from J. M. Dent and Sons for the book which he thought would be published in the spring of 1935. When *Over Prairie Trails* was accepted in 1922, Grove explained that he had a number of manuscripts on hand, enough to supply the trade with one a year for some time. The point of this discussion is that the publication dates of Grove's novels have little bearing on when they were conceived or written, and it is almost impossible to establish a true chronology based on Grove's own evidence. In many cases it seems that they were being written concurrently. In this essay I will impose my own chronology based on a thematic examination of the novels. Grove was interested in the nature of life in America. He came in search of a Promised Land and remained to help chart the complexities of the life he found.

67

In his use of this Promised Land motif, Grove was articulating an essential myth of North American culture. Professor Frye has suggested that literature is "conscious mythology". He explains the point:

> As society develops, its mystical stories become structural principles of story-telling, its mythical concepts, sun gods and the like, become habits of metaphorical thought. In a fully mature literary tradition the writer enters into a structure of traditional stories and images.[2]

In his use of the Promised Land myth, Grove was employing a story which has always had relevance to North American society. From the beginning the New World was viewed as a Land of Promise. Perhaps the first version was reflected by the Spanish Conquistadors who left Spain to find their fortunes in the new land. They accepted native mythology about the existence of great wealth and set out to find the "Seven Cities of Gold", the lost city of Cibola, the wondrous fountain of youth. While these lost cities were never found, the Conquistadors did locate Aztec and Inca gold, and the New World fulfilled the promise of wealth. Once the metaphorical "milk and honey" was found, the procedure was to return to Europe and rejoin the society from which they had been barred for lack of means. The New World was a place where one could "make his pile" and then return to the more desirable milieu of upper class life in Europe. This view of the Promised Land has endured, and it is still not uncommon for Europeans to come to America with the dream of refurbishing a failing fortune.

In Canada and the United States, the promise of quick wealth was provided by the fur trade, plantation crops, fisheries, timber and other raw materials. Thus the first vision of the Promised Land was basically economic in nature. The vision of the Promised Land as a "new Canaan", a place where the new covenant could be fulfilled, developed with the growth of immigration. The immigrant was attracted by the tales of the abundance of the new land. The lower-class immigrants were, like the children of Israel, living under severe conditions in their native lands. They were prey to a variety of tyrannies: conscription, unemployment, low wages, loss of farm land, religious prejudice, depression, famine, population explosion and the ills of industrialization. The New World promised a new life free of the evils of a constricting society, a new chance to achieve salvation. It was the Promised Land of Moses reaffirmed in the New World.

IN 1892, WHEN Frederick Philip Grove arrived in America, the debate over the future of the Promised Land was being conducted by those who favoured agrarian life against those who felt that the new covenant could best be achieved through the advances of an industrial society. Grove felt that the industrial vision provided the least opportunity for man to find his soul. In his work he set out to explore the nature of the Promised Land, and his novels reveal the complexity of his reading of the myth.

In the United States, the period from the end of the Indian wars to 1890 was one of western expansion. Those who rejected a commercial vision of the Promised Land could still head out to the western frontier where free land was available. By 1890, however, settlement had progressed to the point where the Superintendent of the Census acknowledged that "the unsettled area has been so broken into by isolated bodies of settlement that there can hardly be said to be a frontier line."[3] The New World was slowly filling up and a dream of a new kind of Promised Land was usurping the old. While the first dream was still basically oriented around life on the land, the ultimate fruits of the new vision were to be achieved through industrial revolution. The nature of the dream was still essentially religious in its overtones, although the symbolism had changed from the agrarian to the mechanical. The machine was the new Messiah come among men to lead them to a new salvation in the industrial cities of America. The industrial society provided Grove with little substance for his soul, and soon after his arrival he became aware of the inherent flaws in the materially oriented life lived in the cities. His experiences with "getting the best" of the other fellow caused him to question the values of American society. He set out to discover the America of Lincoln and Thoreau and spent the best part of twenty years in agrarian surroundings. He summed up his feelings about the industrial society in an essay published in 1929:

> An industrial society means . . . the reorientation of the immigrants' minds towards a religion, if we may call it such, whose god is a jealous god because he denies the human soul the soil in which it can grow according to laws of its own, his name being a Standard of Living; toward a law which bows before economic obesity; toward aims which exhaust themselves in sensual enjoyment and the so-called conquest of nature. These things have become tools devised by a new, a nascent plutocracy for the enslavement of the mind and the spirit.[4]

Grove very early identified the conflict between the two visions of the Promised Land. In his fiction he set out to explore the implications of this conflict, and his novels reveal his deep understanding of the problems involved. He explored the imaginative force of North American culture and gave it structure.

The motif made its first appearance in *A Search for America* where it had strong autobiographical overtones. The motif which grew out of Grove's own search for a Promised Land was successfully transferred to a fable in the later novels. Briefly stated, the motif starts with a geographical search for a Promised Land where the individual soul can grow according to its own innate rules, but it ultimately becomes a striving for an ideal existence beyond physical environments: the Promised Land vision becomes an unattainable ideal luring men on to a new and better life. Grove expands the point in *A Search for America*:

> When I came from Europe, I came as an individual; when I settled down in America, at the end of my wanderings, I was a social man. My view of life ... had been in Europe, historical; it had become in America, ethical. We come indeed from Hell and climb to Heaven; the Golden Age stands at the never attainable end of history, not at man's origins. Every step forward is bound to be a compromise; right and wrong are inescapably mixed; the best we can hope for is to make right prevail more and more; to reduce wrong to a smaller and smaller fraction of the whole till it reaches the vanishing point. Europe regards the past; America the future. America is an ideal and as such has to be striven for; it has to be realized in partial victories.[5]

Fruits of the Earth and *Settlers of the Marsh* are novels concerned with the taming of the land. Abe Spalding and Niels Lindstedt are economic pioneers, striving to exist in an environment already tainted with the excesses of an industrial society. Grove was well aware that it was no longer possible to escape from the influences of technology, and in his novels his heroes face the problem of living a life based on essentials in an environment bombarded by non-essential materialism. For my purposes, I will refer to these men as pioneers of the first generation. They are the starting point for Grove's investigations.

The next pair of novels, *Our Daily Bread* and *Two Generations*, deal with the conflict between the first generation and the second. In *Settlers of the Marsh*, Niels Lindstedt is concerned with the problem of continuity between generations. He feels his destiny is to set down roots in the new world by engendering a family, and he and Ellen go forward at the end of that novel to fulfil that goal. The continuance of life is necessary for the preservation of the Promised Land dream. In *Our Daily Bread* and *Two Generations*, the continuance of life has been assured. Both John Elliot and Ralph Patterson have produced offspring to carry on after them. In these novels Grove examined the problem of transferring individual visions from father to children.

In these two sets of novels the setting is becoming more and more involved with the problems of materialism. In *The Yoke of Life*, Grove deals with a hero from the second generation. He examines the impact of industrial society upon a young and intuitively sensitive farm boy. Len Sterner is a misfit, unable to cope with either the land or the city. He moves through both, finally rejecting each and returning to the wilderness to die.

The Master of the Mill is wholly concerned with life in the industrial society. Here Grove traces the lives of three generations of men operating in the technological milieu. The novel projects Grove's views into the future of North American society. In this book he considers the question of whether the covenant of the Promised Land could be obtained in the here and now, as the disciples of industrialism were predicting. This novel is the logical conclusion to a series of novels which start with a consideration of the first generation, then move to the second generation's conflict with the first, then to a study of the second generation alone, finally projecting a vision into the future generations. I suggest that an examination of Grove's total vision of life in America within the framework of this chronology gives new insight into his function as a spokesman for North American society. Considered in this order, each novel gains in impact as it is viewed as a part of a larger scheme.

Having examined the seven novels of Frederick Philip Grove according to the above chronology, we may offer some conclusions about Grove's use of the Promised Land motif.

THERE IS LITTLE DOUBT that Grove was influenced by two archetypal figures: Moses and Prometheus. Both displayed, for Grove, man's essentially tragic nature: both are embarked on hopeless struggles against forces they do not understand, knowing they will fail. Each is content to carry the banner for future generations. Moses especially was an important figure in Grove's imagination. Moses knew that the Children of Israel would go on to achieve the Promised Land. He could acquiesce in the knowledge that ultimately his people would enjoy a success he would not live to see. Like Moses, Grove's heroes have epic stature; they are larger than life. Like Moses, they are the leaders in the community. Moses never reached the Promised Land because he was human; he had the human flaw of egotism. Grove's characters suffer from the same fault. Abe Spalding and Niels Lindstedt had to learn to identify themselves with all that was not "I". Abe had to realize that no personal victory was possible in the battle against the forces in the universe which were trying to overcome him. He had to accept the fact that victory came collectively through the continued battle

71

fought by many men through the ages. Niels had to learn that he could not exist in a meaningful way in isolation. He had to learn to live as a social man before his dream of life in the Promised Land had validity. In *Our Daily Bread* and *Two Generations* a similar type of egotism is encountered. The first generation must learn to accept the fact that their personal visions of life are not going to be those of their children. John Elliot must learn to accept the fact that he will never have his children living around him like the patriarchs of old. Ralph Patterson must learn to allow his children to work out their own destinies. Each man makes the mistake of living his life through his children, by this means robbing himself of personal fulfilment. Len Sterner is guilty of moral egotism. He isolates himself from other men with the idea that he is morally superior to them. Edmund Clark is guilty of attempting to change the course of world history single-handedly. He refuses to become a social man; he refuses to give birth to future generations who might carry on the chore he has set out to accomplish. Both Len Sterner and Edmund Clark die with no hope for any continuance of their lives. Each has denied life to future generations.

Central to the Promised Land motif is the importance of land itself. The Children of Israel are in search of a land of milk and honey where a spiritual life based on the essentials is possible. Grove's characters are involved with the land as well. Grove himself was strongly influenced by landcape which was flat, un-relieved, uncomplicated and vaguely menacing. He felt most at home on the prairies and the sea. On these flat expanses, man's contest with nature is reduced to a basic equation: horizontal nature and vertical man. Such landscape helps to simplify life, reducing it to fundamentals. In such a setting it is easier to find the essentials of life; to weed out the non-essentials. Phil Branden goes in search of the real America, and in the early stages of the book his search is geographical. Abe Spalding is looking for land upon which he can carve his own history. Niels Lindstedt comes from Sweden to the land of a million farmsteads. For John Elliot there is no other occupation than tilling the soil. The same holds true for Ralph Patterson. Len Sterner finally is forced to escape to the wilderness in his search for insight. Only the Clarks in *The Master of the Mill* do not reflect a strong affinity to land, though even in that book, Sam Clark becomes a student of botany, creating world-famous gardens on his estate. The mill itself is the link, concerned as it is with converting wheat into man's daily bread.

Most of Grove's characters require the solace of landscape. They must make the symbolic trip to the wilderness to listen for truth. Under its influence they become intuitively aware of the value of their own souls. Phil Branden was the first to go into the wilderness in the search for personal equilibrium. Len Sterner also makes his last trip into the wilds in search of truth. Phil and Alice Patterson experience transcendent feelings from nature while working at the "Sleepy Hollow" farm. The wilderness strips man of his conventions and enables him to see into his essential humanity.

While the land fosters the intuitive process which makes people aware that they have souls, it does not act as a deterministic force. Rather it works as a catalyst, causing spiritual development without becoming actively involved in the process. If Grove believed in any kind of determinism, it was a psychological determinism. "We are what we are." The individual must work out his own destiny in the search for the Promised Land. That destiny is fixed like the image on an undeveloped photographic plate. Life is the developing agent which produces a visible image. Thus man's reaction to life determines whether his destiny will be fulfilled. Central to fulfilment is awareness of soul. Awareness of soul is the ability to identify with all that is outside of self, with all that is not "I". The Promised Land becomes an ideal of what life could be for mankind if all men had awareness of soul. Grove states that the Golden Age lies at the never attainable end of history. We can approach closer and closer to that Promised Land as more and more good prevails through the efforts of an increasing number of aware people, but we can never fully achieve complete realization.

The realization of a goal spells the end of its value as an inspirational force. Grove believed that if God were known he would be dead. From this view Grove developed a paradox basic to his vision of life. Man must have a goal in life to give his existence meaning; he must have a destiny to fulfil. But the completion of that goal or destiny spells spiritual death. Edmund Clark points out that every culture is born with the seeds of death in it. So every man's creative life spawns its own destruction. For the pioneer this paradox works out in the taming of the land. When he has successfully cleared and tamed the land, he has removed the very impetus which gives his life meaning, and he finds himself unable to enjoy the fruits of his labour. The industrialist, fighting to free man from the necessity of working — when and if he accomplishes this aim — will also destroy the very drive which gives him life. In terms of love, if the complete union of personalities were accomplished, the act would destroy the individual longing which fed the love in the first place. It is always, in Grove's world, the striving for a goal that is most significant. Thus it becomes imperative that man choose a goal which will be beyond his abilities to achieve. The battle for the realization of the Promised Land is such a goal.

There is a basic dichotomy in Grove's vision of life. On one hand he saw that man remains today what he was in the time of Moses. The essentials of life never change. Opposed to, and separate from, this essential nature of man lies man's history. Man's nature is timeless; man's cultural experience is within time. Man's history tends to be cyclic, with cultures rising and falling. Each culture is an attempt to realize the Promised Land; each culture gains its impetus through revolution. It finds the old culture stultifying and degenerate. Revolution is necessary to break from the old conventions. The new society, however, never manages to carry its revolution through to its logical conclusions. Man becomes frightened of the implications of his revolution and turns reactionary, reverting eventually to the same state from which he had originally revolted. If a revolution could work out to its logical conclusion, the Promised Land might be obtainable. Man's history then would become part of that timeless force of nature; his revolution would become evolution. While it is the nature of cultures to follow a circular route, Grove did acknowledge the existence of progress. He saw the circular motion in terms of a wheel. While a point on the wheel always returns to the same point on the circumference as the wheel revolves, at the same time the wheel moves ahead. This slow, spiralling progress comes as man learns more about himself and his relationship to others around him.

Just as revolution is necessary in the overthrow of societies, it is also a fact of family life. Children, faced with parents who insist upon forcing their own visions of life on them, must rebel in order to ensure the right of fulfilling their own destinies. Fundamental to this conflict is the role of the wife and mother. Grove places the responsibility for maintaining continuity between the generations firmly on the shoulders of the woman. It is her job to mediate between the father and his children. In the novels where there is no mediating mother, rebellion is guaranteed. Such is the case in *Our Daily Bread* and *The Master of the Mill*. Where a mother is available, compromise is often achieved. *Two Generations* is the best example of this. Grove holds that life proceeds by compromises only. Compromise is the mark of a man who can overrule his own egotism and identify himself with others. This emphasis on man as a social creature is important to Grove. Commitment to the service of mankind is basic to his view of life. In *A Search for America*, Phil Branden goes forth to assist fellow immigrants. Abe Spalding commits himself to public service in his district. Niels Lindstedt must learn to live as a social man. The two Clarks, Sam and Edmund, have idealistic visions of freeing man from toil by supplying them with their daily bread. Grove himself lived a life of commitment to mankind. He taught, often using his own

74

funds to establish classes and equip laboratories. In 1943 he ran for the Ontario legislature as a C.C.F. candidate.[6] His aim as a writer reflects his desire to serve mankind:

> I, the cosmopolitan, fitted myself to be the spokesman of a race — not necessarily a race in the ethnographic sense; in fact not at all in that sense; rather in the sense of a stratum of society which cross-sectioned all races, consisting of those who, in no matter what climate, at no matter what time, feel the impulse of starting anew from the ground up, to fashion a new world which might serve as the breeding place of a civilization to come.[7]

There is a strong stoic influence in Grove's vision of life. He stresses the necessity of living in the present rather than in the past or future. He emphasizes stoic endurance in the face of ultimate failure, seeing this as the heroic stature of mankind. Those characters who live in either the future or the past find their lives slipping by unlived. Abe Spalding experiences this problem. He lives for a future of materialistic success and finds that he has never known his own family. Sam Clark, on the other hand, is bound to the past, shackled by his father's unscrupulous practices. Each day must be lived as it comes. Grove's ideal is a life based on the essentials; on the raising of families, the growing of food, on an awareness of the fellowship of man. The city, for the most part, does not promote this kind of life. There one can become lost in the rush to acquire the spoils of an industrial society. Life becomes a continual race to acquire material goods which once acquired, quickly lose their novelty. The arts, Grove suggests, are eternal. Great music, art, or literature never lose their novelty: they remain fresh and significant. Grove feels that the fundamental function of art is to lead man into the recesses of his own soul. Materialism cannot offer any solace to the soul.

For Grove, the conception of the Promised Land begins as a geographical search for landscape which will allow his soul to grow according to its own innate rules. North America offered him that environment, but he learned that the Promised Land was really an unattainable ideal, yet an ideal which all men could strive to achieve. In *The Master of the Mill* he raises the question as to whether that ideal could be achieved through the Industrial Revolution: he replies in the negative. The ideal must prevail as a vision to spur men on to a better life. Each generation will advance its own conclusions about the nature of the Promised Land, and it will matter little that their observations are at odds with earlier or later generations. The fundamentals of life will remain constant, even though individual visions change. There will be progress; men will gradually become more and more aware of their own souls; the Promised Land will draw closer. Its final attainment will mark the end of history.

NOTES

[1] Frederick Philip Grove, *In Search of Myself* (Toronto: Macmillan, 1946), pp. 351-52.

[2] Northrop Frye, in "Conclusions," *Literary History of Canada*, ed. C. F. Klinck (Toronto: University of Toronto Press, 1965), p. 836.

[3] Quoted by Frederick Jackson Turner, "The Significance of the Frontier in American History," *The Turner Thesis Concerning the Role of the Frontier in American History*, ed. George Taylor (Boston: Heath, 1956), p. 1.

[4] Frederick Philip Grove, *It Needs To Be Said* (Toronto: Macmillan, 1929), p. 145.

[5] Frederick Philip Grove, *A Search For America* (Ottawa: Graphic Press, 1927), p. 436.

[6] Bruce Nesbit, "The Seasons: Grove's Unfinished Novel," *Canadian Literature*, No. 18 (Autumn 1963), 48.

[7] Quoted by Desmond Pacey, *Frederick Philip Grove* (Toronto: Ryerson, 1945), p. 11.

SPIRITUAL ECOLOGY

Adele Wiseman's
"The Sacrifice"

Hélène Rosenthal

ADELE WISEMAN'S *The Sacrifice* is a novel which grows out of the heritage of an historically hounded and dispersed people which has maintained its Jewish identity and survived through a passionate commitment to traditional values. In situating herself within this tradition, the author braves the literary current of the times, in fact, counters it, for she affirms an optimistic faith in mankind's struggle to achieve meaningful self-realization. The power of the novel largely inheres in its finely constructed illumination of this mystery: man and God are indivisible; man and God are opposites; man and God must resolve their paradox by an act of perfect balance and understanding, so that there is no longer any contradiction in the terms "man" and "God". Wiseman reminds us that the Promised Land demands willing sacrifice and that the unity of the tribe is still a model worth pondering.

Events of the last half-century have borne this truth in upon us. As a result of major shocks and crises, we are slowly recovering an intuitive grasp of reality, re-learning the primitive response to environment: what is required for survival. A general concern recognizes the desperate necessity for an ecological balance between man and nature and a moral concern between man and man. The conduct of human affairs must take futurity into account. As in the novel's central symbolic image, we are poised within a "closed circle" where both past and future tremble in the balance, and only an act of faith can ensure the continuity of life. In bringing the myth to life within a modern context of changing social patterns, Wiseman restores the meaning of an Old Testament teaching and allows it to speak relevantly to our times.

Though *The Sacrifice*, at its centre, is personal and metaphysical, true to the cultural history in which the narrative is steeped, it is also social and pragmatic. In an important sense, its wrestling with moral issues derives from its setting. The

77

novel documents a particular aspect of recent history that has universal application. The author recalls to us — through Isaac's factory experiences — that our North American industrial growth is based on a proletariat composed of immigrant labour, in the main, and that our emphasis on material values has its origin in the rise of small capital on its way towards becoming powerful and dehumanized as well as dehumanizing. Abraham's decline in health and status at the butcher shop, where he is exploited by a fellow Jew with enterprising means, documents a classic pattern of capital aggrandizement: the expansion of profit at the expense of people who have nothing to sell but their labour power. And the situation in Chaim's home shows us what effect this material striving has on the family and human relations. In his foolish wife's adulation of their "successful" son Ralph, a rich manufacturer who is ashamed of his father's humble occupation and old country ways, we glimpse the effect of the rising bourgeoisie on moral values; in Ralph's life-style, we witness the loss of the more sensitive human attributes of love and warmth, a loss leading to family breakdown. The effect of spiritual vitiation is misery and alienation. But the author — the Jewish spirit being nursed on dialectic and the conflict of opposites — also shows us that traditional values survive within the new environment: in Ruth, who unselfishly dedicates herself to the future of her fatherless son Moses, and in Moses himself, Abraham's grandson, whose promise as a violinist reflects and carries forward the European culture which is his heritage. Thus, through its intimate presentation of the struggles and assimilations of a stubbornly surviving minority, the novel comes dramatically alive. In her re-creation of such lives, Wiseman has given us the insights of a sociological case-book. As a study in opposing value systems, it is, of course, much more than this.

IN FACT, the novel is a profound meditation upon moral responsibility and the ethics of behaviour. What does it take to become a full human being? How can one truly become a partner of God in shaping the future to some noble purpose? What is the sacrifice this joint effort asks of us? Wiseman raises these questions in the form, it may be said, of a syllogism. The primary premise is the immigrant trauma of uprooting and replanting; the secondary premise is the psychic trauma of a man's passionate pride in conflict with the circumscriptions of his human conditions within these circumstances; the synthesis is the resolution of the basic conflict in terms of both spiritual and practical transcendence.

The nature of these trials is such that suffering becomes a subject in itself. The classical Wandering Jew "running from death and from every other insult", Abraham, reaching a mid-continent destination still short of his goal, suddenly feels he can run no longer, and gathering his family, cries "enough!" In what ironically follows, we are given to see the extent of how much further suffering man may be made to bear. The Biblical story of the testing of Abraham, with its dread demand and its subsequent victory for the cause of Jewish survival, provides the structure and meaning for this examination, as well as the most vivid part of its imagery. Consequently, the particular symbolism of the knife and of its ritual significance is central to the theme of suffering.

Like the other related images with their attendant significations in the book, the knife is ambivalent. It is the means, for Abraham, of making a living; he provides cuts of meat for the hungry: the knife is equivalent to life. But besides being a useful and necessary tool, the knife is also an instrument of death; it is the means of Abraham's initiation into the mystery of death and the meaning it holds for life: first in the abattoir, and later in the apocalyptic encounter fatal to Laiah. The knife has a happier sacramental function as seen in its relation to Chaim, who, as the hero's friend and confidant, is a smaller version of the hero: a semi-comic, pathetic yet sympathetic, foil for the larger-than-life patriarch. Although Chaim uses the knife in his profession of *shoichet*, the slaughter of chickens carries considerably less emotional investment than the slaughter of cattle, though the necessity of "rejecting life after life", even when it is only the life of chickens, gives Abraham some uneasy feelings of distaste for the occupation. However, Chaim is an "educated" man, a *mohel* consecrated in the art and rites of circumcision, a venerated role serving the continuation of Jewish identity since time immemorial.

The larger ambivalence of the knife is resolved in relation to Laiah, in the murder scene. In his soul's torment and delusion, Abraham sees Laiah as an embodiment of the cow he was forced to slaughter in his youth. Laiah's sensuality is full of portent. She exemplifies the double-edged nature of life: she is at once the promise of renewed life for Abraham — its offer of love, however imperfect — and the denial of everything Abraham stands for, in her barrenness and lack of moral commitment. In her the sacramental and practical uses of the knife converge to epitomize the carnal frailty of the mortal condition. Instead of cow sacrificed for human nourishment, she becomes a sort of sacrificial lamb of God, a human surrogate deludedly and criminally rendered up.

Laiah's sensuality is underlined not merely in her ample body and her immoral, sexual indulgence of it, but in the animal suggestiveness of her luxurious red hair and her fur coat. This imagery is linked with Abraham's beard — the beard of a sage or rabbi — which has a special secret attraction for Laiah. It recalls for her the erotic pleasure she experienced as a very young servant girl in Russia at the hands of her master. The first man she had ever known, the movements of his beard "against her naked breasts . . . had traced themselves in fire", and the thought of Abraham's dignified beard and manner titillates her hopes of being rewakened to that "first delight". It is for her the pathetic hope of rejuvenation, of recovering a lost kind of innocence. The near-mystic power of the beard is established in the link with Isaac. The last time father and son are together, Isaac asks to touch his father's beard as he did when he was a child. Mourning Isaac on his sackcloth, Abraham remembers this gesture, the son on his deathbed "touching with wistful fingers and caressing his father's beard, clinging to it as though to life itself". And Abraham feels the beard burn "against his skin as though it were afire". The image, the very diction here, in which are commingled pain and desire, recalls Laiah's sensibility of the beard that had awakened her sexual response to life. Emphasizing the connection, Abraham relives the incident with Isaac yet again, speaking his thoughts aloud to Laiah during his penulti- mate visit to her to deliver her meat order, when she detains him with tea and confidences and betrays him into imparting his own.

Thus, indirectly through the beard, the knife and all it portends of sacrifice is linked to Isaac. He who has to bear the messianic burden of his father's hubristic expectations is led to fulfil them in a bitterly ironic way. There is an additional irony in that he dies a martyr to the religious faith he has all but lost. This ironic twist is characteristic of nearly all the prophetic outcomes, since Abraham, a maker of prophecies, is convinced that he and his have been specially marked for greatness; are, so to speak, the chosen of the Chosen People. Isaac's bitterly realistic prediction that his act of heroism, first hailed as a miracle, would event- ually be denied and his name even besmirched, is the only "prophecy" that is borne out in the manner its maker has foreseen. In comparison, almost none of Abraham's prophecies come true in that way; his refusal to look into the dark places of the heart, his own included, ensures that the prophecies will be fulfilled according to possibilities he cannot foresee or entertain. For Abraham, Isaac is simply the last of his great hopes: "My life", he designates him to Chaim, as the son comes through the "long shadows" of a "beginning" night to meet his father. Thus, when Isaac dies, Abraham's will to live dies also. Now, according to the logic of his own previously expressed insight, nothing but a conscious sacrifice can

80

restore him to a sense of life. This is presaged early in the novel where Abraham decribes his ordeal with the cow in the abattoir:

> Her eye was large and brown and moist, and very deep. It made me dizzy to look. I closed my eyes and fell upon her. Will I ever forget that moment? It was as though I too were sinking with the knife.... Not until I saw the creature was dead did I realize I was still alive. I have wondered since if that was what our forefathers felt when they made the sacrifice to renew their wonder and their fear and their belief....

The description of Laiah in the murder scene is almost word for word the description of the cow given, in part, here. It is almost inevitable then that when Laiah binds herself to Abraham in that totally misunderstood first and final embrace, it is a bond of victim and victimizer as he has already experienced it. The act of sacrifice becomes the act of revelation, born out of the "womb of death", which Abraham now realizes as "the other part of him". He has probed the knowledge that death and life are inseparable and form one meaning. In an earlier, as yet untroubled family setting, he had glowingly and with great insight held forth on the Biblical story of Abraham's sacrifice, for the edification of his grandson:

> God himself is bound in that moment, for it is the point of mutual surrender, the one thing He cannot resist, a faith so absolute...it is like a circle — the completed circle, when the maker of the sacrifice and the sacrifice himself and the Demander who is the Receiver of the sacrifice are poised together, and life flows into eternity, and for a moment all three are as one.

In his own suffering of the vision, he has the same experience or intimation of eternity. Wiseman's interpretation of the Old Testament paradigm of sacrifice brings it in line with the Christian paradigm in the New. The Sacrifice on the cross, with its triumph of Resurrection of the body of Christ, is a promise of futurity based on His having assumed the burden of men's evil; the truly penitent may then aspire to salvation and the "life eternal".

THE JEWISH PEOPLE as the body of Christ: this is what the novel posits in its emphasis on suffering, sacrifice and cyclical continuity. More specifically, we are given Isaac as the all-too-human exemplar. His very frailty — the physical damage done to his heart as a result of the persecutions and trials of his childhood — is symbolic, for the heart is synonymous with goodness and love, and Isaac dies as a result of both these virtues. Yet the irony of his goodness is that indirectly it makes a murderer of Abraham. This other great paradox — the indivisible relationship of good and evil — is, like the relationship between life and death, plumbed in several counterpointing ways.

The first time is when Abraham recounts to Chaim the tragic horror of the pogrom in which he lost his two elder sons. The occasion was the joint festivals of Easter and Passover. Again there is irony in the fact of the sons' goodness in intending to bring joy to their family's Passover observance, but bringing instead agony and loss through their deaths at the hands of the rampaging Christians. Choosing Good Friday, following on Christ's symbolic death, for their massacre and pillage, the Cossacks re-enact the Easter Passion. The Jews are again crucified, as the initial blood-letting on the cross is seen to beget more blood-letting. The observance of the religious occasion merely serves to reinforce the generic sadistic image, so that the old bloodlust is aroused and the Passion of Jesus' inhuman/human suffering is repeated in a recurring nightmare that seems fated. The passage suggests that the presence of a vulnerable victim incites and invites wanton cruelty and is, in this oblique sense, a critical comment on Crucifixion symbolism and imagery. Abraham tells how, after hiding three days and an additional night in the dark, the remaining village Jews ventured forth to close around their wounds and survive. The pogrom was over, or, as he sardonically puts it, "Christ is sated." The bitterness is best understood in the light of the Hebraic vision of sacrifice: when the sacrifice of a son is demanded in the Old Testament, God does not permit human blood to be shed but is satisfied to have an animal's in token of faith.

The emphasis is on the ritual. The fact that the God of the Hebrews does not require the actual deed, but just the obedience and trust, transforms the nature of the sacrifice. It is a psychic one, primarily — one of commitment, not one of human blood — and so the ritual is all that remains of the ordeal. The ram which is substituted for Isaac lacks, in his animal state, the knowledge of God and therefore of free choice between good and evil. He is a surrogate for the principle of man's compact with necessity. Man surrenders a certain part of his innocence, *i.e.,* the protective envelope of his earlier, unaware existence as a child, for the aware and necessarily compromising experience of adult responsibility, as the novel's protagonist affirms in his interpretation of the abattoir confrontation. The Covenant assumes an equal share of responsibility on the side of both God and man; it is an agreement predicated on a mutual concern for the preservation of the species. When Abraham places the future in trust with the only One who can know it, God counters with His own good faith and preserves it. In the sparing of human life, His care is proved. The ordeal is finally a test of man's faith in humanity at large, for if one is not ready to yield life for the sake of an ultimate principle of goodness, then the quality of life is in itself not worth preserving. We are all guilty until we prove ourselves innocent.

However, the fact remains, as the novel confirms in its exposition of goodness, that pure goodness cannot be borne by man, since he is a carnal as well as a spiritual being. Pure goodness invokes its opposite (either polarity cannot exist without the other) and so, since they are abstracts of a human admixture, nature itself tips the scales to establish a balance.

Abraham's tragic flaw, his overriding ambition for his sons, means that he does not allow himself to recognize frailty — physical or spiritual — as having an equal validity with strength. His wife's frailty is the exception: she represents the open wound the family must close around; she is the truly tragic reminder of their helplessness in the face of man's inhumanity to man. As such, she is the passive feminine principle — the *Mater Dolorosa* who, given no other role, can only weep over the body of her dead child.

Ruth, on the other hand, is another matter. She has the role, not of a sorrowing mother, but of a bereaved wife. And she is the product of the new world, an orphan without backward-looking ties. Ruth, like Abraham, is God's partner in the sense that conditions free her to take part, like him, in shaping destiny. Unlike the traditional Sarah, submissive by training and by nature, and so scarred by suffering that she is oblivious and unequal to the demands of the new world, Ruth is her own woman. Rescued from servitude to unloving relatives, given a home in the bosom of Abraham's family, Ruth is on her way to becoming an emancipated woman. The process of this development — the move beyond the purely domestic sphere — is not one of choice, at first, but of necessity, attendant upon economic pressures. But more than that, and this is the moral aspect of her move towards independence, in establishing it she chooses to put her child's interests — the interests of his future world — before her own. She does not seek the personal gratification of romantic love, nor ask to be spared the necessity of making a living by seeking the comforts available to a woman through marriage. Having had a husband she loved, she takes the formerly male initiative in providing for the family upon herself. Since she is not bound, as was Isaac, by the authority of a patriarchal figure, she has something of an advantage. Since she does have a bond with a tradition of suffering and overcoming in the interests of survival, she is responding to the best in that tradition. She is the Jewish mother whose courage and fortitude have been so little appreciated under the barrage of maligning stereotypes in recent contemporary literature.

In a very modest sense, Wiseman is thus one of the first Jewish novelists, perhaps the only one so far, to furnish us with an antidote to the fictions that reenforce that species of American myth which vilifies the humanity of a particular category of woman. She provides a corrective balance to the "complaint" of certain male novelists that it is their mothers who are responsible for their failures as men. But few will see Ruth as a heroine, despite this service, since her author has not asked for any special sympathy for her; Ruth's role in the novel is at best subsidiary, not calculated to win attention away from the main philosophical issues having their locus in Abraham. Nevertheless, in the thematic design, she has an integral purpose: she is the feminine counterpart of Abraham as a working partner of God: she rises to the necessity of assuring a future for the succeeding generation. Dramatically, she plays a profound part in the searing argument with Abraham which exposes him to himself and so sends him headlong into his own inner abyss.

Abraham's failure to understand the widowed Ruth, as she becomes individualized, is just part of his larger failure. He does not see how his struggles and his faith are being vindicated in her since, as a man in the patriarchal mold of his forebears, for him it is the men who must lead. His whole life has been dedicated to the idea that his male issue would redeem the future. With a subtle sort of symbolism, therefore, when he takes a life for the lives that have been taken from him, it is the life of a woman. It is, to be sure, a particularly affronting life: that of a woman who is childless by her choice of a manner of living that is a negation of all he so fervently holds to. When Abraham, in his madness, sacrifices Laiah on the block of his faith in God's love, he is, in effect, denying God: he is forgetting that God did not permit human sacrifice. He is forgetting the specific injunction: Thou shalt not kill. "I did not understand," he realizes much later, addressing the memory of Laiah, though he is talking to Moses in the asylum: "Nothing was necessary. I could have blessed you and left you. I could have loved you. . . . I took what was not mine to take." He now fully appreciates that it was not God who took his sons but human circumstances: man's deluded inhumanity in the case of the first two sons, self-sacrificing devotion in the case of the third. Isaac, by his rescue of the Torah, can now be seen as an exemplum of the Living Word of God.

As a Christ-figure cast in the role of Redeemer, then, Isaac's life is fully achieved when he gives it, though he is in conflict, refusing both the altruistic motive and the temporary glory with which he is invested. Logical in terms of his life, the act which results in his death is also logical in terms of the book's thesis. Isaac becomes the means whereby his father is humbled into accepting the principle of Love and Charity — the New Testament principle that educates and humanizes the anachronism of Abraham's tribal pride.

This is Abraham's "real" coming of age, although, earlier in the story, he feels that the turning point was his confrontation with the necessity of "creating" death in the abattoir:

> Perhaps it was wrong of me to think so, but I have always felt that was my real Bar Mitzvah. When I had my Bar Mitzvah, in the synagogue, with half the town there facing me, and I choking the words in my throat, it was a great moment, and I felt that I was really becoming a man. But it was not until after I had been forced to take a life that I really changed and was no longer a child.

Abraham's third coming of age is interestingly enough linked to the fact that it was the third cow he had to kill, his master having done away with the first two; and it is Isaac, the third son, who is unwittingly sacrificed through Abraham's obsessive pride.

THE IDEA OF TRINITY which is repeated throughout the novel in various and changing patterns of association suggests that there is involved here a play upon the symbolism inherent in the interlocked triangles of the Star of David. Three, of course, is an old magic number which attains holy significance in Christian theology, a theology which is assimilated into the novel's synthesis of the Judaic-Christian heritage. Some examples of these triangular relationships are, first, the model one: "the maker of the sacrifice and the sacrifice himself and the Demander who is the Receiver of the sacrifice", and next the shifting, or interrelated ones: Abraham and his two dead sons; Abraham, Sarah and Isaac; Mrs. Plopler and her two daughters; Isaac, Ruth and Moses — examples which do not exhaust the possibilities. An important aspect of the Star is that, when a line is drawn around its outward points in an equal radius from the centre, a circle is formed. Besides figuring in Abraham's exposition of the moment of sacrifice as a "completed circle", the figure is expanded into a circular sphere in the concrete image of Isaac's dream bubble sequence, which provides a metaphor for his oppressive condition. Since the book completes its own circle by ending as it began, with an arrival, it is easy to see how carefully Wiseman has structured her story. If there is a somewhat cabbalistic notion in the mystic significance of the geometric symbols discernible in the novel, it is there with the full awareness of an author who is sensitive to the wide range of implications drawn in by her subject.

An aspect of the philosophical viewpoint which animates the book and has not yet been remarked upon is its emphasis on the physical, or sensual, side of life. Though inexorably part of the whole, death is negative: "the dark underside". There is a total absence in the novel of the characteristic Christian, or Gentile — meaning non-Jewish — apology for death which extols it as a reprieve from the vale of tears that is this life, and makes the return to one's Maker in a heavenly paradise a life-long goal. There is no preachment, in any of the characters, of virtue for the sake of enjoying a guaranteed existence in a disembodied carefree afterlife. The afterlife of the individual in the main current of Jewish theology is concrete and physical: it resides in the children who carry life forward. The thrust of necessity in the world of the novel is therefore towards a greater appreciation of the sensual nature of man.

When Abraham is fleeing from the horror of a conscience for the first time awakened to a sense of its own guilt, following the quarrel with Ruth, it is "the warm wind of a summer night, tugging persistently at his beard" which pulls him out of a death-like stupor. This wind, which draws him instinctively towards Laiah, "whispered teasingly of life"; it is nature's own voice urging him to seek revitalization. And when he finds himself facing Laiah, when he begins to sense that the situation is forcing him into a choice, he bursts out, protesting:

> All my life . . . I have wanted only one thing: to grow, to discover, to build. . . . I chose the path of creation, of life. I thought that merely in the choosing I had discarded all else. I thought that I could choose. . . . Wherever I look, there is a shadow, a shadow that all my life I did not see, I tried to ignore. The shadow grows about me, filling the corners of my emptiness, darkening my desire. You've waited for me, empty, all this time.

Associating Laiah with the negation of life, Abraham is put to a tortuous test. He cannot help but identify her with the dark, empty places of his desolation — his lost children; and so, forced to a decision by her direct, bodily offer of herself, he embraces her, literally embracing death. Though he accepted his self-surprised presence at Laiah's door to mean that God was preparing to reveal His purpose to him at last, his mind, imprisoned in the past, is no longer able to distinguish that purpose. His alienation from reality is complete. At the climactic moment, having made the ritual prayer for sacrifice over her, he still awaits the definitive Word. Ironically it is supplied by Laiah, who, in the terrible irony of the situation, urges him to get on with it — complete the consummation — believing, all this while, that he sexually desires her. "For God's sake!" exclaims the exasperated woman. As his arm leaps with knife in hand, the truth is revealed to him in an ecstasy:

> ... the Word leaped too, illuminating her living face, caressing the wonder of the pulse in her throat, ... Life! cried Isaac as the blood gushed from her throat and her frantic fingers gripped first, then relaxed and loosened finally their hold on his beard. Life! pleaded Jacob as Abraham stared, horrified, into her death-glazed eyes. Life! chanted Moses as he smelled, sickened, the hot blood that had spurted onto his beard. Life! rose the chorus as the knife clattered to the ground, and the word rebounded ... thundering in accusation against him.

And, as the weight of the butchered body pulls him down, "Live," pleads Abraham, weeping, and begging over and over, "his face against hers. 'Live! ... Live ....' "

The final irony is that Abraham's punishment is life, not the surcease from pain and struggle that death by any means would grant. Still true to the prototype, God does not take a life that is willingly offered. "What right had I to die, like the innocent?" weeps the old man atop Mad Mountain where he has been incarcerated, and where Moses has come to seek a kind of revenge on his grandfather for having shocked and betrayed the family. Abraham can now see God's justice, and is grateful for the opportunity to spend his remaining days making prayerful amends. However, he is too far removed from the ongoing process of life to have more than an intimation that he has come through God's test victoriously. Thus joy comes to Abraham, totally unlooked for, as Moses, moved to tears of understanding, offers his grandfather the free gift of love and forgiveness. It is a sign that God has noted and approved the outcome of Abraham's suffering, an approval that is sealed in the handclasp with Moses. In that confused love-death clasp with Laiah, Abraham had been pressed together "like one" with her. Now he is re-united with the life of humanity as the hand of Moses fuses with his: "one hand, the hand of a murderer, hero, artist, the hand of a man". And this act becomes Moses' initiation, for he has "the strangest feeling of awakening" as it occurs. The book ends with the most optimistic fulfilment of one of Abraham's cherished hopes and prophecies, perhaps the only one to reach such a conclusion. His and Chaim's grandsons become friends through their own perception of each other's differing but desirable qualities, and, finding a common source of sympathy, go forward to meet the future.

Is Abraham a tragic hero? From the evidence of the novel, with its affirmative ending, one has to conclude that he is not, for all his suffering and nobility. The tragedy of human waste, which is at the core of the Greek concept of the tragic, is missing here, though it is implied in the loss of the three talented sons. Wiseman's hero learns, albeit late, from his traditional tragic flaw of *hubris*, and God forgives: an indication that the Hebraic-Christian tradition has deepened our understanding of the need for and nature of goodness in teaching us how to endure and grow. From the difficult fruit of experience comes the knowledge of a new kind of justice. The concern of this justice is for the human family, not only for one's own family or tribe. One may embrace even a Magdalen like Laiah, with love, as Abraham comes to realize, recalling, too late, "I could have blessed you and left you." Perhaps this is the most important discovery of his life, for it enables him to reach out to Moses and so bring about the removal of the last of the shadows which have dogged his strivings. Abraham is, in this sense, Everyman who asks Who am I and Why of existence, and is rewarded with an answer in keeping with the choices he himself has made in determining the shape and direction of his life.

A FEELING OF COMPLETION

Aspects of W. O. Mitchell

W. H. New

"**W**HEN I BECAME A MAN,**"** wrote Saint Paul to the Corinthians, "I put away childish things." In context, this exchange of childish for mature behaviour is related specifically to man's perception of God, but the question of human growth and development, of man's relationship with time during his mortal existence, is one that varies with each society's estimation of what constitutes appropriate reaction and behaviour in childhood and in maturity. The transition itself is many-sided, and when it is recorded in written literature or in folk traditions, it takes on different forms and emphasizes various concepts. In his two novels, *The Kite* and *Who Has Seen the Wind*, W. O. Mitchell makes use of this transition as a means to consider man's awareness of time and perception of reality during his life's span on earth. The two novels explore these questions, however, from different points of view. Though one is an artistic success while the other falls short of this, part of their interest lies in the extent to which they complement each other, and an examination of the intent, method, and accomplishment of the two works leads to a clearer understanding of the questions that Mitchell asks about life and of the answers that he postulates.

Mitchell's first novel, *Who Has Seen the Wind*, is the success. It is a study of the development involved in a boy's increasing conscious awareness of abstraction, a study of Brian O'Connal's transition from the perfection of sensitive childhood, through conflict, to a balance that is achieved in early maturity. In *The Kite*, which fails largely because of technical difficulties, Keith Maclean is parallel to Brian in many respects, but the author is concerned less with the growth of a child than with the effect of continuing awareness of time on an old man, Daddy Sherry, and the late awareness of the truth of emotional abstractions that comes to the apparently mature David Lang.

Brian O'Connal's growth begins in perfection. He is a child, complete in his own environment, when *Who Has Seen the Wind* opens; he meets existence from an awareness of self and by sense perception of the material things around him. For the actual growth to take place, however, this state of harmonious innocence must be disrupted, and it is, by the conflict that is aroused in Brian as he is brought into contact with death. An examination of each of the six death scenes in the novel will demonstrate Brian's changing reactions — his growth — and the extent to which he transcends age in developing to maturity.

Before he encounters death for the first time, Brian is given a dog for a pet, to serve as a diversion from the incipient jealousy he feels towards his younger brother Bobbie and to counteract the fantasy world of R. W. God which he invents to escape the imagined tyranny of his grandmother. When the dog is taken from him because it annoyed the grandmother, Brian seeks another pet in a baby pigeon and inadvertently kills it in his attempt to love. Because death deprived him of the pet he wanted, he cries, and drying tears stain his face when he seeks explanatory knowledge from his father, asking " 'Why does it happen to things?' " (cf. Keith Maclean: " 'Why does stuff have to die?' ") But not till the bird's body ("just like dirt, he thought, like prairie dirt that wasn't alive at all") was placed in the prairie was Brian "aware of a sudden relief"; not till then was "the sadness . . . lifted from him". Immediately following this first contact with death, however, he is reunited with the dog, and he then experiences a "soft explosion of feeling. It was one of completion and of culmination." The sought-after knowledge concerning the abstract is forgotten in the immediacy of the child's egocentric world. "The boy was aware that the yard was not still. Every grass-blade and leaf and flower seemed to be breathing, or perhaps, whispering — something *to him* — something *for him*." (Italics mine.) His world is complete; the truth he knows begins and ends in himself, in sense perception. It is only disturbed when emotion is kindled in him by contact with the implied complements of life and death, with the abstracts that youth does not and cannot comprehend.

The feeling of completion alters in character as Brian grows older, however, for with growth and experience comes an intimation that beyond the private world is a social world and beyond that another, a universal world, wherein Absolute Truth and Basic Reality can be known. But certainty still eludes him.

> The barest breath of a wind stirred at his face, and its caress was part of the strange enchantment too. Within him something was opening, releasing shyly as the petals of a flower open, with such gradualness that he was hardly aware of it. . . . He was filled with breathlessness and expectancy, as though he were going to be given something, as though he were about to find something.

But though the feeling is intermittent, it carries, by the time Brian encounters the second death, a tremendous impact. Brian, Art, Fat, and Bobbie at this time go to the prairie to drown gophers, but when Art begins to torture an animal by pulling its tail off, Brian

> realized with a start that an excitement, akin to the feeling that had moved him so often, was beginning to tremble within him. His knees felt weak with it; the Young Ben could cause it too. The Young Ben was part of it.

Indeed, the very old Young Ben, who was "born growed up", springs into action at this moment, killing the gopher with "one merciful squeeze" and clawing Art in a violent, retributive attack.

Uninhibited and primitive, the Young Ben is a personified eternal in the novel; one with the prairie, he is a sort of incarnate life-urge that in microcosm and in physical terms demonstrates in his attack on Art the potent retributive violence that knowledge of not having acted justly can wreak upon the spirit and mind — the conscience, or the childhood memory of perfect order — of man. Art, who repeated tearfully " 'I didn't do anything to *him*,' " did realize that he was "doing something" to Life: which, however, amounts to the same thing. Bobbie's reaction in this situation is the child's reaction of crying, but Brian's, characteristically, is introspection.

> The feeling was in Brian now, fierce — uncontrollably so, with wild and unbidden power, with a new, frightening quality. . . . Prairie's awful, thought Brian, and in his mind there loomed vaguely fearful images of a still and brooding spirit, a quiescent power unsmiling from everlasting to everlasting. . . . The Young Ben was part of all this.

In introducing characters such as the Young Ben or Saint Sammy, who are in some ways the most vividly drawn of all the people in the book, Mitchell runs the danger of letting his focus shift from the central development. Such a shift occurs in *The Kite* and weakens that book, but in *Who Has Seen the Wind* the focus is fortunately sustained, and because of this, the author achieves a remarkable insight into the operation of his central character's mind. Though much of this novel deals with characters other than Brian O'Connal, Brian's growth to responsibility always remains central, and the various successful and unsuccessful adaptations that the minor characters make in their respective situations of conflict, reflect upon this central growth. Svarich, for example, fails to accept his Ukrainian identity; Hislop fails to accept the existence of opposition in his church and merely resigns. Sean, Digby, and Miss Thompson, however, come to take responsible positions in their own spheres; they act positively to solve the conflict in which they find themselves, and yet they are able at the same time to accept what they cannot control. Brian, therefore, has both examples before him. Also before him are the vividly-drawn Saint Sammy and Young Ben with their strange adaptive abilities, but even they remain minor figures, because they, too, serve to contribute to an understanding of the emotional sensitivity of Brian himself.

After Brian has encountered death for the second time, this sensitivity brings him to a vague awareness of a difference between death inevitable and death avoidable and of the bond of life that joins all mortal creatures. He must then come to a realization that in life there is deformity, but that this can be lived with and even loved. His first reaction to such deformity is one of shock. "The feeling", when he looks at a dead two-headed calf, for example, "was fierce in Brian as he stared down . . . ; he felt as though he were on a tightrope high in the air. . . . It was wrong!" His judgment is based on the still vivid recollection of completion — of perfect order — but the very recognition of deformity leads to a movement away from the complete awareness of this perfection, and the feeling "lacked the sharper quality of the other times". The knowledge of perfection decreases, therefore, to the extent that the knowledge of departure from perfection (deformity) increases.

Later in the novel Brian becomes aware that the deformities men recognize are those that differentiate physical realities from earthly norms, but that some deviations from those norms do not necessitate correction in order that human love can be expressed toward them. On Sean's farm he looks down at a pet runt pig and considers:

> It would always be a runt, he declared, a shivery runt. It had no twist to its tail; it never would have. The world was a funny place. He loved his runt pig that wasn't good for anything. Ab was fussy about Noreen, the snuffiest cow in the herd, with her wheezing and sneezing and coughing. Before Annie's eyes had been straightened he had . . . [loved her too].
> Brian knew then.

But by loving what exists on earth, man moves imperceptibly further and further from instinctive love of antecedent perfection. By consciously becoming aware of love *per se*, as of death, he is becoming increasingly aware of conceptual and emotional abstractions which sensory perception cannot explain.

To the deaths which he has heretofore encountered, Brian has been largely able to maintain an objective attitude. Even towards the baby pigeon, the love expressed was in infancy as well as the child who loved. With growth and with

92

acquaintance with the love object, however, comes a more fully developed emotion, and when that is disturbed, as in the case of the fourth death when Brian's
dog Jappy is killed under the wheels of a dray, the boy's reaction is as profound
as it is subjective. Though he "looked as though he were going to cry", he does
not. Though filled with memories of the dog's life, he also "remembers the stiff-
ness of the body, the turned head, the filmed eyes. He knew that a lifeless thing
was under the earth. *His* dog was dead." (Italics mine.) With this personal
deprivation comes also a knowledge of personal mortality, and the feeling of
completion, once so strong, is lost.

> Somewhere with Brian something was gone; ever since the accident it had been
> leaving him as the sand of an hourglass threads away grain by tiny grain. Now
> there was an emptiness that wasn't to be believed.

IT IS AT THIS STAGE that *The Kite* can be again considered,
for the reader knows of David Lang's childhood completeness only by inference
from his loss of it. As a boy, David had anticipated a day of kite-flying with Lon
Burke, only to be disappointed by lack of space, by bad weather, and finally by
Lon's heart attack, at which time David loses the kite:

> as he walked towards home, the late guilt he felt could not overcome his sense
> of irreparable loss, mortal loss too great for tears. It would never soar for him. . . .
> While he had been fruitlessly searching for his kite, Lon had died.

David tries to fill the void he has now encountered by taking Lon's "explosion-
pills", by experiencing as it were "explosions of feeling", and knowledge of the
pills "soothed and reminded him of when he used to suck his thumb, though he
hadn't done that for years". But this is an unsatisfactory solution, for it is in effect
an attempt to regress to a stage of childhood that he had already left behind, and
so after the pills are used up, the emptiness returns, partly because David has
been using another's remedy, partly because in attempting to achieve a reversal of
time, he is attempting that which is impossible.

The "other sort of legacy from Lon", however, was the encyclopaedia, and by
immersing himself in knowledge, David can grow intellectually and after some
time accept adult occupations in journalism and in the television industry. But
these do not complete him; "In a way it was as though he were being requested
to die — as himself." What he lacks he lost when he never flew the kite: the

elasticity, the acrobatics, that would allow him emotional maturity, that would give him an awareness of life whereby he could realize that social participation does not necessarily mean concomitant death of individuality. His visit to Daddy Sherry is the growth of this awareness.

David does not know what he is looking for when he first heads to Shelby; nor does he understand Mr. Dalgliesh when the latter says, " 'I suppose all of us at one time or another have had something to do with Daddy that's — well especially between ourselves and — and Daddy.' " Like the Young Ben, Daddy Sherry is more in the novel than an individual character; like the Young Ben, too, he is a sort of incarnation of a life urge. " 'He *is* excitement,' " says Harry Richardson; " 'The life force sparkles more through him,' the minister suggested"; and after some time in Shelby, David himself realizes that Daddy "had been too immersed in living to build historical significance out of his days". He too has to have an individual contact with Daddy, with life; he too must find, in living, the completeness that has only been known before in his childhood lack of awareness of anything that might disturb the apparent immortality of the immediately perceived world. David is of course attempting to write and complete a story, but the completion he needs and of which he becomes aware in the old man, is bound with the other need for completion at an emotional level; "the crosswilled old human had completely won him, and somehow — if Daddy were to die now — their relationship would have failed to complete itself."

David's contact with Daddy is the central relationship in *The Kite*, and the growth that occurs through this relationship is David's, not Daddy's. The danger of shift of focus, however, that had been circumvented in the case of the Young Ben and Saint Sammy in *Who Has Seen the Wind*, recurs here with results that weaken this novel. Structurally and thematically, Daddy Sherry is a minor figure, but the vividness with which he is drawn and the frequency with which he appears in the novel combine to draw attention away from David Lang. Neither character is sufficiently created to take a central position therefore, and the novel suffers from the resultant lack of an insight into human behaviour comparable to that achieved in the depiction of Brian O'Connal.

To achieve in *The Kite* the focus he desires, Mitchell has set up reflector patterns in the subplots comparable to those in *Who Has Seen the Wind*; he depicts a series of relationships with Daddy on the part of the Shelby townspeople that should act as reflectors or commentaries on the central interaction. Unfortunately this device fails in operation. Because Daddy figures prominently in each case, and because David himself remains relatively passive during the recounted anec-

94

dotes, the focus shifts to Daddy, and David's centrality is concomitantly diminished. Daddy, however, remains a constant throughout the book, albeit a constant vitality; he does not change. It is David who suffers the development and
who discovers the "answer", achieving completion, at the end of the book and at
the end of his stay in Shelby.

Like David Lang, Brian O'Connal, too, must move from childhood completion
through emptiness to a new completion. The "explosions of feeling" which he
has felt before his "emptiness" do momentarily return after Jappy's death and
before his own final glimpse of the nature of reality. A visit to Saint Sammy on
the prairie, who mystically in age can know (to his own satisfaction) the "maj-
esty of His glory" and "the greatnessa His work", stirs up the feeling once more,
but this time "coloured with sickening guilt". In his development, Brian, again
like David, has been acquiring knowledge, but when that knowledge deals grossly
with the physical facts of birth and life and death, it "spoils" the inherent knowledge of immortality. Brian is in conflict with experience, and more often than not,

it was as though he listened to the drearing wind and in the spread darkness of the
prairie night was being drained of his very self. He was trying to hold together
something within himself, that the wind demanded and was relentlessly leaching
from him.

At this stage in Brian's development, his father succumbs to hepatitis and dies,
and Brian is forced again on a highly personal level to recognize the inevitability
of death — this, however, the death of a human being. Moving as he has been
from childish reaction in emotional situations (the tears of deprivation) towards
more verbal response, Brian "did not feel like crying" at the death of his father.
Tears of relief come only when he realizes responsibility for others and a direction
to take during his own life: his mother "needed him now". Aware of death, he
is maturing; aware of some inevitabilities, he begins to accept what he cannot
control; and some years later his grandmother MacMurray's expected death "did
not come with the shocking impact".

Brian's "growing sense of responsibility" accompanies the growth of this awareness; expressed towards all around him, it is a manifestation of his increasingly
competent and humanistic attempts to rectify the unjust and the improperly
controlled in that part of his environment over which he has influence. But as
the growth takes place, the feeling disappears, and Brian would wonder "with
regret, that he never had a return of the old excitement since he had heard the
meadow lark sing to him the day of his father's funeral". The egocentric world

becomes a sociocentric one with Brian outward-oriented, a transition which culminates in his desire to be a "dirt doctor", in his laying plans for his own future in terms of living in the physical and the social world.

Still seeking certainty in his new role, Brian meets Digby and Palmer in the harness shop and puzzles at the adult difficulties of Berkeleyan philosophy. Digby's first impression that Brian was "not old enough" to understand, that his approach to understanding would be through the child's sense perception of material things, is changed when Brian abruptly tells him: " 'I don't get the feeling any more. I — don't think I will — get it any more.' " At this point Digby makes the judgment which I assume is crucial to the novel. He

> was struck by something more than familiar in the serious eyes under the broad band of the toque with its red pom. . . . That was it — the look upon Brian's face — the same expression that had puzzled him on the Young Ben's; maturity in spite of the formlessness of childish features, wisdom without years. 'Intimations of Immortality,' he thought.
> "Perhaps," said Digby to Brian, "you've grown up."

And yet Brian is certainly different from the Young Ben. Western society defines maturity as responsibility to the social world, as the leaving of petulant childishness for emotional restraint at least in recurring situations, and Brian comes to this, in spite of his years, whereas the Young Ben does not. But for that matter, few of the adult characters in the novel achieve maturity to the extent Brian has done. Bent Candy in his greed and the Abercrombies and Mr. Powelly in their desire for revenge furnish ready examples of pettiness and petulance despite their adult years. Their world, like the child's world, is built around themselves, and basing their actions on material values, they can neither appreciate breadth of mind nor express valid and deep emotion. But the Young Ben and Saint Sammy, though socially immature to the extent that they, too, live for themselves, do possess a maturity of a different kind. Unlike Bent Candy or Mrs. Abercrombie and although their methods of appreciation remain those of sensory perception, their values are non-material. By reason of their primitive awareness of life and death and existence, by their uninhibited passion, by their oneness with the prairie, they have achieved apparently instinctively the egocentric "maturity" of contact with the timeless and immortal.

Brian, however, gives promise of coming to a contact with the Absolute which is comparable to this, but of course his methods will differ. The approach of the Young Ben and Saint Sammy to eternal truths is from a material, a physical point of view. They see the Eternal through the senses, by running *with* the prairie wind and watching coloured butterflies and collecting broken glass and labels, and their appreciation of beauty and truth is as if by instinct, whereas Brian's changed approach, his socially mature approach, is not through sense perception but rather through the more abstract routes of emotion and conscious intellect. Staring out at the prairie when he is twelve, he muses:

> It had something to do with dying; it had something to do with being born. Loving something and being hungry were with it too. He knew that much now. ... Some day, he thought, perhaps when he was older than he was now, he would know; he would find out completely and for good. He would be satisfied.... Some day. The thing could not hide from him forever.

But the day of rebirth to oneness with the perfect and immortal would be a day of death to the physical and mortal, a cycle of existence that is reflected in Mitchell's recurrent imagery of light and dark, summer and winter, growth and decay and new growth.

The realization of the nature of this cycle would bring Brian to the state of awareness — an intellectual awareness — that Digby himself has achieved. Brian does not in the novel come to full knowledge and understanding of the "realities of birth, hunger, satiety, eternity, death". For him are only glimpses, only foretastes of the final order — or perhaps only recollections of early childhood — in Mitchell's terms: "moments of fleeting vision". Maturity involves moving *from* childhood, however, and to acceptance of the responsibilities of a social world. Brian, in achieving the degree of maturity beyond his child's years that Digby recognizes as "growing up", chooses a way of life which is balanced between the isolating extremes of material crassness and private mysticism. And yet he preserves in curiosity and breadth of vision the sympathetic state of mind that will allow at once both acknowledgement of human interdependence and an adult-grown contemplation of the mysteries of existence that activate the world in which he lives. This is the maturity that will allow the new completeness — leading a full life — to replace satisfactorily for the period of mortal existence the old, the childlike awareness of a different order.

DAVID LANG and Keith Maclean and Daddy Sherry are seen in their period of mortal existence, too, and at the end of *The Kite* David realizes that it is Daddy's "awareness of his own mortality" that supplies the completion he needs to live his own life fully. David already has intellect, but as Donald Finlay has told him, intellect by itself is insufficient:

"...intuition is nearer to life than intellect — or science.... That's why we have the arts, isn't it?"

"I suppose."

"It's one of the reasons I'm a minister."

"Just what do you mean by living fully?"

"Expressing your whole potentiality — taking advantage of every bit of elasticity life offers and stretching it to your profit.... Liberty — freedom."

But freedom does not mean indulgence of appetite, nor does it mean disregard of all but the self. Daddy Sherry, for example, has led a full life, has taken advantage of its elasticity, and though in his age he is at times cantankerous, he remains loyal to his ideals (Ramrod Parsons) in spite of the opportunity to turn Paradise Valley to personal material gain. He stays concerned, too, for his family (Helen and Keith), but, as the doctor notes, " 'he steps at will into the past — might even be a form of adjustment for him. His personality may have lost some of its elasticity.' "

Daddy's life, which in Helen's words " 'didn't encourage conformity — it gave him a chance to resist imprint' ", has therefore been a continual expression of individuality within the framework of a given environment. Because it has expressed the potentiality of the man, it has brought him happiness — an awareness of growth and an expectation of the future that will not allow him to die in the spring season. Having achieved the completeness of a full life, Daddy no longer fears death, just as the child, who is unaware of death, also has no fear of it — but different, because the mature approach is a conscious one. No longer fearing death, he must still continue to live fully, however, for once he consciously lets time live for him — once he allows his actions to be governed by the clock — he loses the attunement with immortality that allows him to continue to live. Hence he can say to Keith Maclean:

"Get to ninety-five an' you're immortal again — jist as immortal as you are right now — settin' there ten years old on the top my front porch step...."

The one does not know death, and the other does not fear it and can therefore destroy time by destroying the clock on his one hundred and eleventh birthday. Unlike the others at the Daddy Sherry celebration, Daddy himself cannot partake in any "propitiation of the god of mortality". He recognizes it, and that suffices.

At these celebrations, however, David Lang achieves a new completion of his own, for here he at last recognizes the necessary relationship between the individual and the realities of life and death. Limbo — surrender to the negating power of time — is a kind of death-in-life for the journalist in him, but elasticity of self within his own environment, in place and in time, will allow immortality and let the artist in him create. Recognition of this also allows him to anticipate a full future — out of limbo — with Helen and Keith Maclean.

B OTH DAVID LANG and Brian O'Connal, then, undergo a process of growth and development that results in their increased awareness of realities beyond the physical. But though their situations are in a sense comple- mentary — the sensitive boy balancing emotion with intellect and the man in limbo balancing intellect with emotion — the two novels that explore these situa- tions differ markedly.

In *Canadian Literature* No. 14, Patricia Barclay quotes W. O. Mitchell as saying: "When I wrote *Who Has Seen the Wind*, I didn't have an answer. It was just a question, which is a perfectly fine reason for writing a novel. In *The Kite*, there is an answer. . . ." The answer in *The Kite*, however, which should have become apparent through the situation itself, is made so explicit by the end of the book as to weaken the effect of the central symbol:

> Now he knew what it was that Daddy had for him — the astonishingly simple thing the old man had to say — and had said through the hundred and eleven years of his life — between the personal deeds of his birth and his death, knowing always that the string was thin — that it could be dropped — that it could be snapped. He had lived always with the awareness of his own mortality.

But *Who Has Seen the Wind* approaches the question merely from a different point of view, and the same answer is implicit here in the development that takes place in the novel itself.

The flaws which weaken *The Kite* do not, however, prevent an appreciation of the concepts that Mitchell attempts to convey. David Lang's intellectually competent approach to living recognizes the truth of there being life in art; only when he tempers his objectivity with emotional intuitiveness, however, can he recognize also that there is art in life. His contact with the forces of life when he visits Daddy Sherry in Shelby allows him at last to see the short period of mortal existence as a continuum that does not "arrive at anything" or "echo anything" except what the individual makes of it. If he orients physical reality towards the self only or if he reacts only intellectually towards life, he deprives himself of values that are inherent in more abiding relationships; and if he indulges in emotion only, he again lives in a world populated by self alone. Only by the balance of objective reason and judgment with subjective concern and contemplation can he enjoy the fullness that mortal existence offers. Brian O'Connal's development is also one that brings him to an awareness of the possibilities in mortal life. His maturation takes him from unimpeded emotional indulgence when confronted with death to a balance beyond his child's years that allows him to recognize intellectually the inevitability of death and yet to appreciate through his emotional sensibility the abiding expressions of transcendent perfection. Here, in *Who Has Seen the Wind*, the answer to Mitchell's question is more subtly revealed; partly because of this, and partly because of the novel's unity, its insight, and its world of suggestion, it manifests the strength of certain artistry.

(1963)

ROBERT KROETSCH
AND HIS NOVELS

Morton L. Ross

> Hazard refused to explain what happened next. I begged him
> in the interest of logic, of continuity, in the need to instruct
> and direct future generations, to give me a clue.

THE NARRATOR of *The Studhorse Man* (1969) makes a
plea that echoes through the reviews of Robert Kroetsch's three novels. F. W.
Watt found his first novel, *But We Are Exiles* (1965), both "powerful" and "in-
coherent" and lamented that "the motives and needs of the river-pilot protagonist,
Peter Guy, remain mysterious to the end."[1] J. M. Stedmond felt that two of the
key incidents in Kroetsch's second novel, *The Words of My Roaring* (1966),
were "gratuitous" and a third of "little apparent narrative meaning", speculat-
ing, however, that these incidents "may be intended to add appropriately modern
dark elements to the robust comic scenes".[2] Gordon Roper, discussing *The Studhorse Man*, was moved to apologize for his attempt to explain what was going
on in the book: "My transcendental abstracting may make the book seem
woolly; it is not, . . ." and then explained that Kroetsch was working in a way
"which sends out reverberations like a struck bell".[3] I take these remarks as testimony to the fact that Kroetsch's novels contain, and sometimes only barely contain, a verbal energy which is at once remarkable and elusive — an energy, often
in defiance of logic and continuity, which has provoked the reviewers without immediately satisfying them. What generates much of this energy, and much that is
elusive about it, is Kroetsch's increasingly keen sense of the difficulties in re-creat-
ing experience in language. He has insisted, in an interview with Margaret Laurence, that their function as Western Canadian authors is "in making a new literature out of a new experience". And he goes on to say: "In the process I have
become somewhat impatient with certain traditional kinds of realism. . . ."[4]

Kroetsch's three novels are interesting in part because they record attempts to capture vivid local experience in styles which probe deliberately and step-by-step beyond the conventional realism and regionalism of the short stories with which he began his career. But they are even more interesting because together they dramatize an intriguing interplay of answers to the question of just how experience itself is to be defined. The question is of interest for any novelist — and his answers to it do much to illuminate his work, but in Kroetsch's treatment, matters of craft are deliberately extended to engage analogous human and moral issues, and his novels become graphic parables of the ways in which efforts to gratify needs, even lusts for significant experience, generate moral consequences.

THE SETTING of the first novel, *But We Are Exiles*, is the M.V. *Nahanni Jane* with "one more downriver trip to complete; five hundred miles to run to the Arctic coast; eleven hundred miles to crawl back, bucking the Mackenzie's freezing current, then crossing Great Slave Lake. . . ." The Mackenzie is the novel's most powerful antagonist, its chief characteristic a resistance to human understanding and control. "Man intruded only occasionally on this blur of landscape. . . . The chaos had not yet been resolved into form." Claimed as a highway by men, the river challenges them literally at every turn, "a maze and tangle of channels that confound all but the best pilots; in an epidemic of ponds and lakes and marshes". The best pilots master the river, reduce its chaos to comprehensible form, and it is the pilot's function which is the clue to the task Kroetsch has here set himself — to reduce the endless detail of the river, the minutiae of life on a working river boat, to coherent narrative form. Kroetsch's descriptions of what the discipline of piloting means for Peter Guy, the novel's protagonist, who has spent six years learning his craft, apply pointedly to his own efforts to command his narrative raw material. For example, both the pilot's and the novelist's crafts require the acquisition of a new perspective, a process necessary yet painful because of a certain loss of awe. As a novice pilot, Peter Guy had found the landscape beautiful and mysterious in its natural chaos; he had "thrilled to this new unknown within an unknown", but he quickly discovers that the river yields only to "a man with experience and judgment, who could read the meaning in a shade of colour, who could grip the wheel and guess his way below the surface". Similarly, Kroetsch must discover a way to make his material, originally exotic to the reader, somehow familiar and workaday enough to allow full participation in the plot's adventures without losing a sense of novelty and excitement. The need is for a careful balance. "Boat and river and sky and a thin line of earth and around every bend another bend. All held in delicate and fluid balance by the pilot."

What is best in *But We Are Exiles* is its achievement of such a balance in the organization of external detail. The major quality of the third person narrative voice, scrupulously limited so that it enters only the mind of Peter Guy, and then rarely, is a cool precision which has the effect of unobtrusively instructing and re-focussing the reader's view. Here, for example, is the novel's second paragraph:

> Peter gave a jerk, another, to set the hooks, his stomach going queasy, and now the grappling-hooks and line and whatever it was they had snagged began to come up, heavy, still too far down to be seen in the sun-filtering green and then dark of the water; the line curled dripping around his high-topped boots as if to entangle him; the wet, cold line stiffened his fingers.

The care with which the details are made discrete, then set in a precise sequence; the notation of minute changes in tactile and visual sensations, and the barest hint of the emotions which accompany this simple action are typical of Kroetsch's procedures. In much the same way that Peter Guy learned his piloting from the Indian, old Jonas Bird, we learn from Kroetsch "to know a wind spot from a rock riffle, a boil spot from a hidden boulder", and gradually the unfamiliar world of bollards, ratchets, and sturgeon-head scows, of "crooked backs and chars and inconnu", of the Hume River, Aklavik, San Sault Rapids, and the Ramparts becomes an experienced, if precarious, order which allows us to share genuinely in life on board the *Nahanni Jane*.

But if controlling the chaos of the river with the craft of the pilot is deeply satisfying for Peter Guy, and by analogy allows a solution to Kroetsch's major narrative problem, both can be said to use discipline as a means of escape from another kind of chaos. On the river "the pilot's eyes and hands were in isolated yet absolute command. Pure. He wanted to shout the word. This is mine. Storm, ice, wind, rock — those can challenge me. But here a man is defined free from the terrors of human relationships." Guy has become "a white river bum with a river in his head to keep everything else out" in desperate flight from the shock of his discovery, six years before, of the girl he loves in bed with "his best if very new friend; ... the eloquence of flesh and desire caught dispassionately in the glass mirror inside the door". But escape is finally impossible for Guy; the friend, Mike Hornyak, continues to dominate his life. Now owner of the *Nahanni Jane* and married to the girl, Kettle, Hornyak is killed shortly before the action of the novel begins. The search for, eventual recovery, and final disposition of his body and the presence of his widow complicate the boat's already difficult last trip before freeze-up and become the physical counterparts of the characters' emotions as they attempt to weigh and assign responsibility for the series of events that resulted in Hornyak's death. The situation is resonant and compelling, kept from melodrama by the precise restraint of the narrative voice, and it permits Kroetsch to open such issues as exile from home, the demands of the past as they surface in present guilt, and the nature of collective responsibility. But in the novel these issues are finally and only suggestive because, as representative of "the terrors of human relationships", they remain beyond the limits of a craft that has few resources for controlling them. Like the craft of piloting which for Guy keeps "everything else out", Kroetsch's choice of method leaves the more profound dimensions of his material in the realm of chaos — provocative, but in the last analysis unclear.

The novel's major characters share the reader's uncertainty about their motives and emotions. Uniformly and credibly laconic, they are unwilling or unable to explain themselves. Peter Guy asks Kettle why she had allowed him to discover her with Hornyak: " 'Did you know it was unlocked?' 'Yes.' 'Why?' 'I don't know why.' 'Tell me.' 'I've wondered often.' " Kettle asks Guy to explain the crew's reaction to Hornyak's recovered body which the boat is carrying upriver: " 'Why are they all afraid, Pete?' 'I'm not sure.' 'Are you afraid, Pete?' 'I keep wondering. I don't know.' " The limits Kroetsch has accepted make it impossible for the narrative voice to add very much to an understanding of motive; after a key decision by Guy, the narrator can only report that he made it, "knowing all the time that he did not know why he himself must get back to the boat". Restrained from direct explanation, Kroetsch's method seeks to illuminate inner states by a technique akin to Eliot's objective correlative, a reliance on the precise image of external detail to evoke and thus display the equivalent feeling. The first, tense meeting between Guy and Kettle, after six years and Hornyak's death, is typical. Kettle offers Guy a cup of tea:

Her elbow brushed his bare arm as she turned to give him a mug. She offered him the mug handle first, her beautiful large hands cupping the mug's chipped bottom.

Awkwardly he accepted, her fingers touching his. They were both silent; then into the quiet of the cabin crashed the high-pitched whine of the motorboats that were dragging the river. Peter bent to glance out the back window.

The requirements here are fairly simple, and the arrangement of detail economically and accurately reflects the shy but reawakening sensuality between the two as it is curbed by their turbulent memories of Hornyak, but like most understatement, it leaves the reader to supply the connections which would carry the moment beyond itself to become part of some larger pattern of meaning. Here Kroetsch clearly shares the belief that a novelist's job is to exhibit and not to explicate, and there is even an explicit hint in the novel that meaning can be genuinely located only in the small, overt patterns of human gesture. Kettle and Guy manage to forget Hornyak only after they participate in an Eskimo drum dance in Aklavik. Kettle explains that "dancing says it" and, of a song she has sung, "It's the gestures, really, not the words." Then, to forestall Guy's returning memories of Hornyak, she offers her flesh: " 'Touch is real,' she said. 'Touch is how we can know.' . . . 'I taste you. I smell you. Even in all the darkness.' " But the situation also makes clear that she is expressing only a variation of Guy's repeatedly shattered hope that the immediate, careful gestures demanded by his craft will somehow exclude the chaos of time, love and guilt. And the analogy holds. Kroetsch's choice of a restrained narrative perspective, devoted largely to the precise display of detail and gesture, is simply too limited to contain and shape the potentially rich consequences it sets in motion; yet what is most interesting about the novel is that it offers another mode of capturing experience which is an alternative to Guy's — and to Kroetsch's — effort to confine experience through careful discipline.

Mike Hornyak, less a character than a force in the novel, opposes discipline with appetite. He is defined almost exclusively by his lust for fulfilment. "I know what I want. You see that, Guy? I know till I ache from my balls to breakfast." Like Guy, he seeks to master chaos, but his impulse is to consume rather than to control: " 'Chaos,' Mike said. 'We've got some chaos to contend with. So hand me that bottle under your seat.' " And Kettle can say of him: "He consumed me the way he consumed everything." Present in the novel only in the memories of others, Hornyak comes to represent the disembodied chaos, "the terrors of human relationships", from which Guy seeks to flee. Predatory in life, Hornyak is preyed upon in death as the living invest him with powers mysterious and destructive, yet fascinating and wholly irresistible. In fact, as the novel's epigraph from Ovid's account of Narcissus suggests, and as key incidents confirm, Hornyak is Peter Guy's yearned-for and fated self, the image of consuming energy which causes Guy to move so erratically through the novel: "Running and searching. That was it. He was searching too; even as he fled." As if acknowledging the limits of his chosen method, Kroetsch creates Hornyak as a figure well beyond those limits, a figure who risks all, even to his own destruction, in order to command experience by devouring it. To show the full force of Hornyak's image, Kroetsch finally chooses to enlarge his narrative perspective in order to reflect Hornyak's passionate apprehension of experience, and in doing so, he concludes the novel in a manner well beyond its original restraint, a manner which edges toward impressionistic chaos.

The novel ends as Peter Guy, like Narcissus, confronts his water-held image. Adrift on a barge he has cut loose from the *Nahanni Jane* as she struggles through a freezing storm on Great Slave Lake, released then from his obligation and discipline as the boat's pilot, and alone with the body of Mike Hornyak, Guy returns in memory to the journey west, "wheeling bird-free through the dry prairies", he had shared with Hornyak six years earlier. The memory is recorded as an orgiastic inventory of impressions, the landscape from the angle of a speeding Rolls Royce, a Gargantuan movable picnic, and the wash of a hundred beer parlours between Manitoba and Banff.

> And at Gull Lake a big H turns and turns on top of a big hotel. Turning and turning, an H red on one side, green on the other, like running lights; winding people in off the road. They drank beer at noon. And they looked for the lake at Gull Lake. "Where's the water?" Mike pleaded to a man with a white walking-cane.

Half comic, half frantic in his plea for life-giving water, Mike Hornyak transforms the experience in Guy's memory from spree to quest. The details of experience are still precisely discrete, but their connections have become urgent, random, and paratactic as Guy's hard-won discipline is displaced by his share in Hornyak's desperate and now almost mythic lusts.

The mixture of styles chosen to convey this displacement in turn moves Kroetsch toward a dilemma which he himself phrases in the novel as another of Guy's memories. Guy remembers his father's car "so heavy that when it was moving fast the brakes weren't strong enough to stop it; it rolled and the driver had to wait until it quit. His father delighted in the speed, yet was tortured by the immorality of steering a car that was in fact out of control." Similarly, Kroetsch's problem is to curb the new momentum of the final section into a resolution which will be consistent with the whole narrative. Like Guy's father, he has difficulty stopping it. The experience of the journey west vivid now in memory, Guy at last finds the courage to look at Hornyak's dead face, and the result is his final explosive act:

And the strength born of his heard laughter: the body toppled stiff from the canoe; hit the water; was lost in the snarl and riot of waves. He did not lock the door, and wrapped in the quilt and tarpaulin he lay in the small canoe. Curled in the quilt and tarpaulin he heard the slamming door, hour after hour.... and as it closed he was slammed back into darkness again, the silence again, and the soft delirium of his impassioned motion.

The image is dramatically climactic; something has been resolved for Guy so that he can deliberately take Hornyak's place in the canoe which is both coffin and shelter, but here it stops and the reader is suddenly left to infer the meaning of that resolution. The question of whether Guy survives the experience remains open, but more important is the equally open question of how Guy's final action is to be understood. Is it a final reconciliation between two disparate attitudes toward experience, an acknowledgment by Guy of his essential identity with Hornyak? Or is it a violent usurpation, a repudiation or exorcism of Hornyak's memory and all that it represents? It is impossible to be certain. That the ambiguity of the ending may be intended, that Kroetsch himself may have remained uncertain about the proper interrelationships of discipline and desire in the apprehension of experience is suggested by his next novel, *The Words of My Roaring*, in which he again explores those relationships.

IN *The Words of My Roaring*, Kroetsch re-creates the Hornyak figure in the person of Johnnie J. Backstrom, thirty-three year old Alberta undertaker, novice and underdog Social Credit candidate for MLA from a drought-stricken, depression-locked prairie constituency, a man "six-four in my stocking feet, or nearly so, a man consumed by high ambitions, pretty well hung, and famed as a heller with women". What was shadowy and therefore sinister about the figure in *But We Are Exiles* is dissipated here by letting Backstrom narrate the novel, voicing the plenitude of his experience in a rhetoric which replaces discipline and precision with a roaring excess. The core of Backstrom's character, like Hornyak's, is the compulsive avidity of his desires. "I have a large jaw and mouth, my appetite is healthy. My eyes are twenty-twenty and so eager they hate to sleep. My ears are wax-free and larger than normal. I consume and I consume." Backstrom's frequent announcements of his capacities are little more than boastful articulations of the Hornyak principle, another way to identify Lear's "unaccommodated man", but Kroetsch has also found a style which fleshes the man, which richly and credibly demonstrates how such capacities function to apprehend and organize, and thus to define particular experience. The simplest element of this style is the miscellaneous catalogue, the inventory of what Backstrom consumes.

> Yes sir, I consumed — pineapple squares and strawberry shortcake. Dutch apple pie and hot dogs with raw onions and whisky and ice cream and sour-cream raisin pie and affection and love and saskatoon pie and generosity and deference and admiration and adulation. I consumed and I consumed.

The itemized contents of the church ladies food booths at a local stampede and of the audience response to his inspired political speech are focussed even as they are confused in the capacious alembic of Backstrom's appetite, and the narrative is rich with these catalogues of local life as they pass through his eager eyes and wax-free ears into language.

But it is another, and more subtle kind of inventory which is Kroetsch's brightest achievement in the novel. W. H. New has complained of "the stereotyped catch phrases we keep stumbling into"[5] which for him make Backstrom sound like Holden Caulfield in disguise. New is right in part; the style depends heavily on the well-worn colloquialisms of the region, but he has failed to see the use to which Kroetsch has put them. Consider Backstrom's explanation for driving his hearse into a telephone pole: " 'I had a pretty good jag on. I was drunker than a skunk. I was three sheets to the wind. What a bagful. Right to the gills.' " This is in fact an inventory of the very conventional, once original, still tangy phrases for capturing the extravagant quality of this experience. Here Backstrom is using the clichés deliberately and woodenly in order to bait Doc Murdock, who is both his political opponent and father-confessor, but Kroetsch repeatedly shows us that it is Backstrom's habit to multiply and play with such phrases, and this verbal compulsion in turn convinces us of Johnnie's nagging dissatisfaction with any one of them, his near-desperate urge to name the experience by trying a succession of them. The habit further suggests Kroetsch's own growing impatience with the conventional language of his region. In his modified travel book, *Alberta* (1968), Kroetsch justifies in part his own efforts to catalogue imaginatively the province in which he was born by saying: "The process of naming is hardly begun in Alberta. We who live here so often cannot name the flowers, the stones, the places, the events, the emotions of our landscape; they await the kind of naming that is the poetic act."[6] Backstrom's occasional efforts to be originally poetic are strained, but he is an adept at folk speech and the flair with which he tastes, combines, occasionally surmounts, and often brightens its figures in a headlong rush of language gives a new wit and vitality to the old saws. Here, for example, is Backstrom's description of his escape from an embarrassing political debate with Doc Murdock:

> Why embrace the boot that kicks and stomps and tramples you? I simply fled. I confess — I turned at that moment and I bolted. Why turn the other cheek when you can turn both? I took to my waiting heels. I nearly wore the door frame as a collar when I crashed into the open air. I burst out of that prison like a startled Hungarian partridge. I flung myself like so much dishwater into the darkening street.

But Backstrom's ways with folk speech have a function even more important than their transformation of the commonplace by an excess we can savour even as we discount it. As a disembodied Hornyak shows, the danger with such figures is the more intense their incarnation of voracious appetite, the more they are abstractions — gigantic maws ingesting the world instead of living in it. Without the generous rain of the community's conventional tropes, Johnnie Backstrom might have remained a prairie Whitman, compulsively naming and enumerating his environment in order to make good his boast of containing it. With that rein, Backstrom becomes a credible creature of his time and place. And in fact the community's language is only the most pervasive of the forces which oppose, frustrate, and thus contain his otherwise boundless appetites. The novel's plot is little more than a string of predicaments for Backstrom — a series of conflicts between his desires and the drought-depressed, wife-nagged, prude-laced, hard-headed world they would consume. These range from the petty annoyances of holes in his socks and dents in his fenders, through the minor embarrassments of an erection in church and the purchase of prophylactics over the counter, and through the narrow corners of ordering ten cent beers for twenty-eight voters with only two-forty in his pockets and bidding $128 for a Model-A at a cash auction with even less, to the crowning agony of waiting for the soaking rain he has impulsively promised the constituency in a summer so dry "the fish lose their gills". And here Backstrom is less Hornyak or Whitman than he is Charlie Chaplin, the persistent clown who risks humiliation and defeat because "I wanted to be extravagant once in my life and get away with it. Like a stampede clown, I wanted to duck into my barrel, just in the nick of time. ... But no, instead of that it was the old misery and woe again." Checked again and again by the experience he burns to command, Johnnie's cries of despair are as outrageously lavish as those of his desire: "Gross, gross. My appetites. My longings. My dreams. My deceptions. My fantasies. My bottomless gullet. My grasping huge fists. My insatiable hunger not just for something but for everything. Gross unto death." But this characteristic rush of phrases, lovingly enumerating his capacities even in the act of condemning them, illustrates the quality which makes the character of Johnnie Backstrom a true comic achievement — he is magnificently incorrigible. He simply refuses to digest the repeated doses of humiliation and defeat, and we leave him struggling with the language to retain his momentarily humble conviction that the soaking rain, which arrived before election day as he predicted it would, was not really of his doing.

This quality is further underscored by Kroetsch's subdued, but unmistakable repetition in this novel of the Hornyak-Guy relationship, this time with the consequences of avaricious desire and careful restraint clearly distinguished. Jonah Bledd, the Guy figure, is Backstrom's best friend "who was always steady as a rock; not much given to laughter, but steady, reliable, levelheaded", and, to point the contrast, "I don't believe he ever quite got loaded, and I don't believe I ever quite failed." Bledd's steady restraint in fact proves unreliable; it fails to sustain him through the shock of losing his job and he drowns himself. Doc Murdock, "a harsh judge", and one voice of wisdom in the novel, pronounces Jonah's epitaph: " 'He was afraid to be a fool. So he was a coward instead.' " Kroetsch has clearly abandoned the restraints he associates with Peter Guy and Jonah Bledd, but the risks he runs in rendering experience as it is present to a figure who passionately dares life, even at the continuous risk of being a fool, are correspondingly great. At times Backstrom is out of his author's effective control, and the result sounds too much like a voice that Johnnie himself condemns as "a flatulent windbag", but generally Kroetsch contrives, with a flexible command and mixture of the ribald figures and Biblical echoes of prairie language, to make the words of Backstrom's roaring both credible and engaging. In the process the character becomes memorable, celebrating his experience with comic zest even as it overwhelms him, wisely self-mocking even as he embarks on yet another unwise course.

THE CREATION of Johnnie Backstrom completed Kroetsch's movement from restrained precision as a means of containing experience to more extravagant styles for evoking it. In his next and latest novel, *The Studhorse Man*, the two methods are both present, and the result is an experience both difficult and illuminating for the reader. The novel is ostensibly a biography of Hazard Lepage, a studhorse man dedicated to breeding the perfect line by Poseidon, his great blue stallion. Hazard, like Hornyak and Johnnie Backstrom, is offered as "a man of inordinate lust", "a reckless man", whose motto is upper-case: "NOTHING IN MODERATION", and the problem which seems to face Kroetsch once again is how to order this experience energized by chaotic and imperious appetite without sacrificing its vitality. To do this, Kroetsch uses Demeter Proudfoot, the novel's narrator and Hazard's biographer, but also his frustrated rival in love and at least momentary successor to his mission. Demeter retells Hazard's adventures with all the exactitudes of the biographer's craft; he is indefatigable in his researches into the minutiae of Hazard's past, careful with "mere fact", prodigal with his inventories of localizing detail, and scrupulous in noting that which he fails to discover. Yet his attempts to record a particularly vivid life in a specific time and place are compromised, not only by his frequently lamented inability to collect adequate information, but more seriously by the fact that he is "by profession quite out of my mind".

Demeter's profession alerts us to Kroetsch's hybrid method in the novel: the objective order affirmed by techniques of biography is constantly imposed upon and reorganized by expressions of the biographer's own peculiar appetites — appetites which fuse the pedant's finicky tastes with the libidinous forces alternately stimulated and frustrated by his subject's vagaries. As Demeter put it: "I myself prefer an ordered world, even if I must order it through the posture of madness. It is the only sane answer to prevailing circumstances." Demeter's posture may be further understood as that of a Peter Guy whose defensive sense of craft has been warped by its response to Hornyak's energies, here those of Hazard Lepage, again the sexual rival whose consuming force is both envied and feared, emulated and repulsed by the man of discipline. Demeter's complex response to Hazard, even more than his violent participation in the climactic events of the plot, makes him an intrusive presence in his own narrative; his self-conscious efforts to escape the limits of disciplined biography with the license claimed by the artist as extreme neurotic are engrossing enough so that Demeter's experience constantly threatens to supplant Hazard's as the novel's subject. And this raises the most serious question about the novel, the question of whether the device of a narrator made unreliable by his self-professed madness is designed to realize the chaotic, but integral vitality shared by Hornyak, Backstrom, and Hazard Lepage, or whether Kroetsch's intention is to show it opposing and finally dissipating that vitality. The answer is disturbing, but inescapable, for Kroetsch is clearly exposing Demeter's narrative as a generally successful act of aggression against Hazard, success marked by the fact that Demeter's actions are in large part responsible for Hazard's literal death.

Just as Johnnie Backstrom is most vivid as he engages the dry prairie world of the 30's, so Hazard is most alive in his frantic efforts to find mares for his stallion amid the distractions of Alberta in the late 40's: beer parlours, nearly eight hundred horses loose in blizzard-bound Edmonton, a contest in fancy invective, the RCMP, butchering a pig for a horny widow, a three-day wedding feast, coyote hunters, a poltergeist, and sexual resurrection in an ice-house. These adventures are extravagant to a point just this side of absurdity, yet they remain firmly comic rather than fantastic because they seem grounded in actuality, the flavour of which is most available in Demeter's account when he most effaces himself from it. But Demeter cannot let Hazard speak and act for himself, cannot let Hazard's world emerge from its antic detail. Demeter's logic is that if "prevailing circumstances" are chaotic enough to approach the absurd, then the usual perspectives must be reversed until madness becomes "the only sane answer" to the need for order. As the consequence of such reasoning, Demeter's madness takes the form of a compulsion to transform his subject, to invest Hazard's extraordinary, but still public adventures with his own private and distorting visions of order and significance.

It is this compulsion which becomes an act of aggression by the artist in Demeter against his subject. This action, threatening to dissolve our sense of an actual Hazard, is begun by reference to the limits of biography, the absence of reliable information which prompts and justifies interpretation and speculation, but Demeter is quick to turn these into alleged deficiencies in Hazard which will sanction the substitution of his own experience: "Fortunately my own experience enabled me to flesh out the bones of his nearly dead memory." Demeter's aggression is further betrayed in his habit of providing fastidious alternatives on the few occasions he allows Hazard to speak in his own voice: "the scent of spring was in that yeasty wind, the high raw odour of mares and spring — ... and he said in his crude way, 'that raw bitch of a wind was full of crocuses and snatch.'" Such juxtapositions call attention not only to Demeter straining for eloquence, but explicitly to Hazard's vulgarity, thus preventing the sense of spontaneity which could excuse and even cause our delight in comparable crudities from Johnnie Backstrom. In full flight from Hazard's earthiness, Demeter resorts to a steady inflationary rhetoric which finally comes near the point where words are separated from their references altogether. Secure in his bathtub retreat (which he has chosen) in the madhouse (in which he has been confined), Demeter forgets Hazard and reports his own pleasure in listening to the hockey games. This pleasure consists "not only in the air of suppressed and yet impending violence, but also in the rain upon our senses of those sudden and glamorous names", names then woven into a euphonious and extended reverie. Demeter's retreat here to the sheer magic of sounds is his final escape from the perversion of the biographer's task: "I close my eyes against the books and notes and cards and papers heaped about and upon me. My dull task is itself buried in my name-horde." And the Hazard buried under Demeter's name-horde suggests the full extent of Demeter's damage to him. The expressions of Demeter's madness not only displace Hazard as the novel's centre; they rob him of his particularity and thus of his vitality as a character. What was specific in the biographer's view of Hazard comes to seem specious during the madman's flights into name magic; what seemed fact comes to seem factitious until the Hazard who might have rivalled Johnnie Backstrom's solid earthiness becomes as disembodied as the dead Hornyak — a wavering image created by Demeter's narcissistic contemplation.

It is not difficult to see *The Studhorse Man* as a parable in which Kroetsch deliberately explores once again his own developing conception of the problems, both technical and moral, in capturing the essence of prairie experience in language. And if the novel is properly understood as a display of Demeter's procedures, motivations, and difficulties as an artist rather than as a biography of Hazard Lepage, it suggests that Kroetsch has reached a crucial juncture in his exploration of these problems. He has confessed himself to be restive under the restraints of realism and traditional regionalism — restraints which define the artist's responsibility as mimetic fidelity to some more or less obdurate given existing outside his consciousness. And Kroetsch has reflected his own strong sense of how recalcitrant his material can be, first in dramatizing Peter Guy's struggles to come to terms both with the Mackenzie River and with Hornyak's energies, and then in the physical and social forces which curb and contain the appetites and language of Johnnie Backstrom.

But in *The Studhorse Man*, Kroetsch claims, and then explores, a new freedom. By choosing to demonstrate how an artist's consciousness may intrude upon, even substitute itself for, his material, Kroetsch signals a shift in his interest from a mimetic to an expressive theory of art in which the experiencing consciousness is of more concern than that which is experienced. But that he may be uneasy with the implications of this emphasis seems equally clear. By revealing Demeter's enterprise as an act of aggression, perhaps even of revenge against the disturbing vitality of his subject, Kroetsch sympathetically, yet firmly exposes the moral dangers in an expressive theory, particularly the danger of a final solipsism which seeks language to escape the chaotic world of shared human experience by completely denying it. This exposure must have cost Kroetsch some pain, for it is at the expense of his narrator, a figure who obviously fascinates him and whose transforming imagination he has expended much ingenuity to portray. But the case against Demeter's aggression is honestly and dramatically made, and this suggests that the tension between the experiencing mind and the obdurate, chaotic, vital experience it works to capture, the tension variously developed through the first two novels to the direct and destructive confrontation rehearsed in *The Studhorse Man*, remains still unresolved for Kroetsch, still then a source of motive energy for his future work.

NOTES

[1] "Letters in Canada 1965," *UTQ* 35 (July 1966), 389.

[2] "Letters in Canada 1966," *UTQ* 36 (July 1967), 386.

[3] "Letters in Canada 1969," *UTQ* 39 (July 1970), 344.

[4] "A Conversation with Margaret Laurence," in *Creation,* ed. Robert Kroetsch (Toronto: New Press, 1970), p. 53.

[5] "Clichés and Roaring Words," *Canadian Literature* No. 31 (Winter 1962), 66.

[6] *Alberta* (Toronto: Macmillan, 1968), 83.

GABRIELLE ROY ET LA PRAIRIE CANADIENNE

Marguerite A. Primeau

Il serait facile et tentant de rattacher l'oeuvre de Gabrielle Roy à sa province natale, le Manitoba, et à cette étendue de prairie aux horizons illimités qu'est la plus grande partie de l'Ouest canadien, simplement par le côté paysagiste de la plupart de ses romans. A moins de fausser la pensée de l'auteur, l'on ne peut guère ignorer la place qu'y occupe le paysage. A maintes reprises, celui-ci atteint la stature d'un véritable personnage, parfois bienveillant comme dans *La Petite Poule d'Eau* ou *La Route d'Altamont*, parfois obstacle à vaincre, hostile ou indifférent, surtout lorsqu'il s'agit du paysage de pierre et d'affiches au néon, ou des taudis de la grande ville. Sa présence, quelque modifiée qu'elle soit, est constante; les saisons suivent leur cours régulier d'un roman à l'autre, apportant des bribes de printemps aux rues de Montréal ou un "timide feuillage" aux bords de la Koksoak. Chaque personnage est sensible à leur rythme, même si, tel le caissier Alexandre Chenevert, la réaction est pour le moins inattendue.

> Autour d'Alexandre s'épanouissait donc cette rare détente humaine.
> Mais lui en était loin. Il allait, les mains crispées au fond de ses poches, son col de velours remonté. Comme si Alexandre seul était demeuré en hiver.[1]

Cette attitude envers le renouveau printanier résume tout entier l'humble caissier hypocondriaque, craintif et solitaire, déchiré par chaque nouveau malheur qui s'abat sur le monde. L'hiver est son univers bien à lui; seule l'approche de la mort l'en délivrera.

Pour Pierre, le grand Nord finit par se réduire aux dimensions d'une montagne qui se transforme en paysage intérieur, métamorphose que l'artiste s'efforcera d'approfondir, de cerner, péniblement, inlassablement, pour en faire sa chose, sa création, et cela jusqu'au dernier jour de sa vie.

115

La montagne de son imagination n'avait presque plus rien de la montagne de l'Ungava. Ou, du moins, ce qu'il en avait pu prendre, il l'avait, à son feu intérieur, coulé, fondu, pour ensuite le mouler à son gré en une matière qui n'était désormais plus qu'humaine, infiniment poignante. Et sans doute ne s'agissait-il plus de savoir qui avait le mieux réussi sa montagne, Dieu ou Pierre, mais que lui aussi avait créé.[2]

Poussant encore plus avant l'association de l'homme avec la nature, Elsa l'Esquimaude devient elle-même une "rivière sans repos". Toujours en marche "vent devant ou vent derrière", aussi sauvage que la "sauvage Koksoak", cette femme solitaire que son fils a rejetée et oubliée ne fait bientôt plus qu'une avec la grande rivière qu'elle suit tout au long du jour.

Il est vrai que le paysage décrit minutieusement, parfois même trop méticuleusement, varie d'un roman à l'autre, de celui des prairies à la ville de Montréal et du grand Nord à Paris. Il n'en est pas moins vrai que c'est parce que Gabrielle Roy a su déceler, jauger et apprécier l'apport des grands espaces, qu' elle a pu faire revivre les innombrables facettes de la nature et son étrange symbiose avec l'homme. Si elle n'avait pas passé son enfance et sa jeunesse au milieu de la prairie canadienne, non seulement le cadre de son oeuvre en aurait été appauvri, mais les personnages eux-mêmes auraient perdu de leur humanité.

Sans vouloir minimiser le rôle du paysage sous quelque forme qu'il apparaisse dans les romans de Madame Roy, il nous faut reconnaître dans son oeuvre une seconde influence encore plus marquante de la prairie canadienne. Cette seconde influence nous paraît capitale puisque c'est elle que l'on retrouve au coeur même des personnages; c'est elle qui leur donne leur vérité particulière, vérité qui, en fin de compte, les rattache les uns aux autres.

Il nous suffit de nous pencher sur l'oeuvre critique de Gaston Bachelard et ses études sur la fonction onirique des quatre éléments pour reconnaître que l'élément *terrestre* domine chez l'*homo faber* de Madame Roy. Dans *La Terre et les rêveries de la volonté*, Bachelard affirme que "les bases de l'imagination matérielle résident dans les images primitives de la dureté et de la mollesse,"[3] le *dur* et le *mou* commandant les images premières. Or, les images princeps qui expliquent l'univers et l'homme chez Gabrielle Roy dépendent de cette dureté et de cette mollesse de l'élément *terrestre* et résument d'une part, les personnages féminins, et d'autre part, les personnages masculins.

La dureté et la mollesse des choses nous engagent — de force — dans des types de vie dynamique bien différents. Le monde résistant nous promeut hors de l'être statique, hors de l'être. Et les mystères de l'énergie commencent. Nous sommes dès lors des êtres *réveillés*. Le marteau ou la truelle en main, nous ne sommes plus seuls, nous avons un adversaire, nous avons quelque chose à faire. Si peu que ce soit, nous avon, de ce fait, un destin cosmique.[4]

Ni Rose-Anna ni Florentine (*Bonheur d'occasion*), ni Luzina (*La Petite Poule d'Eau*), n'emploient de marteau, de truelle, ni d'autre outil à usage masculin qui supposent des objets *résistants* à vaincre, c'est-à-dire, empruntant le langage de Gaston Bachelard, des objets portant "la marque des ambivalences de l'aide et de l'obstacle". Ces objets résistants sont invariablement "des êtres à maîtriser"; ils nous donnent, dit Bachelard, "l'être de notre maîtrise, l'être de notre énergie." Pour les personnages féminins de Gabrielle Roy, notamment pour ceux mentionnés ci-dessus, le monde lui-même est un objet *résistant*; il y a toujours un ou des obstacles à vaincre. C'est dans la nature de Rose-Anna, de Florentine, comme de Luzina, de se mesurer avec l'adversaire, autrement dit avec les misères et les difficultés de la vie, de les affronter courageusement, de les surmonter si possible et, dans le cas de Florentine, avec une brutalité lucide. C'est là que se trouve le principe de leur énergie qui fait d'elles des "êtres réveillés" au sens bachelardien. Ce dynamisme issu de la volonté qu'elles exercent toutes trois *contre* les choses (dynamisme plus marqué chez Rose-Anna et Florentine), est fondé à leur insu sur la résistance qu'elles attribuent aux choses, par conséquent, à la dureté des choses, image princeps de l'élément *terrestre*. Ainsi, la pulsion dominante de ces femmes sera elle-même une certaine dureté devant la vie, ancrée sur la volonté de maîtriser coûte que coûte les objets qui leur résistent. Rien chez elles n'est passif ni statique, elles ont "quelque chose à faire"; elles sont propulsées "hors de l'être". Le but à atteindre, qui n'est autre que l'obstacle à vaincre, les occupe en entier et leur donne véritablement "un destin cosmique", même si ce destin peut nous paraître d'un cosmique relatif. Voilà la raison de leur supériorité en tant que personnage sur le personnage masculin qui, passif, rêveur, agissant peu ou pas (du moins dans la plupart des romans), se rattache de ce fait au *mou*, autre image princeps, de l'élément *terrestre*.

Bien qu'à différents degrés, quatre personnages féminins représentent cette image princeps de la dureté de l'élément *terrestre*: Rose-Anna, Florentine, Luzina et Elsa l'Esquimaude. Il faut d'abord noter que, dans son pauvre quartier de Saint-Henri, la citadine Rose-Anna semble beaucoup plus près de la femme habitant un petit village au milieu de la campagne que de la femme de ville. Attachée à son logis, son univers s'y trouve circonscrit; elle se meut à l'intérieur de ce logis, elle en est le centre. Les courses en ville ne sont pas pour elle, sauf lorsqu'il s'agit de se mettre à la recherche d'un autre logement, de visiter son enfant malade à l'hôpital, ou même de trouver un emploi à son mari. Elle se contenterait sans doute de son rôle à l'intérieur de la famille, dans la sécurité d'une maison où elle sentirait qu'elle a des racines profondes et solides, si elle ne devait envisager une migration annuelle et si la nécessité de reprendre constamment les rênes ne l'obligeaient à remplir les fonctions de père et de mère auprès de ses enfants. Femme du peuple, elle n'a tout de même pas oublié ses origines rurales, et lorsqu'il lui arrive enfin de céder à un désir longtemps refoulé, c'est vers la campagne de sa jeunesse qu'elle se tourne.

> Voyons, elle devait être plus raisonnable, ne pas s'abandonner ainsi. Et pourtant, elle se voyait déjà là-bas, dans les lieux de son enfance; elle avançait à travers l'érablière, dans la neige molle, vers la cabane à sucre et, oh, miraculeusement! elle avançait à longues foulées, avec sa démarche de jeune fille svelte, allant, cassant des branches au passage.... Un instinct l'avertissait de ne pas partir si tôt vers le rêve, mais n'était-ce point déjà peine perdue? N'avait-elle pas déjà pénétré dans la forêt embaumée de sa jeunesse? Qui donc maintenant pourrait la tirer en arrière? Car elle voyait poindre le détour du chemin par lequel on arrivait à la ferme, elle était là-bas, elle avait rejeté vingt ans de sa vie et se hâtait vers les sucres. Et elle découvrait sa joie passée comme une chose qui avait dormi en elle, ignorant qu'elle était pétrie de saveur.[5]

L'EAU CLAIRE, L'EAU MATERNELLE représentée par l'érablière et sa sève nourrissante valorise non seulement le renouveau de la saison mais, pour Rose-Anna, est aussi symbole de fraîcheur, de réconfort, de renouvellement. C'est d'eau vive dont elle a besoin; le retour à sa mère et à la campagne de sa jeunesse est jugé en fonction du retour vers ce qu'elle croit être la source d'une nouvelle vie pour elle et les siens. La mère lui fait défaut tout comme l'érablière; l'eau maternelle, par le truchement de madame Laplante, semble peu à peu se solidifier dans l'austérité sans tendresse de la vieille. Et Rose-Anna constate que c'est "la gêne terrible de ne pas savoir défendre les êtres" qui les raidit ainsi. Il ne lui restera donc plus qu'à reprendre la lutte quotidienne tout en sachant que ce n'est qu'un geste futile, qu'elle ne pourra pas aider ses enfants plus que sa mère à elle n'a pu l'aider. Ce qu'il importe de reconnaître dans la vérité toute humaine du personnage de Rose-Anna, c'est qu'elle ne songe pas un instant à se dérober à l'obstacle. Son monde étant "un monde résistant", dirait Bachelard, "un monde à transformer par la force humaine", la lutte est la clef de voûte de toute sa vie; elle ne peut ni ne veut l'éviter. Il n'est donc pas étonnant qu'au plus profond de son désarroi, lorsque tout va à la dérive, elle retrouve en elle-même non pas l'eau vive de l'érablière de sa jeunesse, mais une mystérieuse et inépuisable source d'énergie.

> Ses yeux vinrent courageusement à la rencontre d'Azarius. L'énergie lui revenait en vagues rapides, consolantes. Femme du peuple, elle semblait en avoir une inépuisable réserve. Et c'est à l'heure où elle paraissait souvent le plus accablée que, de cette mystérieuse source, de cette profonde source obscure et jamais vidée, un nouveau flux de force lui arrivait, frêle d'abord, mais grossissant, prenant de l'ampleur, et qui la lavait bientôt de toute sa fatigue comme une onde rafraîchissante.[6]

A première vue, la fluidité poétique de ce passage tend à tromper le lecteur en le portant à croire que la source qui rafraîchit et revivifie Rose-Anna n'est autre que l'eau vive qu'elle avait cherchée en vain dans l'érablière. Bien que ce jaillissement parti du fond de son être, qui donne naissance au dynamisme d'actions décisives et productives, ait la fraîcheur et la puissance de renouvellement de l'eau vive, il ne faut pas oublier que c'est une vague d'énergie qui la soulève, et que l'énergie est le propre des "êtres *réveillés*", des lutteurs, des *durs*. De plus, l'eau comme métaphore a, dans ce passage, une lourdeur particulière. La longueur de la troisième phrase qui en fait presque une période, les nombreuses coupes, le *Et* qui l'introduit, la répétition de certains mots (*de*, *cette*), ainsi que les noms et les adjectifs polysyllabiques, lui donnent le rythme lent d'un liquide qui se solidifie. Nous voici donc ramenés au solide, au *dur*, à l'une des images princeps de l'élément *terrestre*.

"Quand on aura compris que l'outil implique une dynamisation du travailleur," dit Bachelard dans *La Terre et les rêveries de la volonté*, "on se rendra compte que le *geste ouvrier* n'a pas la même psychologie que le *geste gratuit*, que le *geste sans obstacle* qui prétend donner une figure à notre durée intime, comme si nous n'étions pas liés au monde résistant."[7] L'outil que l'on retrouve le plus souvent entre les mains de Rose-Anna n'est nul autre que les ciseaux de la couturière. Ravaudant, taillant de nouveaux vêtements dans du vieux linge, ou préparant la toilette de mariée de Florentine, Rose-Anna dépend à la fois de son aiguille, de sa machine à coudre et de ses ciseaux. Ces derniers nous paraissent particulièrement symboliques. Le *geste ouvrier* qui les commande est celui du sujet qui reconnaît dans la matière un *coefficient d'adversité*; par conséquent, le geste de tailler, de découper, détermine chez Rose-Anna un *coefficient de maîtrise*. En effet, "adresse et puissance ne vont pas l'une sans l'autre, dans l'onirisme du travail," affirme Bachelard. Depuis toujours, les ciseaux de la couturière ont été reconnus comme des symboles de castration, vengeance des "âmes névrosées". Ce serait se livrer à des exagérations grossières que de suggérer que tel et le cas de Rose-Anna. Au contraire, rien de moins névrosé que cette solidité en face du malheur. Rose-Anna n'a ni un tempérament de névropathe ni les loisirs pour que ses préoccupations quotidiennes, ou même son angoisse devant la misère des siens, donnent prise au déséquilibre nerveux. De ce fait, elle est à l'antipode de la névrose d'angoisse d'un Alexandre Chenevert. Cependant, il faut reconnaître que c'est elle le chef de famille, et qu'Azarius est, sinon une nullité complète, du moins un pauvre reflet du *paterfamilias* traditionnel. Le nom de Rose-Anna lui-même, par sa sonorité, par la dureté incisive de ses trois syllabes, ajoute encore à l'élément *terrestre* qui est le fond de son caractère.

Qui dit Florentine dit *rocher*, solidification la plus absolue de la matière terrestre. Encore plus lucide que sa mère, Florentine mesure sans pitié la pauvreté sordide dans laquelle ils vivent. Elle apprécie l'éloquence et les vagues projets de son père à leur juste valeur et, si elle ne lui tient pas ouvertement rancune de sa faiblesse, du moins semble-t-elle le reléguer à l'écart comme un être sans importance. L'exemple de sa mère ne sert qu'à affermir sa volonté de sortir de son milieu, de chercher le bonheur avec Jean, même au prix de sa virginité. Fille de la ville, née à la ville, elle a la dureté de son paysage de pierre. Et lorsque Jean aura fui, la laissant enceinte, sa peur se transformera vite en défi, défi à la vie et méfiance, mais aussi certitude qu'elle saura trouver le salut. Son amour mort, sa jeunesse morte, son coeur "dur comme une roche", elle attendra l'avenir sans desserrer les lèvres sur son secret.

> Et dans son coeur le besoin de vivre subsistant malgré tout s'exprima par une espèce de défi. Tout n'était pas fini. Puisqu'elle n'avait pas de choix à son goût, elle refusait tout ce qui s'offrait à elle, et il devait se produire parfois des miracles, pensa-t-elle, en faveur d'êtres comme elle, fermés et audacieux. . . . Et épuisée, mais quand même résolue, elle rencontra la vie ainsi qu'il le lui apparaissait maintenant nécessaire, avec calme et méfiance, toute sa douleur refoulée et piétinée, sans plus de retour sur elle-même.[8]

Froidement et sans défaillance, elle met à exécution le plan qu'elle a conçu dès le retour en permission d'Emmanuel. Ce ne sera pas sans regrets ni sans souffrances qu'elle se laissera courtiser, mais c'est délibérément qu'elle aiguillonne l'amour du jeune soldat et le désir qu'il a d'elle. Elle joue sur les sentiments d'Emmanuel avec une touche sûre, et c'est en toute lucidité qu'elle se livre aux ruses et aux mensonges qui, en l'attachant à elle, lui apporteront le salut. La bouche dure et le regard volontaire, elle revêt toute seule sa robe de mariée, refusant l'aide de sa mère comme elle refuse aussi d'entendre ses derniers conseils, cette dernière expression d'inquiétude maternelle à l'égard du mariage précipité. La bouche scellée, sans peur et sans faiblesse, elle affronte seule la vie qui l'attend.

> — Laisse-moi faire, dit-elle, je suis capable de m'habiller toute seule.
> Non, elle ne reviendrait pas sur sa décision. Toute sa vie était réglée enfin, une fois pour toutes. Ce ne serait pas ce qu'elle avait imaginé. Mais c'était mille fois mieux que ce qui aurait pu lui arriver. Et elle se hâtait, elle se hâtait terriblement à sa toilette comme pour se créer un être nouveau, une Florentine qui allait affronter une vie étrange, inconnue, et qui arriverait peut-être à oublier ce qu'elle avait été autrefois.[9]

Du rocher jaillit parfois la source vive. Si Florentine est dure et impitoyable envers elle-même et envers la vie, si elle accepte un "bonheur d'occasion" comme échappatoire à une situation où l'attendaient la honte et le mépris, elle n'est pas qu'égoïsme. Depuis longtemps déjà, elle pourvoyait le plus largement possible aux besoins de la famille, remplaçant le père aux lubies coûteuses. Certes, elle se révoltait contre cette vie mesquine, contre son travail pénible et dégradant, elle anticipait une espèce de bonheur chimérique qui la délivrerait, mais tout en voulant à tout prix s'affranchir de sa condition, jamais elle n'a été tenté de se désolidariser des siens. L'aisance, la tranquillité sans émotions violentes qui semblent maintenant devoir être son partage, elle les étend, aussitôt Emmanuel parti, aux siens. Il entre beaucoup d'orgueil dans ce dessein, l'orgueil d'avoir bien mené la partie, de s'être rachetée aux yeux du monde, mais il s'y trouve aussi un sentiment d'affection réelle envers ceux qui lui sont proches et le désir de les aider.

> Toutes sortes de plans s'offraient à elle, toutes sortes de considérations nouvelles, agréables et consolantes. Avec la pension que sa mère toucherait et la sienne, ils pourraient désormais vivre très bien. Emmanuel l'avait priée de quitter le travail, mais elle songeait, âpre au gain: "Je continuerai tant que je pourrai; ça fera ça de plusse."[10]

Il serait simpliste d'anticiper un renversement total de valeurs chez Florentine. Dure elle est, et dure elle restera. Mais même s'il ne lui apporte pas le bonheur dont elle avait autrefois rêvé, le mariage avec Emmanuel offre une possibilité de renouvellement. Il est vrai que l'amour qu'elle lui a juré ne figure guère dans ses projets, mais la haine de Jean a fait place au calme, sinon à l'oubli, de telle sorte qu'elle en vient à penser à son enfant comme à celui d'Emmanuel. Elle a la jeunesse pour elle, ce qui présuppose des changements éventuels, une maturité à atteindre avec l'âge et l'expérience. Saura-t-elle l'atteindre? Nous pouvons l'espérer sans être tenus d'y croire. Pour le moment, elle en est encore à calculer froidement.

> Elle organisait leur vie d'une façon logique, habile, avec un sérieux tout nouveau; elle voyait les difficultés de leur vie s'éloigner, très loin déjà. Ah! oui, c'était vraiment une vie nouvelle qui commençait.[11]

Contrairement à sa mère, Florentine n'a pas de véritables retours en arrière. Leur vie est pour elle presque toujours une suite de "présents" qu'il faut organiser en vue d'un avenir très proche. Comme pour sa mère, ces "présents" sont des obstacles à surmonter ou à contourner, mais plus dure et plus intransigeante que Rose-Anna, elle annihile froidement le passé pour peser les alternatives qui s'offrent à son choix. Le chemin qu'elle s'est tracé occupe toute sa pensée, et l'erreur commise une fois reconnue comme telle et acceptée, une autre route doit être déblayée vers un avenir plus modeste, cette fois, mais qu'elle envisage volontairement en calculant les avantages qui en découlent. Il manque au personnage de Florentine pour être tout à fait sympathique l'interrogation constante de sa mère, ou même les illusions de son père, et le besoin d'être rassurée et réconfortée tel que symbolisé par le retour de Rose-Anna à l'érablière. Le tempérament de Florentine se refuse à de telles faiblesses. Pour vaincre la vie, il faut être de pierre. C'est ce qu'elle est. Voilà pourquoi l'on peut dégager un certain parallèle entre elle et Martha, l'héroïne de Camus dans *Le Malentendu*.

LE PERSONNAGE de Luzina participe à la fois de la solidité de la terre et du bercement paisible des eaux qui entourent cette terre. Pays d'eau et de petits arbres, l'île de la Petite Poule d'Eau signifie donc pour Luzina sécurité, sentiment d'y plonger des racines profondes et tenaces, et le repos des eaux tranquilles. Elle a elle-même "les nerfs tranquilles, l'humeur rêveuse et portée au beau". Loin d'être des rêves d'évasion qui feraient du présent une série d'obstacles à vaincre en vue d'un avenir de bonheur ou de succès problématiques, comme dans le cas de Florentine, ce qui lui donnerait la dureté agressive du rocher, l'activité imaginative de Luzina est un délassement, un arrêt momentané au milieu de la besogne de tous les jours. Elle en est rafraîchie et vivifiée, tout comme l'est son île par l'eau de la rivière. Ses jours s'écoulent aussi paisibles que les eaux de la Petite Poule d'Eau, sauf pour l'accouchement annuel qui la ramène à Sainte-Rose-du-Lac, événement qu'en femme raisonnable et imaginative, elle considère comme des vacances. Un psychiâtre dirait d'elle que c'est un esprit bien équilibré. Sa bonté naturelle, sa propension à mettre en valeur et à profiter de chaque instant, n'enlèvent rien à son tempérament *terrestre*, à la solidité et à la fermeté qui forment, comme chez Rose-Anna, le fond de son caractère. A l'instar de celle-ci, elle considère le monde comme un objet résistant, mais moins hostile. Elle fait preuve de la même initiative et du même courage lorsqu'il s'agit de vaincre l'obstacle, que ce soient les difficultés du voyage à Sainte-Rose-du-Lac, les démarches à entreprendre pour pourvoir à l'éducation de ses enfants ou simplement la nécessité d'apprivoiser une Miss O'Rorke hargneuse. C'est elle qui prend les décisions, qui organise la vie des siens, en somme, qui joue constamment le rôle de chef de famille. Il est vrai qu' Hippolyte, bon travailleur, la seconde en tout; c'est même lui qui découvre parfois la solution au problème qui se présente. Il n'en est pas moins vrai que c'est Luzina qui commande, et que c'est vers elle que se tournent les enfants lorsqu'ils ont besoin de conseils comme de tendresse. Plus tard, ce sera elle aussi qui continuera à les encourager dans les différentes voies qu'ils se sont choisies, loin de la Petite Poule d'Eau. Le père ne remplira toujours qu'un rôle très secondaire.

"Etre réveillé" comme Rose-Anna et Florentine, solide et ferme envers la vie, elle est cependant beaucoup plus malléable. Tout comme l'eau adoucit la terre, la bonne humeur de Luzina, sa sérénité constante, ses joies simples pour ne pas dire naïves, atténuent ce qu'il pourrait y avoir de dur ou d'agressif chez elle. L'ambivalence qu'il faut reconnaître en elle n'est ni une lutte de l'élément *terrestre* contre la "puissance dissolvante" de l'eau, ni un défi à "la puissance absorbante" de la terre qui assèche et solidifie. C'est plutôt une adhésion de son être aux images matérielles qui constituent son univers, images de la dureté d'une terre arrosée par l'écoulement d'eaux tranquilles et nourrissantes; c'est, somme toute, le mariage de l'eau avec la terre. Si l'on pousse un peu plus avant cette comparaison, l'on se rendra compte que Luzina est une pâte qui produit, qui, dirait Bachelard, "manifeste un pouvoir créant". Son paysage aquatique la modèle, mais elle-même, sculpteur à son tour, agit sur les autres, les façonne, fait en sorte que de leur argile surgisse une création vivante et agissante. Son dynamisme, tempéré de compréhension et d'optimisme tranquille, fait nécessairement de sa vie un succès à sa mesure, mais non moins satisfaisant.

Luzina avait dans sa vie lu autant de romans qu'elle avait pu s'en procurer. Presque tous l'avaient fait pleurer, que le dénouement fût triste ou consolant. Simplement c'était la fin en soi de toute histoire qui la portait à un inconsolable regret. Plus l'histoire avait été belle et plus elle était chagrinée de la voir achevée.

Mais dans quel roman, raconté par main d'auteur, avait-elle assisté à un dénouement mieux conduit, plus satisfaisant que celui de sa propre vie et qui eût pu la faire pleurer davantage![12]

Nous avons dit au début de cette étude que, dans le dernier roman de Madame Roy, Elsa l'Esquimaude se définissait comme une "rivière sans repos". Entreprenante et résistante lorsqu'il s'agit de son fils — ce qui implique une certaine dureté — celui-ci disparu brusquement sans fournir d'autre signe de vie qu'un tardif écho de voix gouailleuse, Elsa retourne à la "paresseuse rêverie fluide" qu'elle avait combattue jusqu' alors.

> Peu à peu la vie maintenant sans but d'Elsa commença à se défaire, ce qui en avait été le ressort et constitué le sens s'épuisant à la fin. Par étapes elle glissa dans la fainéantise et l'habitude de toujours rêvasser qui étaient sans doute le fond de son caractère, et qu'elle n'avait surmontées que par un perpétuel élan d'amour.[13]

Parfois les souvenirs la harcèlent, sa peine revient et le désir de "reprendre sa vie en main", de la "conduire vers un but changeant, impossible, toujours incompréhensible". Ces journées d'effort, inutiles parce que sans orientation précise, ne sont qu'une halte momentanée dans le courant qui l'entraîne.

> Toujours solitaire, toujours en marche le long de la Koksoak, elle avait parfois l'impression de descendre elle aussi le cours de sa vie vers son but ultime, vers sa fin. Elle aurait pu imaginer que sa propre existence, issue comme le rivière de loin derrière les vieilles montagnes rongées, coulait aussi depuis une sorte d'éternité. Elle éprouvait parfois comme une hâte d' "arriver" enfin.[14]

Pétrie de terre et d'eau comme Luzina, mais d'une terre froide et aride contre laquelle l'homme doit lutter pour vivre, et d'une eau "sans repos" qui ne saurait lui apporter le calme ou un renouveau quelconque, Elsa est condamnée par la coopération qui s'établit entre ces deux éléments. Pendant les années où sa vie avait eu un sens, cette coopération avait semblé s'équilibrer en elle, la dureté de l'effort quotidien étant compensé par l'affection filiale, si avare qu'ait été celle-ci. Le jeune homme parti, la "puissance dissolvante" de l'eau domine, et le personnage d'Elsa, de dur et de ferme qu'il était, devient un être fluide qui s'apparente de plus en plus à la Koksoak. Sa pensée dérive au fil de l'eau, vagues rêveries où s'entremêlent des souvenirs et un espoir jamais défini; elle coule sans arrêt comme la rivière; elle s'extériorise dans d'interminables promenades sur les bords de la Koksoak. Alors que pour Luzina l'eau avait été un élément adoucissant et enrichissant, chez Elsa, elle est signe de dissolution et de mort. L'eau a miné la pierre et l' "être réveillé" est devenu une morte vivante que ranime à peine un

instant la découverte, au crépuscule, de petits riens: oeuf d'oiseau, galet au reflet bleuté ou "de ces filaments de plante, fins, blonds et soyeux comme des
cheveux d'enfant".

S I LA *prima matéries* de la femme dans l'oeuvre de Gab-
rielle Roy est la dureté de l'élément *terrestre* — malgré le fait que, chez Luzina,
cette matière primitive s'allie à l'élément liquide pour faire d'elle une pâte pro-
ductive, et que l'eau triomphe finalement de la dureté d'Elsa — par contre,
l'image commune aux personnages masculins est celle de la mollesse. Personnages
falots, inquiets, nerveux, souvent à la recherche d'une vérité qui se dérobe, les
hommes s'apparentent tous plus ou moins à ce deuxième élément *terrestre*. Ce ne
sont pas des agissants ni des "êtres réveillés" qui maîtrisent l'objet résistant; ils
sont passifs et rêveurs. Sauf dans le cas de Pierre (*La Montagne secrète*), leurs
rêves n'aboutissent à rien ou, comme pour Azarius (*Bonheur d'occasion*), le but
qu'ils atteignent semble atteint par hasard, au gré du destin. Il suffit de con-
sidérer le rôle secondaire, à peine existant, du père de famille dans *Bonheur
d'occasion* et dans *La Petite Poule d'Eau* pour comprendre la faiblesse du personnage masculin en regard de la femme, surtout de la mère de famille.

L'on pourrait définir le personnage d'Azarius comme l'*homo faber* privé de
l'outil qui lui donne sa raison d'être. Menuisier de son état, Azarius se grise de
mots et de nobles sentiments pour oublier la honte de n'être plus qu'un homme à
tout faire, qu'un homme sans métier. Le *geste ouvrier* lui étant refusé, il est con-
damné à un onirisme passif. Au lieu des rêveries d'un travail qui, selon Bachelard, "ouvre des perspectives à la volonté", et où "s'unissent les grandes fonctions
psychiques: imagination et volonté", il ne reste plus au mari de Rose-Anna
qu'une imagination débridée où se chevauchent projets et échappées impossibles.
Il vit en marge de la vie, incapable de garder un emploi, tiraillé par le regret de ce
qu'il a été et de ce qu'il devrait être.

> Il s'était avancé d'un pas vers ce maçon qui aurait pu être un compagnon des
> beaux jours écoulés. Il levait vers la lumière ses mains de menuisier qui avaient
> aimé le contact du bois franc, et ses larges narines frémissaient à la bonne odeur
> des planches neuves qu'il croyait tout à coup retrouver.[15]

Il faut noter qu'il n'y a a nulle colère dans le personage d'Azarius, ce qui suppose-
rait un penchant pour la lutte et le désir de maîtriser l'adversaire. Il se trouvera

donc impuissant devant la misère des siens jusqu'au jour où l'horreur de leur vie, le destin, son goût des sentiments élevés le pousseront à s'enrôler. Par le *mou* qui est le fondement de son caractère, Azarius est un enfant vis-à-vis de la vie, à tel point qu'il prend pour lui les pensées de Rose-Anna à l'intention de sa fille.

> — Pauvre enfant! soupira-t-elle.
> Et Azarius tressaillit perceptiblement. Il crut un instant qu'elle lui parlait. Autrefois, pour le guérir de ses illusions, pour le consoler de ses défaites, elle lui avait parfois murmuré ces mots en le gardant entre ses bras ainsi qu'un enfant.[16]

Cependant, l'on peut admettre la possibilité que si Azarius n'avait pas été privé de son métier par la crise économique, le *geste ouvrier* qui lui eût accordé une réalité matérielle et un onirisme dynamique lui eût donné la stature d'un adulte.

Alexandre Chenevert, premier personnage masculin de Gabrielle Roy à attirer à lui toute l'attention du lecteur, a pareillement comme base de son imagination matérielle l'image princeps du *mou*. Plus encore qu'Azarius, il est mal à l'aise dans son personnage que, pourtant, il ne peut quitter. Il est vrai que son état physique aggrave ses dispositions à l'hypocondrie qui fait enfin de lui un être tout à fait déséquilibré. Il est aussi vrai que les troubles physiologiques qui l'accablent sont dûs, en partie, à une psychopathie qui relève d'une absence de la dureté de l'élément *terrestre*. Si le temperament d'Alexandre Chenevert relevait, comme chez la plupart des gens, d'une union des deux images primitives du *dur* et du *mou*, peut-être parviendrait-il à assumer sa condition et même à la dépasser, comme dirait Sartre, ce qui lui assurerait une vie beaucoup plus normale. Malheureusement, la prédominance chez lui de l'élément de mollesse et l'absence presque totale de la fermeté et de la solidité du *dur*, le prédisposent à la faiblesse, par conséquent, à l'impuissance. Comme Azarius, il lui sera impossible de faire face à la vie. Il n'aura même pas le réconfort d'une imagination trompeuse ni le plaisir d'être écouté et parfois compris. Son imagination, aussi vive que celle d'Azarius, ne sert qu'à lui représenter dans toute son horreur les malheurs d'une humanité sans défense. Son état de caissier le condamne, du fait même, à un onirisme passif et morbide. Le *geste ouvrier* lui étant refusé, aucune des perspectives de la volonté agissante ne lui est ouverte. Il ne connaîtra ni la résistance de l'objet, ni le plaisir de le maîtriser. En effet, privé de l'onirisme dynamique qui aurait pu transformer sa réalité matérielle, il continue à être ballotté par la vie, projeté d'une inquiétude à l'autre, jusqu'au jour où une maladie inexorable, en le rendant à la passivité qui est sa nature, lui apportera le calme et un peu de bonheur.

Dans cette vie douloureuse qui peut paraître inutile si l'on ne considère le lien qui le rattache à tout homme et son besoin de fraternité qui lui acquiert une noblesse certaine, il y a pourtant une éclaircie. Cette échappée momentanée qu'il appelle ses "vacances" le ramène à la nature, au fond des bois où il découvre la paix du lac Vert. Un instant, cette solitude solide lui apporte le bonheur, mais ce n'est pas de ce bonheur égoïste et indifférent qu'il a faim. C'est d'une fraternité humaine, universelle, qu'il est avide.

> Il pensa aux vitrines de magasins craquant de vivres, à une abondance telle que le pauvre Le Gardeur ne pouvait la concevoir. Il rêva aussi de journaux, de magazines en grosses piles sur le trottoir, apportant les nouvelles du monde. Là était la vie, l'échange perpétuel, émouvant, fraternel.[17]

Cependant, n'ayant ni la solidité, ni la fermeté du lutteur, du *dur*, Alexandre ne saurait combattre franchement en faveur de cette fraternité; il est simplement emporté par la vie comme un fétu de paille qui ne réussit à s'accrocher nulle part.

Malgré son nom suggestif, Pierre (*La Montagne secrète*) n'a pas non plus la solidité du personnage feminin. S'il croit en lui-même et en son destin d'artiste, s'il poursuit inlassablement la création, il est sans conteste un être qui se cherche. Il est en marche du commencement du roman à la fin vers un but de plus en plus insaisissable. On ne pourrait sans fausser la pensée de l'auteur suggérer qu'il est la pierre du proverbe traditionnel. (*Pierre qui roule n'amasse pas mousse.*) Le contraire est plutôt évident, mais il faut tout de même souligner la propension de Pierre à voyager. Au cours d'une vie relativement brève, il parcourt en tout sens l'Ouest canadien, les étendues du grand Nord, pour aller enfin mourir à Paris après avoir traversé plus d'une province française. Les montagnes et les fleuves l'attirent, symboles de dureté et de fluidité, mais qui nous ramènent au *mou*, car l'eau peut dissoudre la terre, comme dans le cas d'Elsa. Tel n'est pas le fait en ce qui concerne Pierre puisqu'il n'abandonne jamais son travail d'artiste, puisque jusqu'à la fin, il cherche sa propre réalité. Mais la montagne qu'il retrouve en lui, "la montagne de son imagination", n'est plus la montagne solide de l'Ungava, mais "de légères petites touches de mauve, autour desquelles devait s'harmoniser l'ensemble des plans et des jeux lumineux, complexe écheveau de coloris, d'ombre et de clarté". De ce jaillissement de l'inspiration, seul demeure "le mauve fragile", image de douceur, de légèreté, qui n'a rien à voir avec le *dur* de l'élément *terrestre*. Chez Pierre, comme chez les autres personnages masculins, l'image princeps est donc le *mou*, signe de complexité inquiète et de la recherche du moi. Au contraire, les personnages féminins, solides dans leur rôle de femme et de mère, se trouvent ancrés dans la dureté de l'élèment *terrestre*.

Il peut sembler difficile de baser sans l'ombre d'un doute la psychologie des personnages de Gabrielle Roy sur des influences précises. Ce serait également un exemple de mauvaise foi que d'écarter la possibilité que l'élément *terrestre* qui domine chez elle et que l'élément liquide qui l'accompagne, soit pour l'enrichir ou lui opposer sa "puissance dissolvante", se rattache instinctivement aux racines de l'auteur, c'est-à-dire à la prairie canadienne où elle est née et où elle a passé sa jeunesse.

NOTES

1 Gabrielle Roy, *Alexandre Chenevert* (Montreal: Beauchemin, 1964), p. 104.
2 Gabrielle Roy, *La Montagne secrète* (Montreal: Beauchemin, 1961), p. 221.
3 Gaston Bachelard, *La Terre et les rêveries de la volonté* (Paris: Corti, 1948), p. 18.
4 *Ibid.*
5 Gabrielle Roy, *Bonheur d'occasion* (Montreal: Beauchemin, 1947), T. I, p. 231.
6 *Ibid.,* T. II, p. 374.
7 *La Terre et les revéries de la volonté,* p. 52.
8 *Bonheur d'occasion,* T. II, p. 371.
9 *Ibid,* p. 476.
10 *Ibid,* p. 530.
11 *Ibid,* p. 531.
12 Gabrielle Roy, *La Petite Poule d'Eau* (Montreal: Beauchemin, 1950), pp. 160-161.
13 Gabrielle Roy, *La Rivière sans repos* (Montreal: Beauchemin, 1970), p. 292.
14 *Ibid.,* p. 301.
15 *Bonheur d'occasion,* T. I, p. 207.
16 *Ibid.,* T. II, p. 483.
17 *Alexandre Chenevert,* p. 250.

PASSAGE BY LAND

Rudy Wiebe

I NEVER SAW A MOUNTAIN or a plain until I was twelve, almost thirteen. The world was poplar and birch-covered; muskeg hollows and stony hills; great hay sloughs with the spruce on their far shores shimmering in summer heat, and swamps with wild patterns burned three and four, sometimes five feet into their moss by some fire decades before, filled with water in spring but dry in summer and sometimes smoking faintly still in the morning light where, if you slid from your horse and pushed your hand into the moss, you could feel the strange heat of it lurking.

In such a world, a city of houses with brick chimneys, telephones, was less real than Grimm's folk tales, or Greek myths. I was born in what would become, when my father and older brothers chopped down enough trees for the house, our chicken barn; and did not speak English until I went to school, though I can't remember learning it. Perhaps I never have (as one former professor insists when he reads my novels); certainly it wasn't until years later I discovered that the three miles my sister and I had meandered to school, sniffing and poking at pussy-willows and ant hills, lay somewhere in the territory Big Bear and Wandering Spirit had roamed with their warriors always just ahead of General Strange in May and June, 1885. As a child, however, I was for years the official flag raiser (Union Jack) in our one-room school and during the war I remember wondering what it would be like if one day, just as I turned the corner of the pasture with the cows, a huge car would wheel into our yard, Joseph Stalin emerge and from under his moustache tell my father he could have his farm back in Russia, if he wanted it. Then I would stand still on the cow path trodden into the thin bush soil and listen, listen for our cowbells; hear a dog bark some miles away, and a boy call; and wonder what an immense world of people — I could not quite imagine how many — was now doing chores and if it wasn't for the trees and the curvature of the earth (as the teacher said) I could easily see Mount Everest somewhere a little south of east. Or west?

My first sight of the prairie itself I do not remember. We were moving south, leaving the rocks and bush of northern Saskatchewan forever, my parents said, and I was hanging my head out of the rear window of the hired car, vomiting. I had a weak stomach from having been stepped on by a horse, which sounds funny though I cannot remember it ever being so. Consequently, our first day in south Alberta the driver had me wash his car and so I cannot remember my first glimpse of the Rocky Mountains either. It was long after that that anyone explained to me the only mountain we could see plainly from there was in the United States.

But sometimes a fall morning mirage will lift the line of Rockies over the level plain and there they will be, streaked black in crevices under their new snow with wheat stubble for base and the sky over you; you can bend back forever and not see its edge. Both on foot and from the air I have since seen some plains, some mountains on several continents; jungles; the Danube, the Mississippi, even the Amazon. But it was north of Old Man River one summer Sunday when I was driving my father (he had stopped trying to farm and he never learned to drive a car) to his week's work pouring concrete in a new irrigation town, that we got lost in broad daylight on the prairie. Somewhere we had missed something and the tracks we were following at last faded and were gone like grass. My father said in Low German, "Boy, now you turn around."

I got out. The grass crunched dry as crumbs and in every direction the earth so flat another two steps would place me at the horizon, looking into the abyss of the universe. There is too much here, the line of sky and grass rolls in upon you and silences you thin, too impossibly thin to remain in any part recognizably yourself. The space must be broken somehow or it uses you up, and my father muttered in the car, "If you go so far and get lost at least there's room to go back. Now turn around." A few moments thereafter we came upon a rail line stretched in a wrinkle of the land — the prairie in Alberta is not at all flat, it only looks like that at any given point — white crosses beside rails that disappeared straight as far in either direction as could be seen. We had not crossed a railroad before but the tracks could no more be avoided here than anything else and some connecting road to the new town be eventually somewhere beyond.

In that wandering to find it is rooted, I believe, the feeling I articulated much later; the feeling that to touch this land with words requires an architectural structure; to break into the space of the reader's mind with the space of this western landscape and the people in it you must build a structure of fiction like an engineer builds a bridge or a skyscraper over and into space. A poem, a lyric, will not do. You must lay great black steel lines of fiction, break up that space with huge design and, like the fiction of the Russian steppes, build giant artifact. No song can do that; it must be giant fiction.

The way a man feels with and lives with that living earth with which he is always labouring to live. Farmer or writer.

(1971)

THE MAZE OF LIFE

The Work of Margaret Laurence

S. E. Read

DR. JOHNSON in his "Preface to Shakespeare" comments trenchantly on the hazards of evaluating that which is new in the realm of the creative arts. "To works . . . of which the excellence is not absolute and definite, but gradual and comparative; to works not raised upon principles demonstrative and scientific, but appealing wholly to observation and experience, no other test can be applied than length of duration and continuance of esteem." Yet the new must be tested and appraised, and esteem or condemnation rendered, long before the passing of the traditional century, "the term commonly fixed as the test of literary merit".

To criticize the writings of Margaret Laurence is to criticize that which is new — very new. Five years ago her name was unknown to the reading public. Today, as the result of the publication of four works, three of which appeared in a few brief months in 1963 and 1964, she is recognized in many parts of the English-speaking world as a serious writer who has already achieved greatly and who gives promise of even greater achievement. I realize, of course, that the excellence of her works "is not absolute and definite", but when I read her pages I feel certain that her means are just, and "Applause, in spite of trivial faults, is due."

Margaret Laurence is a Canadian, born in Neepawa, Manitoba, a very small prairie town somewhat to the northeast of Brandon. She graduated from the University of Manitoba but shortly after found herself in the British protectorate of Somaliland (now part of the Republic of Somalia), the young wife of a British civil engineer. She then moved to the Gold Coast (now Ghana); later, for a brief period, to Vancouver; then back to England. But wherever she goes, she looks, sees, records, studies, and remembers. For she has the eye of an artist and from

132

the world of her experience she draws the materials for the patterns of her writing. And the patterns are many and varied.

Though the establishment of her reputation has been brilliantly rapid, this is not to say that she sprang full armed from the head of Melpomene, or some such suitable muse. From childhood on she has studied and practised the craft of story telling, and readers of *Prism* and *Queen's Quarterly* may recall a few of her short stories published in the late 1950's. But her first novel, *This Side Jordan,* did not appear until 1960, to be followed, after a silence of more than two years, by *The Prophet's Camel Bell* (1963), *The Tomorrow-Tamer* (1963), and *The Stone Angel* (1964). It is on these books that her present reputation rests.

The Prophet's Camel Bell makes the best starting point for an article of this general nature. It most fully reveals the writer herself — her character and personality, her attitudes and opinions, her sensitivity and her reactions to the world around her, her ability to observe and interpret, her approach to the business of writing.

The work itself does not slip easily into any rigid category. It starts like a journal and in some parts reads like a journal. But basically it is a commentary on a people — the Somalis — and on their character, their ways of life, and their literature. It also contains a series of sharp, penetrating sketches of individuals — Somalis, Italians, British. But free of dates and the binding restrictions of time, it has a timeless feeling about it that sets the work quite apart from the usual books of travel and adventure in distant and exotic parts.

Mrs. Laurence was twenty-four or less when she went to Somaliland as the wife of an English engineer, who had been appointed by the British Government to direct the construction of a series of *ballehs* or earth dams along the southern edge of the Protectorate, just to the north of the Ethiopian boundary. The area is known as the Haud. On its northern edge is Hargeisa, the only town of any size, and it is no centre of civilization. The economy of the country is poor; the chief occupation is grazing camels and sheep; the population is almost entirely Moslem; the number of Europeans is very small; and the heat can be extreme. Yet into the Haud Mrs. Laurence went, to be with her husband as he surveyed the project and as he supervised the building of the *ballehs* that were to store water and to bring some assurance of life to the animals and the people of the land. Conditions were tough and the hazards real. Yet it is from this background that Mrs. Laurence drew the fabrics for *The Prophet's Camel Bell;* and — if I may hazard a guess — it is within this circle of time that she began to mature as a writer.

If she had not been herself she might well have become a memsahib, a well behaved, tea-going wife of a sahib. This would have been the right and proper thing to do. But she saw the distance which the memsahibs "put between themselves and the Somalis" and quickly took the unconventional road. Within hours of arriving at Hargeisa she had gone to the town's centre *on foot* ("European women did not go to the Somali town alone, and no European ever went on foot. It simply wasn't done."); she soon entertained Somalis in her house; and before long she moved into the wilderness to live with the working crews. Actions such as these require courage, independence, and perhaps a good sense of humour. Mrs. Laurence has all three.

But she did not do these things just to be contrary. She wanted to learn, to know, and to acquire materials from which books might be made. She not only observed and listened, with keen eyes and delicately attuned ears; she also studied works on Somaliland (for example, Richard Burton's classic, *First Steps in East Africa*), and immersed herself in the language and the unwritten literature of the people. In brief, she became a thoroughly disciplined and hard working scholar and writer.

Two works resulted. The first, *A Tree for Poverty*, a translation of traditional though unrecorded tales and poems, was published by the Somaliland government in 1954; the second, *The Prophet's Camel Bell*, appeared almost a decade later, in 1963. I have not seen the earlier work, but one chapter in the more recent book is entitled "A Tree for Poverty" and contains critical comments on the literature of the Somalis, as well as extended examples of poems and tales. Included are one *belwo*, a short love poem; an extract from a *gabei*, the highest literary form, impressive in proportions and technique; and two thoroughly delightful tales, rapid in movement, rich in humour, and revealing Somali attitudes towards life, death, and Allah.

All in all, the Somaliland venture must have been a rich one for Mrs. Laurence, and by the time she moved from Somaliland into the Gold Coast (still not yet Ghana), she had become a skilled stylist, a sharp observer of landscapes and people, deeply involved in the study of language, folk lore, myths, and traditions. She was ready to begin the groundwork for her volume of short stories, *The Tomorrow-Tamer*, and the novel that brought her initial fame, *This Side Jordan*.

I AM NOT QUITE SURE when the Laurences went to the Gold Coast, but it was in the period of transition — shortly before Ghana became independent in 1957. Certainly the atmosphere of change — of breakdown and building, of white withdrawal and black upsurge, of uncertain conflict and deep-rooted suspicion — runs through all the stories and through the novel, a unifying, binding current.

Ten stories in all compose *The Tomorrow-Tamer*. Nine of them had been previously published in magazines and periodicals from 1956 to 1963. All of them are gems, though some more finely cut than others, and the volume is unified by a common theme — the dying of the old way of life and the birth of the new. *The Tomorrow-Tamer* has been wisely chosen as the core story for the volume. Not only is it the best story, but it best expresses the inevitable conflict inherent in change.

In bare outline the story is simple. A bridge is to be built across the river Owura. The bridge will link the village Owurasu with the outside world. The village is old and primitive, in the grip of the ancient gods and the old super-stitions. The bridge is new, modern, and, to the villagers, a mystery. Will the river god be offended by the structure that slowly begins to span the waters? Will the destruction of the sacred grove bring disaster? At first the young man Kofi is the only villager the council of elders will allow to work with the invading labour force. When no harm comes to him, other villagers are allowed to join in the work. Kofi becomes their leader; then, in his own mind, he becomes the priest of the bridge. He will tend it; fearless, he will tame it. In his pride, he climbs to the highest beam of the great structure, and standing erect on the steel he gazes even higher — into the sun. Blinded by the sudden brilliance, he loses his balance and plunges to his death in the waters far below.

> As for the people of Owurasu, they were not surprised. They understood per-fectly well what had happened. The bridge, clearly, had sacrificed its priest in order to appease the river. The people felt they knew the bridge now. Kofi had been the first to recognize the shrine, but he had been wrong about one thing. The bridge was not as powerful as Owura. The river had been acknowledged as elder. The queenly bridge had paid its homage and was a part of Owurasu at last.

This conflict, clearly symbolic, is repeated with varying patterns in the other stories — at times with humour, at times with a touch of sentiment, at times with irony and bitterness. "The Merchant of Heaven", the tale of Amory Lemon, "proselytizer for a mission known as the Angel of Philadelphia", is a bitter and acid comment on a salvager of souls who is no better than the witch doctor in a bush village; "The Perfume Sea" is a delightful tale of Archipelago, "English-Style Barber European Ladies' Hairdresser", who managed to survive the impact of change by merging his interests with that of his manicurist and beautician and painting a new sign that read:

ARCHIPELAGO & DOREE

BARBERSHOP

ALL-BEAUTY SALON

African Ladies a Specialty

And "The Pure Diamond Man" is a good-fun story of a fast operator, Tettel, who tries to make quick money by selling the secrets of village magic to an amateur anthropologist only to be caught in his own trickery. It is satiric, but not as serious a study of change as the other stories I have mentioned. All in all it is a collection of delightful and brilliantly told tales. I shall say more later about the distinguishing characteristics of the style.

To date, Mrs. Laurence has had two novels published — *This Side Jordan* and *The Stone Angel*. The first (and it is the earlier) belongs to the African period; the second is purely Canadian in its setting.

This Side Jordan continues the theme that runs through the tales. The setting is again Ghana; the time, the transitional period of Ghanaian independence. The action stems from the problem of adjustment — the adjustment of the African to a new-found freedom; the adjustment of the English to a radically and rapidly changing position. The characters are neatly arranged in two opposing groups — Africans on the left, English on the right; and the action is skilfully developed (though at times it seems slightly artificial or contrived) so as to bring the two groups spasmodically together. Irritation, suspicion, anger, even hate are the recurring results when their paths cross.

Johnnie Kestoe, the principal English character, is an opportunist — aggressive, short-sighted, intolerant, and self-centred. As a new employee of the Textile Division of a long-established English firm, he does not understand the world he is in, nor does he want to. Only at the end does he shift ground slightly, but then by necessity more than desire. His dramatic opponent, Nathaniel Amegbe, schoolmaster at Futura Academy (principal and owner, Jacob Abraham), is unqualified, underpaid, somewhat stupid, slightly dishonest, and, still close to the primitive ways and superstitions of the bush village from which he came, confused and frustrated by Christianity, education, and city life. But, unlike Kestoe, Amegbe is something of an idealist, though slightly tarnished, and can dream about, and is willing to work for, a better world in the not too distant future.

136

This balance of opposites is neatly extended to include the two wives. Miranda, the wife of Kestoe, is painfully curious about the African way of life and embarrasses the sensitive Amegbe at every turn. Aya, Amegbe's wife, is ignorant, suspicious, hostile. Both women, as the novel opens, are pregnant; and, as the novel comes to its close, they find themselves together in hospital, each awaiting the common experience of birth. Within hours, to each a child is born — to Miranda, a girl, Mary; to Aya, a boy, Joshua. And with their birth, hope for the future is also born — the new Mary may bring a new love, the new Joshua may well lead his people to "this side Jordan".

Around this central four revolve a half dozen or more other characters — black and white. None is perfect, either in virtue or villainy; all are caught in the whirlpool of change, all are confused, each in his own degree. Some resist and break; some compromise and survive. All are sketched with penetrating insight and considerable sympathy. For — if I read it aright — this is a novel that damns no one completely. Rather it is a novel that pleads for understanding and enlightenment. As such, it was, and is, a successful and exciting work. As such, too, it creates its own limitations — for it is a novel that deals with a problem of a moment, and, with the passing of time, its reason for being will be darkened, and interest in it will decline.

With the writing of *The Stone Angel*, Mrs. Laurence reached full maturity as a novelist. In my opinion she must now be considered as a significant literary artist — on any terms. For here she has created a great central character, untrammeled by bounds of place or time; and has handled her core theme — the aging of a prideful, independent woman — with profound sympathy and telling conviction. This is a novel that should appeal to many readers for many years to come.

The book's jacket describes the work as a "novel with a Canadian setting". True. Part of the action unrolls in Manawaka, a small town somewhere on the prairie; part in a nameless city (Vancouver — perhaps) on the western seaboard. But these settings are condiments. They give flavour or spice, but they are not the essential food. That is Hagar Shipley, an old and stubborn woman of ninety, who is "rampant with memory", but who also finds that each passing day has for her a rarity which must be treasured and admired.

It is the weaving of these past and present strands that makes the final fabric of the work. Through an alternating pattern we are given the story of her life and the account of her last struggle to maintain her independence; and when the weaving is done, we see her as a character portrayed with deep understanding and sympathy. This autobiographical technique — combining as it does reminiscence and stream of consciousness — may produce some flaws and certainly demands suspension of disbelief; but it is handled with skill and daring and produces a fast moving story and a strong feeling of tension.

Hagar Shipley is a Lear-like figure. She is prideful, stubborn, hard, opinionated, and confused. Like her Biblical namesake, she wanders in a wilderness of her own making. Like the stone angel that stands over the remains "of her who relinquished her feeble ghost as I gained my stubborn one", she views her world with sightless eyes, for the marble monument was "doubly blind, not only stone but unendowed with even a pretense of sight. Whoever carved her had left the eyeballs blank." But, like Lear, she — Hagar — through the agony of her last days, achieves vision, understands human suffering, and reaches out her hands in a dying gesture of love.

The time span of the final action is short — a few days. But these days are rich in experience and deep with meaning. They frame her last struggle to retain her independence. Against her are ranged her disintegrating body, a bumbling son, Melvin, and a plotting, offensive daughter-in-law, Doris. Against the attacks of the flesh she is helpless; against the scheming of her human opponents she stands firm. With the sharpness of an old vixen she rightly foresees their plan to place her in "Silverthreads", a nursing home where "Mother will find the companionship of those her age, plus every comfort and convenience," and, with animal courage, she seeks salvation in flight.

Alone, by the edge of the sea, she takes refuge from storm and cold in a crumbling cannery building. She seeks and finds courage not through hymns or the Twenty-third Psalm, but through lines from Keats:

> Old Meg was brave as Margaret Queen,
> And tall as Amazon;
> An old red blanket coat she wore,
> A ship hat had she on.

She reviews the darkest moments of her life — the deaths of her drunken husband and her favourite son John, upon whom she had lavished her affection only to have him become her Ishmael, whose hand was "against every man, and every man's hand against him". Then into the blackness of her night comes a fool — a vague parallel, perhaps, but a parallel none the less of Lear's fool — a tippling insurance salesman, Murray F. Lees. Together they fill their bellies with cheap red wine, then tell, each to the other, sad tales of loss and of sorrow. And to

Hagar, as she listens to Lees and as she receives from him understanding and kindness, comes understanding of self and the realization that tragedy is the common lot of man.

A few days later, after being found by her distraught son and daughter-in-law, old Hagar dies in hospital, but not before she has shown, through acts of kindness to those around her, that she has found a new meaning to life. Through freely giving of self, the old stone angel at last receives eyes and sees with terrifying clarity that she herself has been the cause of her blackened years. "Pride was my wilderness, and the demon that lead me was fear. I was alone, never anything else, and never free, for I carried my chains within me, and they spread out from me and shackled all I touched."

It is the creation of Hagar Shipley that clearly marks — for me at least — the emergence of Mrs. Laurence as a fine novelist. For the first business of a serious novelist is the creation of character. And when any particular character slips, almost imperceptibly perhaps, beyond the realms of obvious fiction into the world of reality then the summit of the novelist's art has been achieved. Such is Hagar. She belongs in that great company that begins with Chaucer's Monk and Pardoner, Prioress and Wife of Bath and stretches through the works of the great down to our present day. At times vicious and vulgar, irascible and prideful, stubborn and independent, she is by no means lovable; but she is capable of profound feelings and in the end demands respect. I'll forget, eventually, Johnnie Kestoe and Nathaniel Amegbe; but I'll not forget the Stone Angel. I may even see her from time to time — on the street, in a bus, or in a hospital ward; for she is timeless and the world is her home.

It is evident from what I have already said that Margaret Laurence can tell a good story — short or long — skilfully handle tense dramatic situations, observe with microscopic eye the societies in which she has lived, and create memorable characters. But she can also write extremely well. Her command of language is sure and controlled. Each word is precisely chosen to produce a desired effect, and each sentence is carefully structured to fit the mood of the moment or the motion of the action. Through her extraordinary powers of observation combined with her sure grasp of words she can transport the reader into far-distant lands where sights, sounds, smells, colours form patterns quite different from those we encounter in our own round of life. Take, for example, a brief passage from "The Merchant of Heaven" where the narrator and Brother Lemon, the evangelist, walk through the streets of a Ghanaian town:

On our second trip, however, he began to notice other things. A boy with sup-purating yaws covering nearly as much of his body as did his shreds of clothing. A loin-clothed labourer carrying a headload so heavy that his flimsy legs buckled and bent. A trader woman minding a roadside stall on which her living was spread — a half dozen boxes of cube sugar and a handful of pink plastic combs. A girl child squatting modestly in the filth-flowing gutter. A grinning penny-pleading gamin with a belly outpuffed by navel hernia. A young woman, pregnant and carrying another infant on her back, her placid eyes growing all at once proud and hating as we passed comfortably by. An old Muslim beggar who howled and shouted *sura* from the Qoran, and then, silent, looked and looked with the un-clouded innocent eyes of lunacy.

Or take the opening lines of "The Tomorrow-Tamer", lines filled with rapid movement, strong colours, and local lore:

The dust rose like clouds of red locusts around the small stampeding hooves of taggle-furred goats and the frantic wings of chickens with all their feathers awry. Behind them the children darted, their bodies velvety with dust, like a flash and tumble of brown butterflies in the sun.

The young man laughed to see them, and began to lope after them. Past the palms where the tapsters got wine, and the sacred grove to Owura, god of the river. Past the shrine where Nana Ayensu poured libation to the dead and guardian grandsires. Past the thicket of ghosts, where the graves were, where every leaf and flower had fed on someone's kin, and the wind was the thin whisper-speech of ancestral spirits. Past the deserted huts, clay walls runnelled by rain, where rats and demons dwelt in unholy brotherhood. Past the old men drowsing in doorways, dreaming of women, perhaps, or death. Past the good huts with their brown baked walls strong against any threatening night-thing, the slithering snake carrying in its secret sac the end of life, or red-eyed Sasabonsam, huge and hairy, older than time and always hungry.

Or again, this passage from *The Stone Angel*, which further illustrates Mrs. Laurence's profound powers of perception, her delicate handling of language, and her ability to penetrate the workings of the mind. Old Hagar, having fled from her family, sits alone in the forest. Her mind wanders freely, the movement is slow, poetic:

Now I perceive that the forest is not still at all, but crammed with creatures scurrying here and there on multitudinous and mysterious errands. A line of ants crosses the tree trunk where I'm sitting. Solemn and in single file they march to-wards some miniature battle or carrion feast. A giant slug oozes across my path flowing with infinite slowness like a stagnant creek. My log is covered with moss — I pluck it, and an enormous piece comes away in my hand. It's long and curly as hair, a green wig suitable for some judicial owl holding court over the thievish jays of scavenging beetles. Beside me grows a shelf of fungus, the velvety under-side a mushroom colour, and when I touch it, it takes and retains my fingerprint. From the ground nearby sprouts a scarlet-tipped Indian paintbrush — that's for the scribe. Now we need only summon the sparrows as jurors, but they'd condemn me quick as a wink, no doubt.

With equal skill, Mrs. Laurence handles the dialogue of her characters. She has a fine ear for conversation, and through the nuances of idiom, the tonal varia-tions that exist between young and old, native and non-native, and the vocabulary differences between educated and uneducated, she keeps her characters sharply apart. She rarely fumbles, for she is a genuine artist in the handling of words. There is little padding. Each word — even each sound — has its place in the over-all pattern. As a result, she is effective, persuasive, and at times deeply moving.

But she is not effective and moving merely because she writes well. In the last analysis, I believe that her potential greatness — a greatness not yet fully realized — lies in the fact that through all her works runs a deep and passionate interest in human beings. From *The Prophet's Camel Bell* through to *The Stone Angel* there is an ever-present call for understanding and tolerance between individuals, of different races or of the same race. In none of her works is Mrs. Laurence just a slick and a brilliant teller of tales, nor a cold, albeit perceptive analyst. She is deeply moved, I am sure, by the tragedies of human existence, by man's constant frustrations as he tries to work through the Minoan maze that is life. She writes because she is impelled to write, not as a propagandist or an orthodox moralist, but as one willing to wrestle unceasingly with the human dilemma. Her far distant ancestor is the unknown author of Job who in his own questioning anguish cried:

> Oh that my words were now written!
> Oh that they were inscribed in a book!
> That with an iron pen and lead
> They were graven in the rock for ever!

(1966)

TEN YEARS' SENTENCES

Margaret Laurence

Almost exactly ten years ago I was sitting in the study of our house in Vancouver, filled with the black celtic gloom which sometimes strikes. I had just received a letter from an American publisher which said, among other things, that their chief reader reported himself to be "only reasonably nauseated" by the lengthy interior monologues of the main character of my first novel, *This Side Jordan*. If I could see my way clear to reconsidering parts of the novel, they would be willing to look at it again. More revision, I thought, was out of the question. I had already rewritten half the book from scratch when I decided, after leaving Africa and getting a fresh perspective on colonial society, that I'd been unfair to the European characters. More work I couldn't face. A quick cup of hemlock would be easier. However, as we were a little short on hemlock just then, I got out the manuscript instead. I hadn't looked at it for months, and I saw to my consternation that the gent with the upset stomach was undeniably right in some ways. I managed to cut some of the more emotive prose (although not enough) and lived to bless him for his brutal criticism.

Ten years ago I was thirty-two years old and incredibly naive about writing and publishing. I had never talked with any publisher face-to-face. I knew only one other writer as a close friend — Adele Wiseman, whose letters throughout the years had heartened me. I had had one short story published in *Queen's Quarterly* a few years earlier, and had been encouraged by Malcolm Ross, the then-editor. I had also recently had a story published in *Prism*, and Ethel Wilson had graciously written to say she liked it — that meant more to me than I can ever express and began a friendship which has been one of the most valued in my life.

Can it only have been ten years ago? What has changed? Everything. The world and myself. In some ways it's been the most difficult and most interesting decade of my life, for almost everything I've written which has been publishable has been written in these years. I've mysteriously managed to survive the writing of six more books, after that first novel. It's been said that for some writers the only thing worse than writing is not writing, and for me this is nearly true, for I don't write any more easily now than I did ten years ago. In fact, I write less easily, perhaps because as well as the attempt to connect directly with the character's wavelength, there is now also a kind of subconscious monitor which seeks to cut out the garbage (the totally irrelevant, and the "fine" oratorical writing which I have come to dislike more and more) before it is written rather than after, and the two selves sometimes work in uneasy harness. Simultaneously, of course, it's had its exhilaration, the feeling that comes when the writing is moving well, setting its own pace, finding its own form. I've learned a few things I needed to know — for example, that the best and worst time is when the writing is going on, not when the book is published, for by that point one is disconnected from that particular thing. I've learned that my anxieties and difficulties with writing aren't peculiar to myself — most writers have the same kind of demons and go on having them, as I do. (This seems so obvious as to be hardly worth stating, but I didn't really know it ten years ago.) I've lived for the past six years in England, and although I've picked up a lot of peripherally useful information about the publishing aspect of books and a sense of the writing going on in many countries, I don't really believe my being here has influenced my writing one way or another, certainly not to anything like the same extent as Africa once did.

This Side Jordan and the two other books I wrote which were set in Africa, *The Prophet's Camel Bell* and *The Tomorrow-Tamer*, were written out of the milieu of a rapidly ending colonialism and the emerging independence of African countries. They are not entirely hopeful books, nor do they, I think, ignore some of the inevitable casualties of social change, both African and European, but they do reflect the predominantly optimistic outlook of many Africans and many western liberals in the late 1950's and early 1960's. They were written by an outsider who experienced a seven years' love affair with a continent but who in the end had to remain in precisely that relationship, for it could never become the close involvement of family. The affair could be terminated — it was not basically for me a lifetime commitment, as it has been for some Europeans. On Africa's side, in its people's feelings towards me, it was, not unnaturally, little more than polite tolerance, for white liberals were not much more loved then than they are now, and with some considerable justification, as I discovered partly from listening to myself talking and partly in writing *This Side Jordan*. Another thing all my African writing had in common was that the three books were written by a person who had lived in Africa in her late twenties and early thirties, and it all therefore bears the unmistakable mark of someone who is young and full of faith. In *This Side Jordan* (which I now find out-dated and superficial and yet somehow retrospectively touching) victory for the side of the angels is all but assured. Nathaniel holds up his newborn son, at the end, and says "Cross Jordan, Joshua." Jordan the mythical *could* be crossed; the dream-goal of the promised land *could* be achieved, if not in Nathaniel's lifetime, then in his son's. This was the prevailing spirit, not only of myself but of Africa at that time. Things have shifted considerably since then.

AFTER I CAME TO ENGLAND, in 1962, I picked up some of the threads of a relationship with Africa, although this time only as an observer and amateur friend, for I had had to abandon every *ism* except individualism and even that seemed a little creaky until the last syllable finally vanished of itself, leaving me ismless, which was just as well. I became extremely interested in contemporary African writing in English. It had seemed to me, a few years before, that if anything was now going to be written about Africa, it would have to be done from the inside by Africans themselves, and this was one reason I stopped writing anything with that setting. In fact, although I did not realize it then, already many young African writers were exploring their own backgrounds, their own societies and people. In a period of hiatus after finishing *A Jest Of God*, I read a great deal of contemporary Nigerian writing and even rashly went so far as to write a book of commentary on it. This book, called *Long Drums And Cannons* (the title is taken from a poem by Christopher Okigbo) I now feel refers to a period of history which is over — the fifteen years in which Nigerian writers created a kind of renaissance, drawing upon their cultural past and relating it to the present, seeking links with the ancestors and the old gods in order to discover who they themselves were. This exploration and discovery ended abruptly with the first massacre of the Ibo in the north, some two years ago. When Nigeria finally emerges from its present agony, it will be in some very different and as yet unpredictable form, and its writers may well find themselves having to enquire into themes they have so far hardly touched, such as the appalling grip on the human heart of tribalism in its hate aspect.

In London, in 1965, I got to know a few Nigerian writers when they visited this country. I remember especially the times I met Christopher Okigbo, and how surprised I was at his external ebullience, his jazziness, so much in contrast to his deeply introverted poetry. And I remember, after having read Wole Soyinka's plays and seeing *The Road* performed here, having lunch with Wole and hearing him talk about the travelling theatre company he hoped to get going (he had already set up two theatres in Nigeria, the first contemporary theatres there). How much everything can change in a couple of years! Chris Okigbo is dead, fighting for Biafra. Wole Soyinka, undoubtedly the best writer that English-writing Africa has yet produced, and one of the best anywhere, has been in a Federal jail in Kaduna for more than a year. Chinua Achebe, that excellent and wise novelist, isn't writing for himself these days — he's doing journalism for Biafra, and all one can hope at the moment is that he manages to survive.

I guess I will always care about Africa. But the feeling I had, in everything I wrote about it, isn't the feeling I have now. It would be easy to convey the impression that I've become disillusioned with the entire continent, but this would be a distortion. What has happened, with Africa's upheavals, has been happening all over the world. Just as I feel that Canadians can't say *them* when we talk of America's disastrous and terrifying war in Vietnam, so I feel we can't say *them* of Africans. What one has come to see, in the last decade, is that tribalism is an inheritance of us all. Tribalism is not such a bad thing, if seen as the bond which an individual feels with his roots, his ancestors, his background. It may or may not be stultifying in a personal sense, but that is a problem each of us has to solve or not solve. Where tribalism becomes, to my mind, frighteningly dangerous is where the tribe — whatever it is, the Hausa, the Ibo, the Scots Presbyterians, the Daughters of the American Revolution, the in-group — is seen as "the people", the human beings, and the others, the un-tribe, are seen as sub-human. This is not Africa's problem alone; it is everyone's.

When I stopped writing about Africa and turned to the area of writing where I most wanted to be, my own people and background, I felt very hesitant. The character of Hagar had been in my mind for quite a while before I summoned enough nerve to begin the novel. Strangely enough, however, once I began *The Stone Angel*, it wrote itself more easily than anything I have ever done. I experienced the enormous pleasure of coming home in terms of idiom. With the African characters, I had to rely upon a not-too-bad ear for human speech, but in conceptual terms, where thoughts were concerned, I had no means of knowing whether I'd *come* within a mile of them or not. With Hagar, I had an upsurge of certainty. I wouldn't go to great lengths to defend the form of the novel, at this distance, for I know its flaws. The flashback method is, I think, a little overworked in it, and I am not at all sure that flashbacks ought to be in chronological order, as I placed them in order to make it easier for the reader to follow Hagar's life. But where Hagar herself is concerned, I still believe she speaks and feels as she would have done. She speaks in the voice of someone of my grandparents' generation, but it is a voice I know and have always known. I feel ambiguous towards her, because I resent her authoritarian outlook, and yet I love her, too, for her battling.

I didn't know I was changing so much when I wrote *The Stone Angel*. I haven't ever decided beforehand on a theme for a novel (I know that where *This Side Jordan* is concerned, this statement sounds untrue, but it isn't). The individual characters come first, and I have often been halfway through something before I realized what the theme was. *The Stone Angel* fooled me even when I had finished writing it, for I imagined the theme was probably the same as in much of my African writing — the nature of freedom. This is partly true, but I see now that the emphasis by that time had altered. The world had changed; I had grown older. Perhaps I no longer believed so much in the promised land, even the promised land of one's own inner freedom. Perhaps an obsession with freedom is the persistent (thank God) dance of the young. With *The Stone Angel*, without my recognizing it at the time, the theme had changed to that of survival, the attempt of the personality to survive with some dignity, toting the load of excess mental baggage that everyone carries, until the moment of death.

I think (although I could be wrong) that this is more or less the theme of my last two novels as well. *A Jest of God*, as some critics have pointed out disapprovingly, is a very inturned novel. I recognize the limitations of a novel told in the first person and the present tense, from one viewpoint only, but it couldn't have been done any other way, for Rachel herself is a very inturned person. She tries to break the handcuffs of her own past, but she is self-perceptive enough to recognize that for her no freedom from the shackledom of the ancestors can be total. Her emergence from the tomb-like atmosphere of her extended childhood is a partial defeat — or, looked at in another way, a partial victory. She is no longer so much afraid of herself as she was. She is beginning to learn the rules of survival.

In *The Fire-Dwellers*, Stacey is Rachel's sister (don't ask me why; I don't know; she just is). Her boundaries are wider than Rachel's, for she is married and has four kids, so in everything she does she has to think of five other people. Who on earth, I asked myself when I began writing this novel, is going to be interested in reading about a middle-aged housewife, mother of four? Then I thought, the hell with it — some of my best friends are middle-aged housewives;

I'm one myself, but I deplore labels so let's just call one another by our proper names. I was fed up with the current fictional portraits of women of my generation — middle-aged mums either being presented as glossy magazine types, perfect, everloving and incontestably contented, or else as sinister and spiritually cannibalistic monsters determined only to destroy their men and kids by hypnotic means. I guess there are some women like the latter, but I don't happen to know any of them. There are no women like the former; they don't exist. Stacey had been in my mind for a long time — longer than Rachel, as a matter of fact. She's not particularly valiant (maybe she's an anti-heroine), but she's got some guts and some humour. In various ways she's Hagar's spiritual grand-daughter. When I finally got going at the novel, I experienced the same feeling I had had with *The Stone Angel*, only perhaps more so, because this time it was a question of writing really in my own idiom, the ways of speech and memory of my generation, those who were born in the 20's, were children in the dusty 30's, grew up during the last war. Stacey isn't in any sense myself or any other person except herself, but we know one another awfully well. She is concerned with survival, like Hagar and like Rachel, but in her case it involves living in an external world which she perceives as increasingly violent and indeed lunatic, and trying simultaneously within herself to accept middle age with its tricky ramifications, including the suspicion, not uncommon among her age-peers, that one was nicer, less corrupt and possibly even less stupid twenty years ago, this being, of course, not only a comprehension of reality but also a mirage induced by the point-of-no-return situation.

With this last novel (which interests me more than the others, because I've just finished it and am not yet disconnected) the writing is more pared-down than anything I've written yet, but the form itself is (or so I believe) wider, including as it does a certain amount of third-person narration as well as Stacey's idiomatic inner running commentary and her somewhat less idiomatic fantasies, dreams, memories.

A strange aspect of my so-called Canadian writing is that I haven't been much aware of its being Canadian, and this seems a good thing to me, for it suggests that one has been writing out of a background so closely known that no explanatory tags are necessary. I was always conscious that the novel and stories set in Ghana were *about Africa*. My last three novels just seem like novels.

Over ten years, trying to sum up the changes, I suppose I have become more involved with novels of character and with trying to feel how it would be to *be* that particular person. My viewpoint has altered from modified optimism to modified pessimism. I have become more concerned with form in writing than I used to be. I have moved closer (admittedly, in typically cautious stages) to an expression of my own idiom and way of thought. These are not qualitative statements, of course. I don't know whether my writing has become better or worse. I only know the ways in which it has changed. Sometimes it seems a peculiar way to be spending one's life — a life sentence of sentences, as it were. Or maybe not a life sentence, because one day I won't have any more to say and I hope I'll know when that time comes and have the will power to break a long-standing addiction. (How is that for mixed metaphors?)

I've listened to the speech of three generations — my grandparents, my parents and my own, and maybe I've even heard what some of it means. I can listen with great interest to the speech of a generation younger than mine, but I can't hear it accurately enough to set it down and I have no desire to try. That is specifically their business, not mine, and while envying them meanly, I also wish them god-speed.

At the moment, I have the same feeling as I did when I knew I had finished writing about Africa. I've gone as far as I personally can go, in the area in which I've lived for the past three novels. A change of direction would appear to be indicated. I have a halfway hunch where I want to go, but I don't know how to get there or what will be there if I do. Maybe I'll strike it lucky and find the right compass, or maybe I won't.

(1969)

THAT FOOL OF A FEAR

Notes on "A Jest of God"

George Bowering

MANITOBA was taken from the Cree, and the name means God's country. Neepawa means land of plenty. Margaret Laurence sets many of her stories in Neepawa, Manitoba, and calls the town "Manawaka". For a person such as Rachel Cameron, aware to much of irony in her life, the Cree names for her home might be taken as a jest of God. Anyone knows that in novels set on the Canadian prairie, place is a determinant, sometimes even a character. Margaret Laurence has been lately speaking of a sense of form for the novel. She would begin with a sense of form for the place. Not simply the flatness and the river, but also, in *A Jest of God*, the changing advertising signs over the front door of the funeral parlour Rachel nears as she is walking home. In the mid-fifties, when I arrived in rural Manitoba, I was told that this is God's country. You must be joking, I replied.

The town is split into two parts, each making the other feel guilty, and so is Rachel. Manawaka speaks with two voices, Scots-Canadian and Ukrainian. Rachel speaks with two voices that are unheard except when she speaks in voices, as in the tabernacle, or later in the ecstatic utterances concerning her experience of Nick. One gets the sense of place correctly when one gets the language right. Margaret Laurence is the rare Canadian writer who shows a care for the novel as good writing, language shaped to find literature. Serious writers know that the "content" of their work is no reality — all content is made-up or referential. In your language, in your voice, you can strive to make a record of the real, at least in so far as the written word may be taken as score for the tongue's workings.

In *A Jest of God*, seen as formally failed by some nineteenth-century reviewers, Margaret Laurence assays a responsive vocal style, the voice in the ear pursuing

Rachel's mind even into the deep places where the most superior fiction (Joyce, Beckett, etc.) comes from. Instead of doggedly getting on with the "story", the draggiest part of a book, the writing begins in its place and expands outward from the keystone province.

From my reading I have a nice visual sense of the place, looking out from those eyes. It is not the narrator's grabbing control of her scene, because she doesn't have it as a prospect. That way vocal: instead of a sifted and settled version of Rachel's summertime adventure we get close with her most private mind in the present tense. We hold a present, and it is tense. If we can do so, we should read the book aloud.

Then we may hear Rachel's tense mind as she sits for the first time in the Pentecostal tabernacle. The reality is tolled by the music, as in poetry:

> Oh my God. They can sit, rapt, wrapped around and smothered willingly by these
> syllables, the chanting of some mad enchanter, himself enchanted?

The rime tells the time. Here is a rare privilege in our fiction, the enjoyment of hearing the mind moving, rather than being on the receiving end of recollection, arrangement, description, and expression.

So I praise the process, beginning with place and voice, leading to that third thing hard to name, something like the risk or gift of getting naked, so that your nakedness may touch something that is not yours. The form of the novel, first-person and present tense, works as Rachel's opening-out does, to get naked. Margaret Laurence shows uncommon courage making this book, to confront social and deep personal stupidities and fears in the womb of her narrator. There is no prince charming waiting at the neck of the womb, but we onlookers are led to see Rachel finding herself, who had always been appalled by open utterance, expressing her desires physically, with tenderness and violence that both frighten and liberate her sensibilities to an extent. To an extent we are not urged to believe but simply allowed to witness.

MANAWAKA is in the brown middle of one of the world's widest countries, a long way from exotic, or so it would seem for anyone desiring elsewhere. Rachel has a mind, that is more important than any reviewer has noticed, and she feels as if her mind has already removed her from her town, as if the town is holding her by circumstances opposed to her mind. In this way she is fixed there by her mind. We are introduced to this state of mind as she listens to the children's skipping songs in the spring of the book, as Rachel's ears pick them out:

> *The wind blows low, the wind blows high*
> *The snow comes falling from the sky,*
> *Rachel Cameron says she'll die*
> *For the want of the golden city.*
> *She is handsome, she is pretty,*
> *She is the queen of the golden city ——*

and a paragraph later we are similarly introduced to a sensing of the town's mindless dislike for the exotic, as the children sing:

> *Spanish dancers, turn around,*
> *Spanish dancers, get out of this town.*

But poor Rachel is not allowed even to associate herself with the Spanish dancers, who are hated not only for their strangeness, but also for their grace. She sees herself as an awkward crane-like creature, or a streak of chalk, or a "tin giant".

Writing as she does, from inside Rachel's neurotic head, Mrs. Laurence feels that she has to go to some objective means of presenting the town's kitschy insularity, and the entrapment of dreams. So she presents to the reader sitting behind Rachel's eyes a number of ikons such as the children's skipping songs. When Rachel goes to the teenage hangout, the Regal Café, she sees venerable Lee Toy, "his centuries-old face not showing at all what he may think of these kids". Lee Toy is still sending money to his wife in China, a woman he has not seen in forty years. Rachel knows that like him she is isolated and secret, but fears that unlike him she is not relentless. Lee Toy's patient resistance is shown in the two pictures on his café's wall: a Coca-Cola poster and a painting, "long and narrow like an unrolled scroll, done on grey silk — a mountain, and on the slope a *solitary* and *splendidly plumaged* tiger". (Italics mine.) The painting is that old Romantic trick, the dream stuff, in this case delicate and exotic.

So that when Rachel has her self-induced masturbation dreams, the image must be removed from the town that has taught her repression. The faceless fantasy-lover enters her in a forest or on a beach. "It has to be right away from everywhere." At one time it is a gaudy Hollywood orgy in ancient Egypt, Rachel as both escapist and voyeur, dreamy outsider in a tangle of flesh.

When she does finally lie naked with a man, they are on the ground outside the town, but more important, her lover is a Ukrainian immigrant's son, whom she tries to picture as an exotic barbarian rider from Genghis Khan's hordes. This lover has a face, of course, one that interests Rachel because of its slavic near-oriental cast, a face unlike the Anglo-Scottish faces of her ancestors. Mrs. Laurence makes much of the hold maintained by her people's ancestors. In *A Jest of God* that notion makes up a good portion of the sense of place.

Manawaka is a symbolic Canadian town, originally Scottish, with a patina (or mould, depending on your side of the tracks) of more recent eastern European immigration. Mrs. Laurence simply sees the Scottish side teaching emotional repression, but also that Rachel's notion of the exotic in the poorer section is a normal stereotype.

Thinking on another ikon, the sign over the undertaker's door, Rachel remarks on how it has been replaced and reworded more than once through the years in order to soften the idea of death, at least for the Scottish Protestants of the town:

> No one in Manawaka ever dies, at least not on this side of the tracks. We are a gathering of immortals. . . . Death is rude, unmannerly, not to be spoken to in the street.

Spanish dancers, get out of this town. Rachel's closest ancestor is her mother, who runs about tidying the house every night so that it will look "as though no frail and mortal creature ever set foot in it". When Mr. Cameron the undertaker had been alive, Mrs. Cameron had put doilies on all the furniture so that his corpse-touching hands would not touch the place of her habitude. She apparently felt the same way about his touch on her body, an interesting fear of the touch of both death and life, a double fear that her daughter has picked up. It is only after she allows herself to be touched, and after she then inaugurates the touching, that she takes some open-eyed control of her own life, and even over that of her mother.

Previous to that time, we may see Rachel's curious suspension in her attitudes toward the two churches. She can feel superior to the uppity Protestants who want their church to be bloodless and quiet, but she herself squirms with embarrassment at the very thought of being seen in the Pentecostal tabernacle. When she is in the middle of the famous service at the tabernacle, she suddenly associates the loud singing with her childhood dream of the horsemen of the Apocalypse. At that time her mother had wakened her to say, "Don't be foolish — don't be foolish, Rachel — there's nothing there." Mrs. Cameron goes to her church every Sunday morning and there is nothing there, and she is no fool, has no chance now of becoming a fool, God's fool or her own. Later, when Rachel goes to her doctor with her fear of becoming a mother and finds that she has a uterine irregularity, she thinks:

> I was always afraid that I might become a fool. Yet I could almost smile with some grotesque lightheadedness at that fool of a fear, that poor fear of fools, now that I really am one ...

really am the town fool, the object of its children's songs, and its potential teacher, not satisfied to be its grade two teacher.

The untaught town is realized by its language, the reported clichés of mother May's card-playing cronies: "I guess they must keep you pretty busy, all those youngsters" — poor vision of the teaching process — and "Well, I think it's marvelous, the way you manage" — no insight into Rachel's problem with managing. This catching of ordinary real dialogue is Margaret Laurence's first easy accomplishment, the stuff her earliest writing was based on, and useful here as the antagonist to Rachel's interior verbal trouble, just as the town is that speaks that way. At the extreme, Mrs. Laurence manhandles it into unconscious irony versus Rachel's overconsciousness, as when, speaking of a movie, one of the old women says, "The one next week at the Roxy is *The Doomed Women*. I can't imagine what *it* can be about."

The town teaches not only repression but also the desire to put up a good appearance. Constantly the town is accurately described to show that the outsides of buildings are misleading declarations, as Rachel's appearance might be. The quiet brick houses are too big for their remaining occupants. "Nothing is old here, but it looks old." Hector, the current undertaker in the building with the rose window, is the agent of the people's wishes to have someone unfamiliar and well-dressed take care of confrontation with a crisis in life. For him it is a business; as in the Scottish church it is the business to make a good appearance. Here is the cheapened hold of the ancestors. Calla's mother named her after the lily, probably because both sound and picture gave the appearance of prettiness, but Calla is not conventionally pretty. The calla lily is the symbol of death — death and a good though not exuberant appearance, basic white, like the town. But Calla rejects the mortuary flower and paints her door a lilac colour, thus offending her neighbours, as Nick's father would have if he'd left his house painted the bright colours he wanted. While flinching at the openness, Rachel tells Nick that she has always envied it, thinking of the Ukrainians as "not so boxed-in, maybe. More outspoken. More able to speak out. More allowed to —

both by your family and by your self. . . . In my family, you didn't get emotional. It was frowned upon."

Part of rachel's quandary springs from the condition of her female-dominated world, a world that mitigates, by its condition, against her growing naturally out of her adolescence, perhaps. That condition traps her as much as the isolation of the shrinking town. Most of the males she sees are no help because they are remote or they are symptomatic of the town — Lee Toy, Hector the undertaker, Willard the school principal, the teenage boys in the coke cafe. Only James Doherty and Nick, two figures of outward, offer any surcease or hope.

James' mother, to begin with, is atypical of the mothers in Manawaka. She lets her son run free in nature when he is supposed to be suffering under the town's indoctrination in school. When she casually touches him, arousing Rachel's jealousy, he squirms away, and his mother "smiles, not unpleased that he wants to be his own and on his own". One feels that this mother would not urge her child to believe that there is "nothing there" in his dreams.

The danger and sadness of corrupting youthful optimism was a theme running through Mrs. Laurence's African stories. Rachel sees that she, desiring to be a mother especially to her favourite pupil, is in danger of fulfilling the role of typical Manawaka mother; and her relationship with James is more complicated than that. She knows that children can quickly detect falseness in their teachers, and become adversaries. She has a rather strong fear of becoming James' enemy, so she becomes his tormentor, because she also knows that if she shows her liking and admiration of him, he will be made to suffer by his classmates, who have been taught by their community to detest and ridicule tender human touch. So she hits him with a ruler (for a moment unable to rule herself) or speaks sharply to him: "It's so often James I speak to like this, fearing to be too much the other way with him." She projects on to him her longing to realize her uniqueness: "Looking at his wiry slightness, his ruffian sorrel hair, I feel an exasperated tenderness. I wonder why I should feel differently toward him? Because he's unique, that's why." (None of us is unaware of the sexual attraction, but that's not my direction here.) But a paragraph later she betrays her mind-forged manacles when she thinks of Calla, "If only she looked a little more usual." But she allies herself with James' uniqueness and independence of imagination, comparing him favourably with the majority of the pupils, who are given a "free choice" drawing class and have to wait for suggestions, their own (sad) houses, what they did last weekend. James draws a splendidly complicated and efficient spaceship, a vehicle to get him away from here, in all senses. Rachel may at times identify with James, or feel that she tacitly collaborates with him against the town's trap, or see him as potential wish-gratification, as parents normally do. "He goes his own way as though he endures the outside world but does not really believe in it," she thinks. Before she observes the unassuming rebellion of his mother Grace, she simply envies her, thinking that "she doesn't deserve to have him."

But, curiously, James also focusses the realistic part of her mind. Ordinary repressed people like Willard can go ahead and strap a boy like James, protesting that it is a duty he doesn't relish, but Rachel considers that she at least realizes her odd sexual botherings while ordinary people do not. *"I am not neutral — I am not detached — I know it. But neither are you, and you do not know it,"* she imagines herself saying to the young married-man principal. (Such realization is often missed by readers of Rachel's book.) From that realization to directness of expression is where Rachel will have to go when she gets close to Nick, but she finds it taught by Grace during a scene in which she talks to James' mother about his truancy. Rachel offers the woman an excuse so that she can "save face", but Grace simply admits that she sometimes allows James to run around in nature instead of going to school. Rachel is so startled that she doesn't know what to say, strange position for an authority-figure to find herself in. She has found out that this mother simply loves her son, and wants for him what she would want in his place. Rachel's own mother characteristically says that she simply cannot understand why Rachel would want to do certain things, generally things that contravene the mother's poor wishes. So when James later hides from Rachel what he is drawing, she makes an "open utterance", striking him on the face with her staff of office, her ruler. Her response is similar to the end of the tabernacle scene — she is not sure she can distinguish between her spoken words and those she bottles-up inside. She is not sure she can watch her words.

As far as the community is concerned, little James has a lot of the Old Nick in him; and for Rachel, the older Nick is a kind of extension of what the son-surrogate James presents to her confusion. At first Nick, the boy who escaped the town, intensifies the normal battle within her. In their first conversation he simply asks, "Been here long, Rachel?" and before speaking her hesitant answer, she thinks: "There is something almost gentle in his voice, and suddenly I long to say *Yes, for ever*, but also to deny everything and to say *Only a year — before that, I was in Samarkand and Tokyo.*" He, on the other hand, is immediately open; he begins to tell her his family stories right away — he is the Ukrainian milkman's son. Rachel thinks: "He's easy to listen to. Easy as well, it almost seems, to reply to. If only it could be that way." She is, then, still thinking of herself as the acted-upon, the conditioned. Nick will teach the teacher to act upon her world and her words. As a beginning, she finds herself, unlike herself, pouncing for the telephone so that her mother may not beat her to Nick's voice.

Nick provides a curious balance for Rachel's incipient schizophrenia. His twin brother died as a boy, so that he is survivor of that relationship as well as his upbringing in the town. "I wanted to be completely on my own. And then it happened that way," he says. Now his closeness will offer one of Rachel's selves an opportunity to assert itself free from its unidentical twin. One might also remember that Nick's brother had been the more approved by his parents, just as Rachel's complying self is approved by her mother and the other controllers.

Nick suggests what he may do with Rachel, when on entering his parents' house with her, he goes to the windows and opens the curtains, to let the sun in. (She later refers to Nick as the sun.) We have earlier been told that Rachel's home is surrounded by the ancestors' trees to protect it from eyes (including the sun's) outside. Windows let light in, and they also let eyesight out. When Nick then enters her body and leaves his sperm there, she curiously thinks of herself in language that might speak of a house: "the knowledge that he will somehow inhabit me, be present in me, for a few days more — this, crazily, gives me warmth, against all reason." However, it is also language that could describe a disease, the dis-ease that Rachel is filled with when she imagines her body and her self occupied by foetus or tumour, or the eccentricities of advancing age and the town's influence. Reason, indeed.

Contrary to the invasion is Rachel's excursion, the risk she learns to take for the first physical love that comes to her in her thirties. She reaches out to him now; it is she who goes first to the telephone. She suggests to Nick that he could teach in Manawaka instead of Winnipeg, and is at once struck by her openness, her loss of pride: "No, I have no pride. None left, not now. This realization reaches me all at once calm, inexplicably, and almost free. Have I finished with facades? Whatever happens, let it happen. I won't deny it." Here is a lesson she is learning from Nick, from time, and from her reading of St. Paul up in Calla's room. (Paul said to allow yourself to become a fool in order to find wisdom.

That is, share in God's joke, don't be its butt.) The next time they are alone with one another's bodies, it is she who reaches out to touch first, to ask for it, and, of course, it is he who moves away first afterwards, saying that he is not God, that he can't solve anything. Finally, in the hospital in Winnipeg, the little tumour, which like a child she takes as a personal gesture from fate, departs, and with it goes Nick's inhabiting of her. Now she can move into that house, and when she does she arranges the furniture as she wants. Literally, she packs up and moves to Vancouver, where fools may live in God's grace, making their own traditions.

I SEE THE CHANGE in Rachel's consciousness as a result of her getting in touch with her body, that part of self the Scottish Christians preferred to cover with rough wool and to forget. Rachel's mother, poor dear, was mortified that her husband made his living by handling bodies, and kept his hands off hers. The first thing we see of Rachel is that she is displaced from her own body — on the first page of the book she imagines her eyes looking from a pupil's desk at Miss Cameron, the "tin giant". Odd metal for "the queen of the golden city". At other times she pictures her body, seen in fugitive reflections from hall mirror or street window, as a "stroke of a white chalk on a blackboard" (again two-dimensional, like tin), a "goose's feather", a "crane of a body", either bird or construction machine, such juiceless things.

We are also quickly introduced to her fear of aging and dying, especially poignant because she hasn't gone through all the steps of the life cycle thought appropriate to a woman of her age. The mature part of her consciousness joins with her immaturity in looking for the signs of her becoming an eccentric old woman. But her mother treats her as if she were "about twelve". Rachel is displaced from her womanhood's age as well as from her body: "What a strangely pendulum life I have, fluctuating in age between extremes, hardly knowing myself whether I am too young or too old." There is an operative irony in the fact that the story is being told in the present tense.

Rachel seems to prefer her inside to her outside, because it is abstract and hidden from outsiders, hence untouchable for two reasons. But her desire to be opened does battle with her sense of good taste and behaviour. While discussing the misdemeanour and punishment of James, she concentrates her glance on her own nicely manicured fingernails with their colourless polish, and realizes that she desires to touch Principal Siddley's furry hands though they repulse her. She makes "reasonable" excuses to soften the guilt of her masturbation. She blames her rising during the climax of the tabernacle scene upon the touch of her neighbours who lifted her to her feet as a consequence of their movement. She is relieved by her own anger when Calla's kiss scares her away from her friend. Characteristically she tries to pass her fear of self-exposure off as disgust. About the people in the tabernacle she thinks: "How can they make fools of themselves like that, so publicly?" To become a fool one must cast off fear, not disgust, sometimes the Protestant fear disguised as disgust. If you like your inside better than your outside, there should be no obstacle to revealing it, certainly no reason for poor snobbery.

Taste is another idea that confuses things for Rachel. How can she be sure that her response to the awful beehive hairdos of the town girls is not simply a mixture of her snobbery and her alienation from the present? She is jealous and hurt when she thinks that these empty-headed sillies are probably being touched by boys in farm fields and Fords every night. Later, Rachel sees herself as graceless and hasty in her scramble to get her clothes on after her first pastoral scene with Nick.

Anyway, shortly after seeing the young beehive heads on the streets of town, she goes to sleep, and before conjuring her erotic onanist images, she is assailed by a vision of herself trapped by time, a giant clock:

> The night feels like a giant Ferris wheel turning in blackness, very slowly, turning once for each hour, interminably slow. And I am glued to it, or wired like paper [two-dimensional again], like a photograph, insubstantial, unable to anchor myself, unable to stop this slow nocturnal circling.

In one sense time must simply be co-operated with — it is the earth, after all, that circles slowly and endlessly in the dark, the earth that Rachel has not moved over. But time, or the using of it, can also be a control device for the good folks of town. There is a second scene in which Rachel catches herself staring at Willard's hands — "with them he touches his wife" — and she quickly looks at something else, the familiar royal blue Bank of Montreal calendar, which "is not so frivolous as to display any picture". The hands and the calendar act dramatically here as objective correlatives of the conflict in Rachel's consciousness. But to this point Rachel is still caught being favourable to the closed attitude. When Willard takes off his protective glasses and shows a look of vulnerability, Rachel feels almost affectionate, and moves backward instead of towards him.

During the tabernacle scene, too, Rachel is embarrassed by vulnerability that leads to people touching one another even in spirit. Calla explains that the "deep and private enjoyment" of making "ecstatic utterances" leads to a sharing of the ecstasy among people who have got together. This is a pretty obvious comparison with sexual experience, as are the words of the hymn the congregation sings: *"In full and glad surrender, / I give myself to Thee."* Mrs. Cameron's church, by contrast, is then seen as antagonistic to both spiritual touch and sexuality, a place where people present only their protective coverings to one another, and probably to the Holy Ghost. "I don't think it would be very nice, not to go. I don't think it would look very good," says Mrs. Cameron to her daughter. Futhermore, she says it would not be nice for Rachel to go in her orange scarf, because it is too bright. The old woman would be "shocked" if her minister ever spoke to his God with emotion or sincerity, as if God were actually there. Even this church's Jesus is beyond and out of touch:

> ... a stained glass window shows a pretty and cleancut Jesus expiring gently and with absolutely no inconvenience, no gore, no pain, just this nice and slightly effeminate insurance salesman who, somewhat incongruously, happens to be clad in a toga, holding his arms languidly up to something which might in other circumstances have been a cross.

This is another of the many pictures Rachel's eyes and mind fall upon, the reflectors Mrs. Laurence is fond of holding up for the mind she has chosen to write from inside of. For instance, compare that Christ with the image of Rachel the lapsed Protestant when she is around Pentecostal Calla: "I hold myself very carefully when she's near, like a clay figurine, easily broken, unmendable," something you ask your visions not to touch.

Part of the time Rachel feels like a rube, unenlightened, and much of the time she is bookish, as if that separates her from her environment, for good or for bad. But small towns usually contain a few bookish rubes, the untouchables, who are not the same as the town fools. When Nick gets through to Rachel, she turns against her bookishness, rejecting the words of "some nitwit in Shakespeare", but the words still come. Rachel perhaps sees herself as a character in a novel; she is unfortunately analytical. She is prepared, because she knows herself as someone like Willard does not, to know it all.

But she has to learn that touch can come before and lead towards knowing — "yet I've touched him, touched his face and his mouth. That is all I know of him, his face, the bones of his shoulders. That's not knowing very much" — and even that touch touches both ways, both people at once, so that knowing yourself

happens from the skin inward. That touching of two makes "possession" irrelevant, her mother's phrase, "*a woman's most precious possession*", something to
reject in oneself. Her mother said of her father, "he was never one to make many
demands upon me." In contrast, Rachel finds "this peace, this pride", when her
body is touching Nick's. They are most un-Protestant feelings for the soul. So also
is her new way of viewing. She finds herself fixing on "a leaf with all its veins
perceived, the fine hairs on the back of a man's hands", rather than accepting the
Protestant and spinsterish "abstract painting of a world".

Not only does touch lead to knowing, it leads to wanting to know, by touching: "Then I want my hands to know everything about him, the way the hair
grows in his armpits, the curve of his bones at the hips, the tight muscles of his
belly, the arching of his sex." It is here that she is inevitably touching herself,
getting past the two-dimensional pictures of her own body.

Now, too, her obscure sex-fantasies are being replaced by dreams of herself
in bed with actual Nick, and the scene is no longer distant unnamed beaches,
but "a Hudson's Bay point blanket on the bed, scarlet", something real to anyone
who has felt such cloth on his bare skin. During the same daydream, Rachel
notices that her cloudy fears have been touched away: "I've felt a damn sight
better since I stopped considering my health." This is not to say that Rachel is
cured, but she is changed, and that is very much to the point for the woman
halfway through her life who could have settled for declining sameness in the
small isolated town. Still she fantasizes, but now about marriage, and now the
fantasy is rejected not so much from shame and guilt, but from a sense of reality.

Now she does not hurry past the mirror. She stops to look into it and sees
actual woman, with blood running in actual veins. With a similar courage she
descends for the first time to the funeral chapel below-floors, and makes another
open utterance: "Let me come in," directionless, or towards the site of her
father's peculiar laying on of hands. She feels some small surprise that she will
do such a thing, but sloughs it off: "Suddenly it doesn't matter at all to me."
When Hector tells her that her father chose a life in which he need not touch
living flesh, she first says why mourn, then changes it to why cease from
mourning.

In the following scene, Rachel goes to see Calla, and is now disconcerted to
see the fear she has instilled in the woman who would like to touch her. To
find herself capable of such control now that she has learned how good it is to
abandon oneself to two-way touch is source for a new kind of guilt, but one that
leads to instruction. It is echoed in the words of St. Paul, as read here by Calla,

who does not realize their immediate application: "*If any man among you thinketh himself to be wise, let him become a fool, that he may be wise.*"

That is a version of Margaret Laurence's theme.

Rachel has pondered it another way just before hearing those words. She thinks that "if you think you contain two realities, perhaps you contain none." I like to think that the operative word here is "contain". Reach out, Rachel, fill yourself up. Something has to give. "My trouble, perhaps, is that I have expected justice. Without being able to give it," she admits to God, who is not there, of course. She is going to lose Nick, but it was his body her fingers pushed against to send feeling back into her own.

One of the lovely things about Margaret Laurence's novel is the gradualness of change. It is not that Rachel realizes steadily. Her early weakness and confusion, her thirty-five-year old character traits are still there at the end of the book. They are just not so bad now. They are accompanied by the later knowledge and experience that alternate with them in her mind, and modify them somewhat. For example, when Rachel goes to the Parthenon Café to think about her pregnancy, her tired mind talks to Nick. At first she wants him to be there so that she can see him and speak with him, not asking to touch him. But two pages later, after she has faced herself in the middle of crisis, thinking of abortion, she admits that she could forego speaking with him if she could hold him and lie down beside him. Touch is the first thing she wants now. She manages to go again to Calla, to touch her with an admission of her trouble, to establish greater intimacy than they have ever known. At the same time, Rachel decides to shake her mother's formerly awful control: "My mother's tricky heart will just have to take its own chances." There is confiding and confidence, outside and inside.

Margaret Laurence has spoken of Rachel's experience as part victory, part defeat. The woman has managed to step outside her own mind for a little, to see the eyes looking back as not totally stupid nor totally ridiculing. While Dr. Raven is touching her womb to find life or tumour, Rachel has a moment of seeing the real world, one in which any individual person has to make his own way. Dr. Raven, the old family friend, is "one well-meaning physician who wants to help me pull myself together and yet can't help having an eye on the clock, the waiting room still full". All life goes on, everyone's, and time is not just a tyrant tying lonely Rachel to some monster clock. He hasn't the time to concentrate on her.

So Rachel steps into the middle ground she could not reach earlier because of the grip of her ancestors. Whereas she had formerly been seen by her mother as child, by herself as aging spinster, and perhaps by the reader as arrested adolescent, she now becomes woman and mother in a weirdly symbolic birth scene. After the tumour is removed and she is lying in the Winnipeg hospital bed, she hears herself saying "*I am the mother now.*" She is referring largely to the relationship between herself and old Mrs. Cameron. She will complete the age-old cycle, becoming the mother of her ancestors, those people we all see as children, socially or historically. When Rachel begins to assert herself and take over control of the family affairs, including especially the leaving of the old town, her mother makes the complaint of all children being moved, that she cannot stand to leave all her playmates. Her mother says to Rachel, "you're not *yourself*," and either she is or she is not.

Rachel has changed somewhat, and change is life, as they say, though not often enough in Manawaka. When she encounters Nick's parents on the street back home, she is surprisedly open in introducing herself to them. But as Mrs. Laurence cautions, this is a story of real life, not a Hollywood movie set in New England. When she speaks to Nick's parents and finds that Nick lied to her about his being married, we have another in a series of unsurenesses about misunderstandings; we still have a woman near middle-age, waving her hands at the mist of life and its meetings. I am changing and coming into focus, but who am I?

ONE OF THE REASONS for my attention to *A Jest of God* is the seriousness of the work as literature. Margaret Laurence is an unusual bird among Canadian novelists, in that she works on the premise that form (not "structure") matters pre-eminently in the endeavour to simulate reality. What happens, happens *in* the writing, not in front of it. One sees through the eye, not with it. Mrs. Laurence is not talking *about* life; she is trying to re-enact the responses to it. I differ from most commentators in praising the success of the present tense and the interior, confused, first-person narrative. The subject of the book is Rachel's mind, and the realism consists in our separation from it by virtue of its unsureness and confusions. That separation brings us so close. Because we are in the position of wanting to talk to Rachel.

We are early convinced of a verisimilitude of thought, while being introduced to young James in the classroom. Rachel's mind is on him, asking herself why she speaks so harshly to him in particular when it is to him that her feelings go out most longingly. Then before thinking on him some more, she asks herself why she didn't bring a coat to work, as the spring wind makes her shiver, and a cold will pull her down so surely. We know then that in some way her spinsterish fear of aging and getting cranky about her declining health is related to her desire to love a son, especially one who exhibits the independence of mind that Rachel has betrayed in herself.

Mrs. Laurence engages the reader continuously this way, inviting and obligating him to evaluate Rachel's thoughts, not simply to receive them toward a narrative completion. We remember that we are at all times privy to Rachel's speaking to herself, and must, for instance, evaluate her adjectives. When she says to herself, "My great mistake was in being born the younger. No. Where I went wrong was in coming back here, once I'd got away. A person has to be ruthless. One has to say *I'm going*, and not be prevailed upon to return," a reader may want to substitute "courageous" for "ruthless". Yet the reader is still the half of the dialogue who is holding his tongue. He should extend to her some of his imagination, *i.e.* sympathy; he should not condemn her, or her vision of reality. Somewhere between that "ruthless" and "courageous", or whatever the second adjective may be, rests the real. The real is like the real in real life — it is mainly encountered in dialogue, encountered but never totally characterized in words.

Similarly the reality of character is found in how the person talks more than in what he says. Mrs. Laurence engages this poetic discovery as a literary approach. So the language with its rhymes and cadences reveals the condition of Rachel's shocked mind as she finds herself speaking ecstatically in the tabernacle:

> Chattering, crying, ululating, the forbidden transformed cryptically to nonsense, dragged from the crypt, stolen and shouted, the shuddering of it, the fear, the breaking, the release, the grieving —
> Not Calla's voice. Mine. Oh my God. Mine. The voice of Rachel.

What I mean to say is that Mrs. Laurence does not seek to use words to explain (L. *explanare*, lit., to make level) the important things that are happening. Take for instance Rachel's words on her wishing that something bad will happen to her mother:

> You mean it all right, Rachel. Not every minute, not every day, even. But right now, you mean it. Mean. I am. I never knew it, not really. Is everyone? Probably, but what possible difference can that make? I do care about her. Surely I love her as much as most parents love their children. I mean, of course, as much as most children love their parents.

163

Rachel's mind picks things up and lays them down like a distracted woman walking through a department store. As we have seen, she gets a purchase on her life after she discovers that she is no longer the child, but something like the new mother. In the passage just quoted, Mrs. Laurence does not introduce the product of Rachel's mind. She shows the motion of the machinery. No fooling.

One small section of the novel is told in the past tense, the first four pages of chapter eleven. It is the scene in the Winnipeg hospital, a scene that is both interlude (the only time told outside of the little town and Rachel's day-to-day confrontations with its people), and dramatic keypoint. The past tense both fills in the news and provides a sense of Rachel's mind taking control of her situation, especially striking after ten chapters of up-close hesitancies in the immediate present.

Certainly when one speaks to God one has to use the present tense (*cf.* Stacey, in *The Fire Dwellers*), as Rachel does at the end of chapter nine, through her irony, declaring her decision to have a child of her own for a change. If God is alive he may or may not be having his little joke. If this happens in the present tense, it happens to you, and that makes it more important than funny. God's jests are not just vocal — the word is made flesh, *i.e.* the eternal present. It is in understanding this that Margaret Laurence chose wisely to write in the present tense, to present the fool made wise by folly.

God's grace shines on fools. Poetry is hospitable to the fool's tongue, and *vice versa*. Rachel's acceptance speech is poetry:

All that. And this at the end of it. I was always afraid that I might become a fool. Yet I could almost smile with some grotesque lightheadedness at the fool of a fear, that poor fear of fools, now that I really am one.

(1971)

THE HOUSE ON
THE PRAIRIES

Susan Jackel

G IVEN THE RELATIVELY RAPID SETTLEMENT of Canada's prairie region and the opportunities open to individual enterprise during the formative years of Western society, the frequent moral examination of materialism in prairie fiction up to 1935 is understandable; so is the altered mood of prairie novelists after the economic and spiritual trials of drought and depression in the thirties. The broad outlines of this shift from social commentary to character study can be indicated in a few paragraphs. What will be noted at greater length in the following pages is the consistency with which one symbol — the house — speaks for the changing attitudes of Western writers over half a century, from Nellie McClung in 1908 to Margaret Laurence in 1964. In brief, the significance of the word "house" begins from a straightforward reference to the physical structure which provides shelter, and by association extends to the money needed to build and support it, and develops into the broader concept of a family establishment, a continuing blood line which inherits both material and cultural acquisitions. This development reflects a recurring theme in the fiction of rural Western Canada: that of the family as the basis of social organization and the source of moral values.

The fiction of "settlement", *i.e.*, those novels which concern themselves with the development of rural society in the Canadian prairies, falls into two main phases: the morally-directed fiction of writers up to and including F. P. Grove; and the psychological enquiry of novels which followed Ross's *As For Me and My House* (1941). Until the late 1920's the rural West built up a social ideal that was rampantly acquisitive, to which many prairie writers responded by insisting on the superiority of spiritual resources over material ones. Ralph Connor and Nellie McClung pictured the spiritual poverty of the material life, while showing how those who were poor but selfless — the Sky Pilot, Shock McGregor,

165

Pearl Watson, Maggie Corbett — could lead their misguided neighbours back to the true path. In Martha Ostenso's *Wild Geese* the curse of Mammon is less explicit; nevertheless, the novel is constructed in such a way that Caleb Gare's death could easily be interpreted as retribution for his perverse search for wealth and power. In the novels of Grove, the corrupting influence of wealth is an inescapable theme, particularly evident in the two novels of the southern prairies, *Fruits of the Earth* and *Two Generations*. Abe Spalding is the materialist who comes to see the futility of his possessions; John Elliot, Spalding's moral opposite, subordinates financial success to his ideal of family life. This ideal is undermined by Elliot's inability to arouse love and respect in his children, but also by what Grove saw as the spirit of the age — financial and moral irresponsibility.

To this tradition of moral writing in prairie fiction R. J. C. Stead contributes an interesting variation. He too warns against the dangers of dedication to material success: see, for example, John Harris and Hiram Riles in *The Homesteaders* and Dave Eldon in *The Cowpuncher*. However, Stead sees ambition as a danger only if allowed to crowd out the more important task of "widening one's horizons", Stead's shorthand formula for increased mental, social and cultural activity of all descriptions. For Stead, full participation in life is the moral good; he values material ambitions in so far as they lead outward to wider horizons. Dennison Grant, the philanthropic idealist, represents Stead's only unabashed indulgence in Utopian moralizing; in his other novels Stead points up the restrictions of poverty, leading his heroes through the temptations of Mammon to the appreciation of the finer life which financial security permits.

In the novels published after Grove, however, this insistence on the moral use of Mammon has faded into the background, to be replaced by greater emphasis on character study. The West had grown up during the thirties; the rapid expansion of the century's first three decades and the questions which this phase presented belonged to a by-gone age of adolescence. The concern of fiction writers became not, how should the young sensibility be guided, but, in what form has the adult Western character emerged? Grove had spoken (in *In Search of Myself*, pp. 224-7) of the pioneer "race", made up of certain types of men and women who were particularly attracted by the challenge of pioneering; in *Fruits of the Earth* he referred to the "distinct local character and mentality" of the residents of Spalding District. With Ross's *As For Me and My House,* Grove's generalized interest in prairie psychology became the primary concern of most Western writers.

The two phases of rural prairie fiction here distinguished, the preceptive social fiction up to Grove and the analytic psychological fiction of 1940 and after, are intended only as broad categories; however, their over-all accuracy is illustrated by a survey of the various uses by Western writers of one major symbol, the house. The presence of the house as symbol is surprising only in its ubiquity, for a moment's reflection on the nature of settlement on the plains will indicate how natural is the symbolic use of this physical object as a means of expressing certain themes. As Stead and Grove show more explicity, the provision of shelter on the prairies was equivalent to proclaiming one's social status: the settler could initially build a sod hut at no expense, progress to a lumber shack with lean-to additions at a cost of perhaps forty dollars, and finally, should he prove to be a financial success, announce his wealth with the building of a "New House".

The erection of the New House became more than a question of comfortable housing in almost all the pre-World War II novels, for it was to reflect as well the state of the soul: a moral wrong was committed when a settler demanded from the soil wealth and grandeur, in the form of extravagant housing, instead of a modest living for himself and his family. This view, while again most evident in the writing of Stead and Grove, can be traced back to Nellie McClung's first novel in the first decade of the century. After 1940, with the shift from social concerns to individual characterization, the house/home theme reflects more closely relations within the family group. It is a truism that Canadian writers prefer to examine the relations between generations rather than between individuals of the same generation, and this preference is particularly marked among prairie novelists. In the Western fiction of the past quarter-century the house frequently symbolizes the dominant power within the household, the character who asserts, implicitly or (as is more often the case) explicitly, "This is *my* house." This tendency culminates in Sheila Watson's *The Double Hook* and Margaret Laurence's *The Stone Angel*, where the house is seen to be expressive of the very existence of the central characters. In these novels the "new place" takes on a more clearly symbolic aspect, representing the human need of hope for the future. The word "house" thus progresses in meaning from the moral significance of absorption in material possessions to an inquiry into the rights and responsibilities of individuals within the family.

NELLIE MCCLUNG first employs the house as a symbol of spiritual values in *Sowing Seeds in Danny* (1908). The Motherwells live in "a large stone house, square and gray, lonely and bare". Mrs. Motherwell protests when the visiting Pearl Watson opens a window, saying, "There hasn't been a window open in this house since it was built." Mrs. Motherwell did not always have a soul of "dull drab dryness", for her avarice developed only after she had become mistress of the big stone house. Late in the story Mrs. Motherwell is made to feel remorse for her selfishness, and, making more explicit the equation of Mrs. Motherwell and her house, Mrs. McClung entitles the chapter which deals with this temporary reformation, "A Crack in the Granite". Mrs. McClung's symbolism is never subtle (*cf.* the poppies in the same book); we can see her use of the house as evidence that it is a symbol which comes readily to hand.

R. J. C. Stead makes more extensive use of the house as an indication of moral health. In *The Homesteaders*, Stead's second novel, the Harrises' first house is a sod hut, humble perhaps, but "absolutely the product of their own labour". The Harrises prosper, as do their neighbours; yet amid the advance of "civilization and prosperity",

> There were those, too, who thought that perhaps the country had lost something in all its gaining; that perhaps there was less idealism and less unreckoning hospitality in the brick house on the hill than there once had been in the sod shack in the hollow.

Idealism is a virtue in Stead's novels: Dennison Grant, in the novel of that name, plans and builds his house to express his own ideals. The house is modest in size, yet sun-lit, airy and gracious, with a whim-room to allow for the exercise of impulse and imagination.

Although Stead's moral framework is essentially romantic, his eye for everyday facts of life on the prairies has given him a considerable reputation as a realistic writer. One commonplace in Western life which Stead deals with in *Grain* is the fact that the farm wife often has to wait for a decent house until the debts on land and machinery are paid off — an eventuality which might be postponed until her children have grown up and left home. The most persistent disappointment in Susie Stake's life is the house which Jackson promises will be built "next year, if the crop comes off".

> There was a cheerful virility about [Jackson], and when he had promised Susan Harden a frame house with lathed and plastered walls and an upstairs she had said yes, not for the house, but for himself. But that was before he left the East, when he and his hopes were young. Gander was driving a four-horse team before the ribs of his father's frame house at last rose stark against the prairie sky.

By the time the New House is built, when Susie Stake is forty-five, she has "ceased to be an optimist". However, as Jackson Stake points out to his rebellious son, who sneers at "that log shack we eat and sleep in", "Lath an' plaster don' make a home, an' sometimes poplar logs do." It is not the house itself that is important, but the spirit of contentment and family unity within.

In Martha Ostenso's *Wild Geese* the New House exists only in Martin Gare's dream, a dream which will continue to be frustrated as long as his father lives:

> Martin loved the land, but there was something else in him that craved expression. It had been represented by the dream of the new house, the dream of the thing that was to be made by his own hands, guided by his own will. Now that, too, was gone. Nothing to do now but toil on without a dream. It might have been kinder of Caleb to have deceived him until the end of the harvest — there would then have been a vision to ease the burden. A false vision was better than none.

Here the New House in its very absence symbolizes Caleb's maniacal determination to chain his family to the soil, his conviction that thinking is a threat to having and therefore must be rooted out as one would root out a dangerous weed. In other novels of this period the New House is an outward manifestation of wealth and power; in Miss Ostenso's novel its denial is a symptom of avarice and tyranny.

With F. P. Grove we return to a more conventional use of the house as representative of the moral condition of the novel's characters. Grove seems to be particularly conscious of the symbolic expressiveness of the house. Pacey notes, for instance, how in *Our Daily Bread* Grove equates the disintegration of the house with John Elliot's gradual decay; when Elliot's children gather at his deathbed, they are "horrified" at the condition of the house and of the aged man within, as if only the sight of the physical structure of their former home can make them see clearly the man they have treated as a thing. In *Fruits of the Earth* the house becomes the dominant symbol. Grove explains that his conception of the novel took shape after he had come across a huge farmhouse which had been abandoned by its owners. This house, in the back of Grove's mind while he wrote, represents the tragic experience of Abe Spalding, heroic pioneer.

To Abe the building of the New House means the culmination of his labours, to be not just a house but a mansion. The contrast between Abe's longing for pre-eminence in the district and his wife's more moderate aims is shown in their attitudes to the proposed house: "When Abe said that ... one day he would build her a house which was to be the envy of everybody, she could not summon any enthusiasm; she wanted comfort, not splendour; convenience, not luxury." The house also represents Abe's patriarchal ambitions. In answer to Ruth's ques-

169

tion, "What is it all for?" he says, "To build up a place any man can be proud of, a place to leave to my children for them to be proud of." However, the building of the house is put off until twelve years after the Spaldings' marriage, leaving Ruth to cope with four small children in a two-room shack. By the time the house is built Abe can no longer give her a home; he can only give her all the labour-saving devices money can buy. As far as the neighbours are concerned, moreover, the huge edifice that Abe erects is "Spalding Hall", the ancestral seat of the great lord.

After the death of his favourite son, Abe questions the meaning of his achievement. He looks at his brick house and notes that already nature is reclaiming her own. His attitude to the house changes:

> When, these days, he approached his place, the place built to dominate the prairie, he succumbed to the illusion that he who had built it was essentially different from him who had to live in it. More and more the wind-break surrounding his yard seemed to be a rampart which, without knowing it, he had erected to keep out a hostile world. Occasionally the great house seemed nothing less than a mausoleum to enshrine the memory of a child.

Because the house serves to emphasize Abe's isolation from the rest of the community, his pride in it as a status symbol becomes meaningless and empty; so too does his patriarchal ambition when the child who was meant to inherit the house dies.

Abe Spalding's desire for a house of which he can be proud, as a material possession signifying his success to the world, and which he can leave to his children as a tangible representation of the family line he hopes to establish, combines the two symbolic meanings of the house earlier distinguished. Ross's *As For Me and My House* is typical of prairie novels since 1940 in its use of the house in relation to the family group. Certainly Ross employs the confining and depressing aspects of the Bentleys' house in Horizon to emphasize the repression of their lives there, but these details are used realistically rather than with primarily symbolic intent. "The house of Bentley", however, is a semi-ironic reference to the internal tensions which exist behind the false front Mrs. Bentley so painstakingly erects. The title itself suggests the domestic conflict around which the novel centres, for although the text ("As for me and my house we will serve the Lord") is Philip's introduction to his professed creed, he is unable to believe in it himself. Mrs. Bentley, on the other hand, is the speaking voice in the novel, and the logical referent in the reader's mind of the pronoun "my". Finally, when one considers that Mrs. Bentley rather than her husband makes all the major decisions, the controlling power in "the house of Bentley" is left in little doubt. Like Greta Potter and Hagar Shipley after her, Mrs. Bentley tells the reader, "This is *my* house," although not in so many words.

Nellie McClung's inclusion of the house among her few symbols was, it was suggested, a sign-post that such an object formed obvious associations in the reader's mind, for Mrs. McClung desired above all that her message be clear. Similarly, although for different reasons, its prominent use in Edward McCourt's *Home is the Stranger* is a sign that the concept of the house as representing the establishment of family roots is a congenial one to Western fiction. Published in 1949, two years after McCourt's critical study of Canadian Western fiction, *Home is the Stranger* offers its own commentary on what McCourt found to be the prominent features of prairie fiction to that date.

McCourt first considers the house as home. When Norah Armstrong first sees the prairie house that is to be such a pain-filled home to her, she is amused by the figure her imagination makes of it: " 'Jim, it's human! It's alive!' " she laughs, thinking that it looks like a funny old man. Moving in, she feels that "fear and insecurity were at last vanquished." Norah has to learn to be at home with fear and insecurity, for they accompany her to this house and invest its "aliveness" with a terrible malignity.

In the Armstrongs' future there is also a New House, which they plan to build some day. This plan represents Jim Armstrong's fundamental ambition, that of establishing roots in the West. Jim and Norah are the second generation; Jim envisions sons and grandsons to carry on. Then, with the existence of family traditions, there may come the spiritual traditions which constitute a culture: " 'The house of Armstrong,' Jim said. 'And maybe, if we stay long enough, the gods will come.' "

Brian Malory is the advocate of "culture" in its more obvious forms. He insists that Armstrong House be built facing the river, so that it will have a view of something besides unrelieved prairie. But "he was not just arguing about the proposed site of a house. Some principle was involved, for the time being obscured by irrelevancies." The principle is that of the North American contribution to the cultural heritage of the western world, and according to Brian this contribution can be represented by the sound of that great material invention, "water flushing down a toilet bowl". The modern North American house becomes for him the symbol of all that is lacking in our spiritual life. " 'We're a people without anything to pass on to the next generation,' " he says. " 'Not a book or a picture or a symphony. Or a faith!' " Only indoor plumbing.

In *Home is the Stranger* McCourt brings together several familiar themes to form a new synthesis. Cultural traditions — the coming of the gods — are made the moral good; North American materialism is detrimental to this process because it concentrates on bodily comfort rather than intellectual creativity; therefore, the house as a physical structure is of doubtful value in society. On the other hand, the house as representative of a family heritage, of a continuing blood line, contributes to the stability and traditionalism of society, and is therefore of prime importance to the cultural maturation of the West.

Two WESTERN NOVELS of the past decade, Sheila Watson's *The Double Hook*[1] and Margaret Laurence's *The Stone Angel*, carry this process one step further by analysing relations between successive generations within a family in terms of the houses they occupy. The struggle between generations expresses itself in a fight for possession of the house, a fight embittered by the reluctance of the older generation to give way to the newer one.

In the novels referred to so far, the house has had both a realistic and a symbolic role; for that matter, the symbolic role has often been merely to suggest a readily-recognizable pattern of life, as when Nellie McClung, Stead and Grove question the rewards of material success. In *The Double Hook* the house, as we might expect, takes on a predominantly symbolic value. The control of the house and its inhabitants lies at the root of the Potters' "trouble". For one thing, control of the house means privacy, protection from Mrs. Potter's prying eyes. Greta snaps at Ara, "You've got your own house. I want this house to myself. Every living being has a right to something."

For Greta the house also represents the thin rope of power she wields over James. Greta announces their mother's death by claiming possession of the house: "Get out, she said. Go way. This is my house. Now Ma's lying dead in her bed I give the orders here." But it is a "rebellious house", doomed to destruction. To James, the house is a curse, as he dwells under the successive tyranny of his mother and his sister. Knowing that her rope of power over James has been broken by Lenchen, Greta burns the house with herself inside, and when James sees the charred ruins, his relief is instantaneous:

> He felt as he stood with his eyes closed on the destruction of what his heart had wished destroyed that by some generous gesture he had been turned once more into the first pasture of things.

I will build the new house further down the creek, he thought. All on one floor.

In the new house will live the new generation, born of Lenchen and James.

Margaret Laurence's use of the house as symbol in *The Stone Angel* is frequent and expressive. Hagar's house comes at last to represent as does no other object the spiritual revelations of the dying woman. Hagar recounts her life in terms of the houses in which she has lived: the Currie place, solid and pretentious, as befits the town's leading merchant; the Shipley place, gray, unpainted, the scene of her greatest pleasures and her greatest sorrows; the Oatley place, "like a stone barn", where she worked as a housekeeper, although as a girl she had pitied her Aunt Doll, thinking, "how sad to spend one's life caring for the houses of others."

The first half of the narrative is given the nominal setting of Hagar's own house in Vancouver. That it is more than just another house to Hagar is made clear when she realizes that her son and daughter-in-law want to sell it. " 'You'll never sell this house, Marvin. It's my house. It's my house, Doris. Mine.' " Thinking of her house and of the "shreds and remnants of years . . . scattered through it visibly" in the form of furniture and personal possessions, she tells the reader: "If I am not somehow contained in them and in this house, something of all change caught and fixed here, eternal enough for my purposes, then I do not know where I am to be found at all." The house and its contents become the external manifestation of all that her experience has made her. She declares that she is "unreconciled to this question of the house, my house, mine"; however, she bows to the inevitable, saying, "We drive . . . back to Marvin and Doris's house."

Shorn of the home she feels she has earned, Hagar hides in an old cannery with an adjacent house. Remembering the Shipley farmhouse, she notes, "This house of mine is gray, too. . . . I find a certain reassurance in this fact, and think I'll feel quite at home here." Her reaction to her new dwelling contains the same intention of starting over which James had felt in *The Double Hook*, but with sadly ironic overtones:

> To move to a new place — that's the greatest excitement. For a while you believe you carry nothing with you — all is cancelled from before, or cauterized, and you begin again and nothing will go wrong this time.

The house as symbol has been effectively used by a number of major writers of English and American fiction: one thinks of Dickens, Poe, Hawthorne, Henry James and Virginia Woolf among others. However, these writers have used the physical structure of the house to express highly individual themes. Poe's import and technique, in "The Fall of the House of Usher", for example, can be readily distinguished from Virginia Woolf's in *To the Lighthouse*; the houses in *Bleak House, Great Expectations* and *David Copperfield* represent a variety of themes. The unanimity with which prairie writers interpret this symbol is one element of the "regionalism" of their fiction, inasmuch as the house seems to represent inevitable associations in the minds of both Western writers and Western readers. To them the house stands first for material security and later for cultural security, in a land where both have been hard won. In two writers of the past decade, however, there has been an extension of previous symbolic patterns: both Sheila Watson and Margaret Laurence associate the New House with the unknown future rather than with the social realities of the past and present. Hagar Shipley's consciousness that we are never "turned once more into the first pasture of things" exhibits Mrs. Laurence's more conservative and (for this reader) more satisfying attitude to life.

(1969)

NOTE

[1] Because the setting for this novel originated in Mrs. Watson's experiences in the Cariboo District of British Columbia, this cannot properly be called a prairie novel; nor, since it is, by the author's own definition, an anti-regional novel, should it be classified under the slightly vaguer heading of Western novels. (See John Grube's introduction to the NCL edition.) In atmosphere, however, it is closer to the prairie provinces during the drought years than to the mountains, forest or seacoast more typical of British Columbia; and if parody of the regional novel was intended, it is offset by the naturalistic details on which Mrs. Watson insists of creek, hill and drought-parched land.

WIND, SUN AND DUST

Donald Stephens

TWENTY-FOUR YEARS AGO what is perhaps the best Canadian novel was written: Sinclair Ross's *As For Me and My House*. Up to that time the only writers who could be viewed with any assurance were Morley Callaghan, Frederick Philip Grove, and probably Laura Salverson; since then only Mordecai Richler and, of course, Hugh MacLennan have added to the store of better Canadian novels.

In his novel Ross has caught an essential part of the Canadian scene: the small midwestern town. But it is more than just the place that Ross captures; it is the time of the thirties, a time which many Canadians remember and cannot forget. It is a time, too, that younger Canadians constantly hear about: the drought and wind and dryness of that decade. Ross has recorded that time, and adds a dimension to the memories and dreams of people who cannot, and will not, forget the thirties.

Horizon, the town that is the setting for the novel, could be any place on the prairie in the thirties; yet again, it can be anywhere at any time. It is bleak, it is tired, it is horribly true; and yet there is an element of the flower blooming on the desert, and the flying of feeling that transcends all, that gives to *As For Me and My House* a prominent position in Canadian letters. This is a novel which, despite its Puritanism, its grimness, its dustiness, gives to the reader many of the elements of optimism and romanticism so often found in Canadian literature.

Writes Mr. Ross, in the words of his narrator, Mrs. Bentley:

> They're sad little towns when a philosopher looks at them. Brave little mushroom heyday — new town, new world — false fronts and future, the way all Main Streets grow — and then prolonged senility.... They're poor, tumbledown, shabby little towns, but they persist. Even the dry years yield a little wheat; even the little means livelihood for some. I know a town where once it rained all June, and

175

that fall the grain lay in piles outside full granaries. It's an old town now, shabby and decrepit like the others, but it too persists. It knows only two years: the year it rained all June, and next year.

This is very good writing; in fact, one is first captured by the writing in the book. There is an exact vividness, pure diction choice, observation that is accurate, and a rhythm that is controlled. Everything seems to move at its own pace, and yet the tension of the characters renders vividly the actual setting:

It's an immense night out there, wheeling and windy. The lights on the street and in the houses are helpless against the black wetness, little unilluminating glints that might be painted on it. The town seems huddled lest it topple into the wind. Close to the parsonage is the church, black even against the darkness, towering ominously up through the night and merging with it. There's a soft steady swish of rain on the roof, and a gurgle of eave troughs running over. Above, in the high cold night, the wind goes swinging past, indifferent, liplessly mournful.

The people who inhabit this landscape are described to the reader too, and they dissolve into actual highpoints within the landscape. The minister is shown in many aspects, an individual in every respect, yet typical in his pursuit to live on an inadequate salary that is never paid up. There is his wife, the main character and narrator of the novel, a sensitive woman who is bothered by the role of propriety that she must always play. There is the inevitable woman who is president of every organization that she can get her hands on, the perpetual president who is "austere, beyond reproach, a little grim with the responsibilities of self-assumed leadership — inevitable as broken sidewalks and rickety false fronts". There is the doctor's wife who "simply wasn't meant" for life in a small town, and the spinster choir leader who likes the old hymns, sung slowly. Yet they are not types, though they are marked by typical characteristics; rather, each has his own special and very real reality.

Such is Ross's artistry that no doubt any but the most shallow of readers is affected by his portrayal of the desolate life in a prairie town. His simplicity of style and intricacy of mood create a prairie so immense that it virtually stuns the mind. The physical limitations of existence in Horizon pummelled by the visitations of a cruel God — though He is never blamed for what goes on — are clearly etched in the mind by the almost unbearable monotony of wind, sun, snow, and drought. It is a place with a past and a future, but with no real present, no rock into which to drive a spike which sanity can grasp to pull itself from the mire of despondency. Environment plays a strong role in the story, an environment that is at once uncluttered and cluttered. The intellectual celibacy

176

of the townspeople is made poignantly clear in the light of their ceaseless, numb battle against the overwhelming odds of the climate.

The sky and the earth fuse into a huge blur, a haze which envelops the town and its people and stills all but the faintest murmur of hope for the future. There is a vivid immobility that lies stark against the dullness of the endlessly shifting dust. The theme is of the prairies during the thirties — the unrewarded, unremitting, sluggish labour of men coupled with the loneliness and nameless terror of the women — and is the only action upon the stage that Ross presents before his reader. There is a feeling approaching claustrophobia, yet the vastness soars over the people. There is everywhere an almost unreasonable acquiescence in the inevitable, but what the inevitable is no one can foresee with any accuracy, and so they never really ask what it may be. Perhaps the new year will be better than the last, but the reader is led to wonder if fulfilment will come to those who wait. Perhaps they wait endlessly. The only tie with the outside world is the railway, and it, too, is hidden by the dust. Perhaps these people do not care for the outside world, yet the false store fronts belie their unconcern with what is outside their immediate vision. These people are not hard to imagine, but they are very difficult to understand, and consequently difficult to accept.

Roy Daniells, in his introduction to the New Canadian Library *As For Me and My House*, calls the novel an exposition of the Puritan conscience. Indeed it is, for everywhere there are the unmistakable signs of Puritanism: the standards are rigidly set; the struggles, the tenacity of people in so bleak a circumstance, the horror of hypocrisy and of sexual sin. Jealousy, failure, slow realization of forgiveness, possible redemption and reconciliation after anguish and torment, all take their places in the lives of these tenacious people. The problem of fighting versus flight, and the all powerful will of God remain in the foreground; the nerves of all the people of the town remain taut to the breaking point.

INTO A TREACHEROUS ATMOSPHERE like this Ross introduces his main characters. He does not immerse them totally, but rather just dips them into this sheep-dip of futility and sets them into a corner to let the bitter juices seep into their absorbent beings. Perhaps he has not dipped them for long enough, or again, too much, for none of the characters seem to rise out of the story as individuals of total belief. They are at once types and individuals, yet never really discernible as one or the other. Despite this vagueness, the characters can be analysed; unfortunately, with varying degrees of accuracy.

Ross chooses a woman's point of view for this novel, and obviously has tremendous insight into a woman's mind, and this particular woman's troubles. Before a reader can understand the other characters in the novel, he must examine Mrs. Bentley. She is the narrator, and if the reader takes her at her literal worth, then all the characters become exceptionally clear. But she is a paradox, and there becomes the necessity to probe beyond what she says superficially and to make conjectures as to her real meaning. Mrs. Bentley — she has no first name in the novel — is the main character, for it is through her eyes and sensitivity that the whole story is seen and felt; and she is the one who grows with the action.

She becomes through the novel an epitome of a type of woman; she displays intelligence, responds to situations with courage and sympathy, and displays a vague hope for better times (typical of prairie women of the period: clever, hardworking, hoping). Yet she is individualistic in that she rebels against the stifling pressures of propriety imposed by the town. Though she does not want impropriety, she scoffs at the pretentious airs that the citizens of Horizon so capably put on. She lives in a semi-vacuum, drawing from her stored-up intellectual resources what her husband and the other citizens fail to give her.

However, she is not as strong a person as she would have the reader believe. And this is Ross's point. Assailed by doubt she seems to hang on by sheer stubbornness. Everything she sees before her is thin, disheartening, dull and bare. There is an inert and chilly stillness to the life she leads, and it becomes evident in her thoughts. Yet, what kind of person is she? She seems to be strong, if what she says in her diary is to be taken literally. Her strength, however, comes from the knowledge of the falseness and the sham of the life that she and her husband lead. With this strength comes a certain smugness. She is smug about the falseness of the store fronts, and she is certainly smug about her awareness that Philip is a hopeless failure, a compromise. She knows the discrepancy between the man and the little niche that holds him, but does she not also feel a trifle too satisfied with her dominant position in the family? It is, after all, she who is forced to makes excuses for her husband's lapses. It is her plan to move to the bookstore in the city and her decision to adopt Judith's baby. Though she abides by her husband, she is the one who makes the major decisions, she is the one who fights the internal battles for both of them, and it is because of her inner strength that they emerge triumphant.

She, like all the characters in the book, is hurt too easily, yet she is too enduring. She can see all things clearly and objectively because she is a stranger and
cannot fit into the town and share its frustration. This is her futility. Since she
is outside of Horizon's influence, she can, for the most part, be cool, logical, and
even somewhat caustic about its workings. Even at that she finds it easier to maintain face with the people of Horizon than with the cowboys at the ranch in
Alberta, where they go for a brief holiday.

Her relationship with her husband is very unsatisfactory — to both of them.
She appears to be constantly saying "Poor Philip", and by virtue of this negation, enhances her own virtuous qualities of wifehood. Her theme of "poor
Philip" eventually grates sharply upon the reader's nerves. She protests too much
his innocence thereby attempting to absolve herself and him of blame for their
torturous predicament. That she possesses an optimism for his future and hence
her own is often negated by her emphasis on his moral and spiritual degradation.

She does not reveal enough to the reader for him to deduce anything other
that what she wishes him to deduce. She plays her cards too close to her vest.
When Mr. Downie, the visiting parson, is there, she says that she "glanced at
Philip, and wished for a moment that I were the artist with a pad and a pencil
at my hand". She does not tell us, however, how Philip looked; is he rebelling
against the grace, has he made a momentary reconciliation with his God, or is
he once again "white and thin-lipped"? She whets the curiosity, then proceeds to
another topic totally unrelated to Philip's appearance.

She almost envisions herself as a goddess, all-seeing, but fearful to tell or show
the reader lest he recognize yet another flaw in either herself or her husband.
Ross's stylistic brevity does not make sufficient amends for Mrs. Bentley's brevity;
the reader can make only his own hypothesis concerning their deeds, motives,
and the subsequent results. She says that "there is not much he keeps me in the
dark about" — yet she does not know about the affair with Judith — and by
chance finds out about it.

Contrasted to these ambiguities, she exhibits a good many favourable and
worthy characteristics (if we are to take her account of her affairs as unassailable).
She is candid and receptive. She has a capacity to see and comprehend a whole
situation; she can criticize, objectify, and finally accept, even if her acceptance
is often darkened with grave doubts. Perhaps her major redeeming feature is her
earnest desire for reconciliation with her husband, but even this raises the question of whether she is secure in her faith or merely in a blind alley with no other
way out.

Philip never really emerges as a character, but then maybe that is his condition. He is contrived, far too mechanical to be other than fragmentary; he is a moody, frustrated, baffled seeker of prestige, either intellectual, paternal, or sexual. He is a failure, a hypocrite caught in a web of his own weaving. The frustrations and defeats of his own life etch his mind as the windblown sands furrow the brows of toiling farmers. He flinches from any contact with the world, and a word from his wife causes him to wince, look at her, and retreat to his study. His only lifelines are his pictures, and they only reflect his morbid character. At first, sympathy and pity can be extended to Philip, but after a time irritation sets in with disbelief hard on its heels.

Is he the frustrated artist? Is he, rather, a weak, spineless hypocrite who cannot face what life puts before him? He is neurotic — far more than his wife — but do we know "why" he is? It is never solved. We tire of the statement that Philip needs only the opportunity to prove himself. He must show, eventually, that he is, if not deserving, then at least desirous of this opportunity; he does not exhibit this; as a result he is shallow, drab, partial — a skeleton of an individual.

To Philip, the only part of his life that is real is his pictures. From the rest of life he withdraws into his study, there to withdraw further within himself. Any flareup — real or imagined — results in his retirement to the study, white-faced, thin-lipped and haggard from a nameless exhaustion. He continually responds to an overture with a hurt, flayed look. So drab and colourless is his character that even the dog, El Greco, assumes more reality.

Mrs. Bentley explains his faults by saying that he expected too much, and when it was not forthcoming he was caught with his moral and intellectual fibres around his ankles. Surely in twelve years a man can make some attempt at pulling himself out or else reconcile himself to his fate. If he had been the frustrated artist, he would have found some relief, some compensation in his work. If Philip has found any of this, he does not reveal it to his wife's discerning eye. His relationship with his wife is such that it pleads the question of whether he wants a wife or a friend. After his constant rejection of her, the answer is somewhat obvious.

He is resentful of his wife and of Paul; their resourcefulness and his blind resentfulness and the guilt of his own hopeless inadequacy prompt him to make the accusation of a love affair between Mrs. Bentley and Paul Kirby. Beneath his futile anger lies a boy's emotion seen in the many sulking retreats to the study. He constantly shams a fit of pique and sulks to cover any gesture of generosity. He is a puzzle, never to be solved.

Other characters serve to contrast the principals. Paul Kirby serve as a foil for both Bentleys. For a time a love interest seems to be developing, but it is foredoomed to oblivion and never gets under way. He serves Mrs. Bentley as relief from the monotony of Philip and the solidly aligned faces of Horizon. Nonetheless, his constant philological demonstrations are the only facet really revealed. He is perhaps the least faceted and least successful characater in the story. He seems to have been brought in only for relief, when another page of Philip's sulkings and Mrs. Bentley's wanderings threaten a total suspension of belief.

Steve is opportunely introduced. He is the hope the Bentleys have been seeking; his exit almost extinguishes any hope that the reader and the Bentleys share. He is the simplest character in that he is typical boyhood. He is belligerent, sensitive, and frightened. His temporary importance to the plot cannot be overlooked; he is the image for what the Bentleys have wanted, but his worth to Philip is threatened by his growing disregard of him. The attachment to Mrs. Bentley further drives home to Philip his own inadequacies as a father and a man, and eventually sinks him to a new low of regard for himself and his wife.

Judith West is also shallowly drawn. She lives in a vacuum, beautiful, different, somewhat of an eternal rebel. She displays the inner torments that also rack Philip, thus giving them their common ground on which to create. To Philip she is the rebel with whom he can identify. To Mrs. Bentley she is the potential and then the real "other woman" against whom she must pit her wiles. It is strange that Mrs. Bentley, with all her astuteness, cannot see the supposed power of attraction between Philip and Judith.

Sinclair Ross gives variety in character; not all the characters are those on the racks of internal torture beaten by the overwhelming powers of nature. For variety, Ross injects the potent serum of Mrs. Bird, the rebel of Horizon, and she often successfully gives a pause to the reader; she represents the acceptance of Horizon on her own terms; though she fits into the group, she retains her own individual and special verve.

In general, the characters are made subservient to the environment of the story; the limitations of Ross's vehicle hamper the full realization of these characters. The only way the reader can realize the portent of all the characters is to let his imagination have full rein. Despite the shallowness of the characters, they are interesting, and at an intense, rather than a cursory, examination.

It is, then, the characters who make *As For Me and My House*. The place belongs to the history of Canada, the prairie town that is for the most part gone from our midst; no longer do people have to rely on the railway to communicate with the rest of civilization; the isolation is gone, through super highways and television. The time, too, belongs to history; the thirties, the depression, are only ugly dreams which man hopes will not become another reality. But the people remain the same. We are all typed in some way, and we all, too, hope that there is something individualistic about us that separates us from the crowd. But only rarely are we separated, and only rarely do Sinclair Ross's people separate from their world. And this is the way people are; this is why the reality of Ross's fictional world elevates his novel to a lasting and prominent position.

(1965)

SINCLAIR ROSS'S
AMBIVALENT WORLD

W. H. New

O NE OF THE MOST HAUNTING phrases in all of Canadian fiction has to me always been the last line of Sinclair Ross's *As For Me and My House*. The ambivalence of it puzzles, irritates, confuses. When Philip Bentley at that time protests that to name his illegitimate son Philip would be to raise the possibility of not knowing which of them is which, his wife — the central character-narrator — writes in her diary: "That's right, Philip. I want it so." And so the novel closes. At first that "*I* want it" seems to reveal a great deal; it speaks the voice of the manipulating woman who has already almost destroyed her husband by confining his artistic talents, and who even now does not let up. For Philip in such a climate to leave Horizon and the ministry and run a book-shop somewhere appears still to be his wife's decision, and the future seems bleak indeed.

The picture's other side — for it has one — is, though not exactly rosy, certainly less bleak. If we can accept that Mrs. Bentley's final remark is a sign of a new-found humility — 'I *want* it so" — and this is certainly the received interpretation[1] — then she and Philip have some hope of escaping their hypocrisy towards themselves, towards each other, and towards the towns to which they have been inadequately ministering. Both views are reasonable. This one is supported by the climactic scene in which the storm in Horizon blows down the buildings' false fronts and Mrs. Bentley angrily reveals to Philip that she knows that their adopted baby is really illegitimately his own. The other view acquires its credibility from the book as a whole, from the character we see self-revealed in the pages of her admirably constructed diary. For Ross has consciously constructed it after all; the calendar system itself is enough to tell us that. But what does he really want us to think at the end then? Which view of his character does he want us to accept? There is a third possibility: that it is neither the one nor the other view, but the ambivalence itself which is the desired aim — not based on an indecisiveness about who his character really is, but emerging out of a carefully constructed web of viewpoints, Mrs. Bentley's and ours, pitted ironically against each other so that we come to appreciate not only the depth and complexity of the narrator and her situation, but also the control in which Ross artistically holds his words.

The scene which gives us some indication of this lies between the storm scene and the final words of the novel. It is their last Sunday in Horizon, and Mrs. Bentley writes:

> After three or four years it's easy to leave a little town. After just one it's hard.
>
> It turns out now that all along they've liked us. . . . Last Friday they had a farewell supper for us in the basement of the Church, made speeches, sang *God Be With You Till We Meet Again,* presented us with a handsome silver flower basket. It's the way of a little Main Street town — sometimes a rather nice way.
>
> It's blowing tonight, and there's dust again, and the room sways slowly in a yellow smoky haze. The bare, rain-stained walls remind me of our first Sunday here, just a little over a year ago, and in a sentimental mood I keep thinking what an eventful year it's been, what a wide wheel it's run.

It is the first time she has ever complimented the townspeople or found anything attractive about the small town way of life. But is she sincere now or has she, since the storm, learned another hypocrisy? That ambivalence again.

The importance of this episode for the novel as a whole is not just the revelation of the new attitude, but the image which follows it, that of dust and rain, for if the imagery is structured as well as the events of the novel, it should serve to support the themes and to confirm our interpretation. The simple "polar opposites" view of Mrs. Bentley, that is, as being *either* success *or* failure at the end of the novel, would be supported if a strand of "polar opposites" imagery ran through the book, distinguishing truth from falsehood, good from bad. The false-fronted stores come at once to mind — yet after they have fallen we are still left with ambivalent scenes. The dust and rain, then, would seem to fulfill the function of delineating opposites, but they are even more deceptive than the false-fronted stores, and to force them into this technical role would be to distort what Ross intends. To illuminate this question, however, forces us back into the novel.

THE OVERALL IMPRESSION left by the book is certainly one of aridity: of dust and heat, the Depression on the prairies and the drought which went with it.[2] And accompanying the unproductivity of the land is the dryness of the people: Mrs. Bentley, who cannot bear a child; Philip, who does not believe in his church and cannot comfort the people; the people themselves, who in Mrs. Bentley's eyes cannot appreciate anything or anyone beyond their own restricted world. Yet this directly conflicts with the view of them she gives us at the end of the book, so obviously "in Mrs. Bentley's eyes" is the operative phrase here. By extension, we suspect all of her affirmations, finding in them partial truths that ring ironically against the complex realities Ross ultimately allows us to glimpse.

So it is with the dust and rain, which reveal the complexity that several separate points of view create. The image becomes one not of affirming polarities of good and bad, but of exploring what is real in the world. Mrs. Bentley's view is thus not the only one we are conscious of, for the technique of the book, Ross's words in Mrs. Bentley's diary, establishes a linguistic tension that allows us to view the narrator with distance, objectivity, dispassion: and so perceive the irony and ambivalence — the "jests of God", in a sense, if we can anticipate Margaret Laurence — which characterize reality in Ross's world.

Although from the very beginning, that is, we come up against Mrs. Bentley's explanation of things, the false fronts and social attitudes of Horizon, the first detail of weather we see is not one of dryness but one of a "soft steady swish of rain on the roof, and a gurgle of eave troughs running over". April rains are usually a symbol of hope, of nurture for new growth, of Christian sacrifice and forgiveness, but here in this "disordered house", they (ostensibly for the first time) leak through the roof and stain the walls. Obviously the rain in reality does not serve to refresh, just as the "Christianity" hypocritically uttered by Philip or by Mrs. Bentley's townspeople is powerless to affect the environments through which they move.

We see this most clearly in the Partridge Hill episodes. In this little country town, beyond Horizon, the people are experiencing their fifth straight year without a harvest, yet they continue to place faith in the ministerings of the Church. Sardonically, in June, Mrs. Bentley writes, "This was the day out at Partridge Hill we prayed for rain." The Church ceremony is thus reduced to pagan ritual, and she and Paul Kirby, the equally sardonic schoolteacher, "tie" in their reaction: "Surely it must be a very great faith that such indifference on the part of its deity cannot weaken — a very great faith, or a very foolish one." It is just this ambivalence, explicitly enunciated here, expressing at once the impossibility of taking sides and the human inclination to do so, which the book communicates throughout.

Paul's continuing habit of uttering etymological facts, which seems almost gratuitous in the novel at times, is not thematically unrelated. He has already

185

told us, for example, "*pagan*, you know, originally that's what it meant, *country dweller*", and in June in Partridge Hill this echoes through the scenes we see. Paul's problem is that he cannot live outside his world of arid facts. Whereas he thinks he knows what's around him and withholds himself from it, others are encountering, experiencing whatever is there. The problems that others (like the farmers) do have, however, emerge not just physically from the encounter (the drought, the land), but from a state of mind in relation to the experience that is not unlike Mrs. Bentley's or Paul's own. Mrs. Bentley later wonders if she is "the one who's never grown up, who can't see life for illusions"; the farmers for their part live in one sense in a dream world that does not recognize the present, for it acknowledges only two times, the good harvest and the possibility for one, "the year it rained all June, and next year".

April rains, for the Bentleys, then, had been destructive; June rains do not exist. The persistent faith in rain seems ironic, therefore, and with this in mind we move back to Mrs. Bentley herself. She likes water, wants it, apparently needs to go walking in the rain, for example, and so heads out in it whenever possible. Even snow will do, though then reality gives way "to the white lineless blend of sky and earth". "Horizon" seems itself to be reality, therefore, just as the present is reality, and like the farmers with their belief in June rains, she comes headlong into conflict with it. Once in a recital she played Debussy's *Garden in the Rain*; now she tries to build one, but water is scarce and all that blooms is a single poppy — while she is away.

Similarly, her view of her husband is founded in this dream of fruition. That he is an artist is what *she* says, but whether or not he indeed has talent, he lacks the milieu that might foster greatness. She sees his artistry, moreover, in terms of her own image, just as he (with his "sons", Steve and young Philip, as well as with his God) creates in his:

> It's always been my way to comfort myself thinking that water finds its own level, that if there's anything great or good in a man it will eventually find its way out. But I've never taken hold of the thought and analyzed it before, never seen how false it really is. Water gets dammed sometimes; and sometimes, seeking its level, it seeps away in dry, barren earth. Just as he's seeping away among the false fronts of these little towns.

When Philip is ill, too, it is she who says he has nausea — causing Paul to flinch, because his etymological sensibility is outraged. *Nausea* "is from a Greek word meaning *ship* and is, therefore, etymologically speaking, an impossibility on dry land".

186

That Philip needs a change of environment is true, but again it is Mrs. Bentley who voices the desire, even acts it out when she walks recurrently down the railway track as far as the ravine. When Philip goes with her, she locates her wish in his eyes, and finds the possibility of escape — the possibility of a fruitful, ordered future — in the train to an outside world.

> At last we heard a distant whistle-blade, then a single point of sound, like one drop of water in a whole sky. It dilated, spread. The sky and silence began imperceptibly to fill with it. We steeled ourselves a little, feeling the pounding onrush in the trestle of the bridge. It quickened, gathered, shook the earth, then swept in an iron roar above us, thundering and dark.

Paradoxically the train comes from, passes through, and heads for "Horizons", which are realities, not dreams, and must be faced. The "water sickness" is in a sense Mrs. Bentley's, not Philip's; therefore, a function of her perhaps unconscious dream and a further indication of her imposition of her own point of view onto the world around her.

WHAT ROSS DOES to communicate these ironies and ambiguities is to blur the edges of his images. Absolutes do not exist. For all that the recurrent water images seem to accompany an inability to come to terms with reality, that is, the water is not itself "bad" — it only becomes so when in a person's viewpoint the dream it represents stands in the way of altering the present. When the dream and the reality come into conflict, the water takes on the characteristics of the desert, the arid land. At the ravine, thinking of Judith, Mrs. Bentley writes:

> Philip and I sat in the snowstorm watching the water rush through the stones — so swift that sometimes as we watched, it seemed still, solid like glass.

Later, knowing of the affair between Judith and Philip, she notes:

> The rain's so sharp and strong it crackles on the windows just like sand.

The similes work in the opposite direction as well. At Partridge Hill, "There was a bright fall of sunshine that made the dingy landscape radiant. Right to the horizon it winked with little lakes of spring-thaw water." But we also hear of "dust clouds lapping at the sky", of "dense, rigid heat" and "planks of sunlight". We're told that the August heat "was heavy and suffocating. We seemed imbedded in it, like insects in a fluid that has congealed." This last image recurs again when Philip seduces Judith, and Mrs. Bentley wakes, listens, and knows:

"like a live fly struggling in a block of ice". For her, during the winter that follows, "The sun seems cold." These are not all working to say exactly the same thing. There are times, apparently, when the dream serves a useful function in the mind of a people, but again, when the reality — "Horizon" — is obscured, the dream is frozen, becomes as hard and apparently sterile as the dust and sand.

The ambivalence we are left with at the end of the book is not absolutely resolved by these observations, but they bring us closer to understanding it. In presenting and exploring a single point of view, *As For Me and My House* runs the danger of seeming shallow, of allowing no aesthetic distance from which we can respond *to* the narrator as well as participate in her verbal reactions to the world. Fortunately Ross's technique, his control over the words he allows Mrs. Bentley to use, creates the ironic tension which raises the book from a piece of "regional realism" to a complex study of human responses. Mrs. Bentley herself is all too prone to approve or condemn, but Ross would have his readers avoid this. By his images and through the other characters, he shows us, in fact, how Mrs. Bentley's polarization of Horizon (this world, arid, sterile, bad) and the Bookstore (dream, water, fruitful, good) is invalid and gradually breaks down. That she and Philip ultimately do leave to try to set up the bookstore is perhaps cause, therefore, for us to see her as a failure, continuing as the manipulator she has been before.

But then we still have her compliment about Horizon's townspeople to contend with, and her acknowledgment in the same breath of both the dust and the rain stains. Here she seems to be aware of reality at last; if so, her future might hold at least some success. But reality to Ross is still not clear cut, and that the book should end so ambivalently seems ultimately part of his plan. The ambivalence is founded in his imagery, founded in the lives of the characters and the nature of their world, germane to the whole novel, magnificently distilling what it has tried to say. When we become conscious of this, we become not only involved in the book, but like the people of Horizon, no matter how apparently sure of themselves, still sensitive to doubt and so to reality as well.

(1969)

NOTES

[1] See Roy Daniells, "Introduction" to *As For Me and My House*, 1957, v-x. Cf. Warren Tallman, "Wolf in the Snow," in George Woodcock, ed., *A Choice of Critics* (Toronto: Oxford, 1966), pp. 53-76.
[2] See Donald Stephens, "Wind, Sun and Dust," *Canadian Literature*, No. 23 (Winter 1965), 17-24.

NO OTHER WAY

Sinclair Ross's
Stories and Novels

Sandra Djwa

> This is a fundamentalist town. To the letter it believes the Old
> Testament stories that we, wisely or presumptuously, choose to
> accept only as tales and allegories.

As a NEWFOUNDLANDER, I have always felt a great fond-
ness for the writings of Sinclair Ross. I do not quite understand the nature of the
attraction, whether it is his concept of a prairie nature — hard, with overtones
of fatalism — which corresponds to my own view of Newfoundland, or whether
it is simply his wry observations of the circumlocutions of the Puritan way — a
sensibility which also strikes a familiar note. In any event, whenever the term
"Canadian novel" comes to mind, I find myself gravitating towards Ross and
particularly towards his sometimes puzzling first novel, *As For Me and My House.*

Reading through *Queen's Quarterly* of the late 30's and early 40's, it is not
too difficult to recognize branches of the novel. Here are the familiar characters
and concerns of Ross's world: the Steves, the Philips, the Pauls, the young boy
with the horse ("A Day with Pegasus", 1938); the chance intrusion of the artist
into the prairie town ("Cornet at Night", 1939); the paralyzing lack of communi-
cation between husband and wife ("The Lamp at Noon", 1938, "The Painted
Door", 1939); or, for that matter, between friends ("Jug and Bottle", 1939)
which leads inevitably to further betrayal; the "unappetizing righteousness" and
pansy-embroidered motto, "As For Me and My House We Will Serve the Lord"
of "Cornet at Night".[1] Here, too, in the short story, as in "No Other Way", first
published in *Nash's* magazine (London, 1938), is the unmistakable silhouette of
Mrs. Bentley. Older, more haggard than the protagonist of *As For Me and My
House*, Hatty Glenn is equally dependent on the love of her still-elusive husband
of over twenty years.

Reviewing the short stories and novels, I seem to find that character recedes into the emotional landscape; the primary impression is of those short paragraphs which establish the natural landscape and its relation to a perceiving consciousness. Throughout Ross's work, there is a sense of a bleak, hard nature — the loneliness and isolation of the prairie winter, the indifferent sun which scorches the summer wheat. Against this nature, man is insignificant:

> In the clear bitter light the long white miles of prairie landscape seemed a region strangely alien to life. Even the distant farmsteads she could see served only to intensify a sense of isolation. Scattered across the face of so vast and bleak a wilderness it was difficult to conceive them as a testimony of human hardihood and endurance. Rather they seemed futile, lost, to cower before the implacibility of snowswept earth and clear pale sun-chilled sky. (*Lamp at Noon*)

Mrs. Bentley, looking across the open prairies and towards the Alberta foothills, recognizes both man's insignificance and his need to project human meaning into the natural landscape:

> We've all lived in a little town too long. The wilderness here makes us uneasy. I felt it the first night I walked alone on the river bank — a queer sense of something cold and fearful, something inanimate, yet aware of us. A Main Street is such a self-sufficient little pocket of existence, so smug, compact, that here we feel abashed somehow before the hills, their passiveness, the unheeding way they sleep. We climb them, but they withstand us, remain as serene and unrevealed as ever. The river slips past us, unperturbed by our coming and going, stealthily confident. We shrink from our insignificance. The stillness and solitude — we think a force or presence into it — even a hostile presence, deliberate, aligned against us — for we dare not admit an indifferent wilderness, where we may have no meaning at all. (*As For Me and My House*)

This is a nature against which man must struggle — not just to become a man — but simply to exist and perhaps, if he is particularly fortunate and determined, to exist in some meaningful way. Most of these stories are a legacy of the drought years of the thirties on the prairies — the depression moving imperceptibly into the war years. Even in Ross's second novel, *The Wall*, where the protagonist, Chris Howe, is given an urban childhood, the primary emphasis is still placed on the essentials of survival: "to outwit, score, defeat, survive — Boyle Street had permitted nothing else." However, as is later suggested in this novel and throughout the first novel, existence of some meaningful way becomes the ultimate goal. For Philip Bentley this search for meaning involves the attempt to find dignity and purpose in nature and in himself through his art:

Tonight Philip made a sketch of Joe Lawson. . . . He's sitting at a table, half-hunched over it, his hands lying heavy and inert in front of him like stones. The hands are mostly what you notice. Such big, disillusioned, steadfast hands, so faithful to the earth and seasons that betray them. I didn't know before what drought was really like, watching a crop dry up, going on again. I didn't know that Philip knew either.

In many of the short stories and also in some of the entries in Mrs. Bentley's journal, human action is presented as the reaction to natural events. The young farm boy of "One's a Heifer" is sent out into the open prairie because a blizzard has caused the cattle to stray; Ellen, the young wife of "The Lamp at Noon", is driven to madness by the incessant wind and dust beating against the walls of the house and stable, "as if the fingers of a giant hand were tightening to collapse them". This reaction to the natural event can precipitate a quarrel, most often between husband and wife, sometimes with a young boy as the interested bystander, and the development of the plot quite often lies in the working out of the emotional tension that has been generated by the conflict.

Because this conflict is intimately connected with the struggle for survival, the tragedy of these stories is that there is often no possible reconciliation of any kind. When an author's horizon is composed of "the bare essentials of a landcape, sky and earth", there are no compromises open: if land and weather fail man, the struggle for survival can only end tragically, the extent of the tragedy being largely determined by the strength of the person concerned. Will, the young farmer of "Not by Rain Alone", has a moment of bleak recognition when he suddenly sees the future which must surely lie ahead of himself and his sweetheart, Eleanor:

He was thinking of other dry spells — other wheat that had promised thirty bushels and yielded ten. It was such niggard land. At the best they would grub along painfully, grow tired and bitter, indifferent to each other. It was the way of the land. For a farmer like him there could be no other way. *(Lamp at Noon)*

As in the poetry of Pratt, this struggle against nature becomes a test of endurance in which only the very strong such as Paul of "The Lamp at Noon" survive, but with such heart-breaking self awareness as to make it almost unendurable, while those who are weaker, such as his wife Ellen, are destroyed. As Laurence notes, Ross's men seem to know by instinct and by habit that strength, if not actual, at least apparent, is demanded, and each of them refuses to communicate to his wife those admissions of failure and of helplessness which would undermine the appearance of strength until the final, irreversible betrayal. John, the good but stolid farmer of "The Painted Door", is simply unable to communicate; his wife's tragedy is that she can see but not accept the fact until it is too late. Paul of "The Lamp at Noon" cannot accept his wife's anguish; even after the final devastating betrayal when he realizes that compromise with the land is no longer possible, when his crops are completely destroyed and he is stripped of "vision and purpose, faith in the land, in the future, in himself", he is still attempting to find a way to withstand his wife and to go on: "For so deep were his instincts of loyalty to the land that still, even with the images of his betrayal stark upon his mind, his concern was now to withstand her, how to go on again and justify himself." For a farmer such as Paul or Will or the John of "A Field of Wheat", there is "no other way" than to go on, and this continued struggle against tremendous odds becomes a revelation of the real self, as is suggested in Ross's description of the stripping down of Paul's character to "a harsh and clenched virility ... at the cost of more engaging qualities ... a fulfillment of his inmost and essential nature".

For other characters of Ross's fictional world, the stripping down which leads to self discovery is equally important. Often made in terms of a sudden discovery of one's essential nature, it delimits the path that this nature must follow. For the country boy of "Cornet at Night", a chance meeting with a musician, Philip, makes him aware of his vocation as an artist: "This way of the brief lost gleam against the night was my way too. And alone I cowered a moment, understanding that there could be no escape, no other way." (*Queen's Quarterly*, Winter 1939-40) For the Bentleys, the gradual stripping away of the "false fronts" of dishonest life leads to the realization that they must get away from the kind of world that the small town of Horizon imposes, to a community where essential self can be safely revealed: "I asked him didn't he want to get out of the Church, didn't he admit that saving a thousand dollars was the only way."

Ross's earliest references to the "way" which character and environment impose are found in his first published story, "No Other Way". Hatty Glenn, the female protagonist of this story, is a simpler character than Mrs. Bentley, as she is most strongly motivated by the habit of parsimony. After a lifetime of "grubbing" while her husband "schemed", she is weather-beaten while he is still comparatively attractive; to make matters worse, he now ignores her. In a moment of insight, she recognizes that nothing in the world can better her relationship with her husband, and that for her there is "no other way" than to continue along in the same tragi-comic fashion:

> She glanced over her shoulder and saw the half-chewed turnips being slobbered into the dirt. December — January — a pail a day.

And then in a flash she was clutching a broom and swooping into the garden. "Get out, you greedy old devils! After them, Tubbie!"

Butter twenty five cents a pound. There was no other way. (*Nash's*, Oct. 1934)

In Ross's more sober stories, character and environment can combine like a vise to grip a character and set up a course of direction that even repeated failure does not change. His characters appear to be driven, like those of Grove in *Settlers of the Marsh*, to act as they do until one or another of a partnership is destroyed. When Paul is finally willing to make some compromises with the land, he finds his wife mad and his child dead. Having betrayed her husband, Ann of "The Painted Door" has a revelation of his intrinsic strength and determines to make it up to him. He, however, has already walked out into the blizzard where he freezes to death. Coulter, the inept recruit who has been repeatedly befriended by the soldier narrator of "Jug and Bottle", is accidently let down by his friend. Crushed by an overwhelming burden of guilt and despair, and with no one to turn to, Coulter kills himself: ". . . caught helpless in some primitive mechanism of conscience like a sheaf in the gear of a thresher, borne on inexorably by the chain of guilt to the blade of punishment". (*Queen's Quarterly*, Winter 1949-50) Many such scenes of human despair and futility suggest that the President of the Immortals also has his sport with the people of Ross's prairie. Mrs. Bentley comments on this when observing the work-torn country congregation which is still waiting and praying after five years without a crop: "And tonight again the sun went down through a clear, brassy sky. Surely it must be a very great faith that such indifference on the part of its deity cannot weaken — a very great faith, or a very foolish one."

O~N THE WHOLE~, despite the suggestion of naturalism, particularly in the metaphor used to describe Coulter, Ross is not a naturalist in the sense of Norris's *The Octopus* or even in the modified sense of Stead's *Grain*. There is a strong streak of determinism running through Ross's work, but it is most often kept firmly within a Christian context through a respectful address to "Providence", albeit with some irony as suggested by the title, "Not by Rain Alone", of one short story where the crops fail. Philip of *As For Me and My House* ". . . keeps on believing that there's a will stronger than his own deliberately pitted against him . . . a supreme being interested in him, opposed to him, arranging with tireless concern the details of his life. . . ." The good man of "The Runaway" finds himself troubled by God's justice, especially when the scales are eventually weighed in his favour: "What kind of reckoning was it that exacted life and innocence for an old man's petty greed? Why, if it was retribution, had it struck so clumsily?" (*Lamp at Noon*)

The whole question of the ways of the Old Testament God to man is an important one for the characters of Ross's fictional world and particularly in relation to the first novel, *As For Me and My House*. Here this question carries with it that latter-day Puritanism of the psychological search for self, often expressed in terms of the "way" that must be taken. As in Rudy Wiebe's novel of the prairies, *Peace Shall Destroy Many*, Harold Horwood's description of Newfoundland, *Tomorrow Will Be Sunday*, or Margaret Laurence's *A Jest of God*, the novel presents a world in which the outward representations of Christianity are without real meaning — simply empty forms without spirit — and in which characters must learn to reject the false gods without before it is possible to find the true God within and, as a sign of this, an authentic sense of direction.

Ostensibly, the "way" of *As For Me and My House* is the Christian way indicated by the title. But this structure is steadily undercut through the central metaphor of the "false front" and through explicit statement until we come to see the Bentleys metaphorically as pagan priest and priestess ministering to an Old Testament World. It is not until the novel has moved full cycle through sin, sacrifice, and repentance, that there is a pulling down of the old false gods and a revelation of the true self. In this sense the novel is, as is suggested by Roy Daniells in his fine introduction to the New Canadian Library edition, the struggle of the Puritan soul to find the way. At the beginning of the novel, Mr. and Mrs. Bentley, the new clergyman and his wife, are hanging out their shingle, "As For Me and My House . . ."; at the end of the book they are taking it in. In between, the process of the novel has involved a shedding of their defenses, a breaking down of the hypocritical "false fronts" behind which they have hidden both from each other and from the townspeople.

The metaphor of the "false front" is probed in basically psychological terms. Philip Bentley, aware that his new role as minister is hypocritical, is tortured by his own dishonesty. Unable to draw or paint constructively, he is reduced to turning out drawing after drawing of self-analysis: Main Streets with their false-fronted stores, all "stricken with a look of self-awareness and futility". In the journal entries which make up the novel, his wife admits that there is something in Philip's art which "hurts", but as she finds it easier to live in Horizon she refuses to sympathize: "False fronts ought to be laughed at, never understood or pitied. They're such outlandish things, the front of a store built up to look like a second storey." Yet when she erects her own false front against Main Street, she discovers that she is just as vulnerable as Philip:

> Three little false-fronted towns before this one have taught me to erect a false front of my own, live my own life, keep myself intact; yet tonight again, for all my indifference to what the people here may choose to think of me, it was an ordeal to walk out of the vestry and take my place at the organ.

The Bentleys also erect facades to hide from each other. He has attempted to mould himself into the ordered life which she considers practical and in so doing, is alienated from her, while she takes up the role of the hard-working woman of the manse, inwardly chafing but outwardly content with her husband's meagre tokens of affection. Without any hope for the future other than a parade of Horizons, each like the one before, Philip turns on his wife as the major instrument of his imprisonment, punishing her through the withdrawal of his love. The novel is orchestrated by Philip's emotional withdrawals, "white, tight-lipped", and the closing of his study door which shuts out his wife while she, in turn, escapes into the night, the granaries, and the railroad tracks.

There is a strong emphasis on the build-up of emotional tension throughout the novel. In comparison with the suffocating atmosphere of the house with its ever-present aura of sexual tension, even the bleakness of the prairie landscape offers a kind of freedom. We are told again and again that one or the other attempts to escape the claims of intimacy by pretending to be asleep when the other finally comes to bed. This situation continues until finally they make up and the process begins again. It is this heightening and release of emotional tension which would seem to characterize the novel's form: the first half develops through a cycle of wind and drought chronicling Steve's coming and going, and the eventual rains where the Bentleys are reunited; the second part of the novel works through the darkness and despair of winter, ending with the death of Judith and the birth of her child in April.

In the first chapter, we are introduced to the Bentley's ostenible Puritan ethos: the shingle, the statement of Philip's creed, and the bargain by which the Bentleys co-exist with the townspeople: "In return for their thousand dollars a year they expect a genteel kind of piety, a well-bred Christianity that will serve as an example to the little sons and daughters of the town." But we soon discover that this "well-bred Christianity" is form without spirit, the false front of a behaviour without belief; it is a modern form of paganism in which the forms or conventions of faith are perverted into a substitution for faith itself. This is explicit in the extended metaphor at the conclusion of the first chapter where the clergyman and his wife are ironically identified as the "priest and priestess" through whom the people make offerings to the small town gods of Propriety and Parity:

> ...the formal dinner of a Main Street hostess is invariably good. Good to an almost sacrificial degree. A kind of rite, at which we preside as priest and priestess — an offering, not for us, but through us, to the exacting small-town gods Propriety and Parity.

In this metaphor, they are revealed as handmaidens to the Puritan false gods of behaviourism — the mechanical acts of behaviour which remain after the true religious spirit has gone out of action. "Propriety", the well-bred Christianity which Mrs. Bentley cites, is the outer form of circumspect behaviour which replaces spontaneous action grounded in love; "Parity", social prestige, is that form of behaviour which results in the establishment of a village elect (notably the trinity of Mrs. Finley, Mrs. Bird, and Mrs. Bentley) and the exclusion of the damned (such as Judith and Steve) on grounds of social elitism rather than in terms of the true Christian love which results in brotherhood and justice. In this schemata, everything is turned upside-down; consequently, when justifying the adoption of the Roman Catholic orphan, Steve, to the Protestant church elders, Mrs. Bentley can see herself as the devil's advocate:

> So I parried them, cool and patient, piety to my finger tips. It was the devil quoting scripture, maybe, but it worked. They couldn't answer.... He [Philip] looked on, flinching for me, but I didn't mind. I'm not so thin-skinned as he is anyway. I resigned myself to sanctimony years ago. Today I was only putting our false front up again, enlarged this time for three.
> Philip, Steve, and I. It's such a trim, efficient little sign; it's such a tough, deep-rooted tangle that it hides.
> And none of them knows. They spy and carp and preen themselves, but none of them knows. They can only read our shingle, all its letters freshened up this afternoon, *As For Me and My House — The House of Bentley — We Will Serve the Lord.*

In this context, the supposedly Christian structure of the novel is ironically reversed. In Joshua, the source of the original quotation, a choice has been made by the Israelites. They have rejected the pagan gods of the Ammonites and chosen the true God, Jehovah. In the first chapters of Ross's novel, it would appear that the Bentleys have chosen the pagan gods, but the development of the novel leads to some new possibility characterized by a new honesty, a child, and "a stillness, a freshness, a vacancy of beginning", suggesting a movement from the Old Testament to the New. In the larger metaphoric framework of the book, this development is characterized by the storm that sweeps through the town of Horizon, demolishing most of the false-fronted little stores on Main Street.

Philip's first sermon in a new town is always "As For Me and My House We Will Serve the Lord." Mrs. Bentley explains that it contains Philip's "creed": "The Word of God as revealed in Holy Writ — Christ Crucified — salvation through His Grace — those are the things Philip stands for." However, soon it becomes clear that Philip does not believe the Christianity he preaches. As a young man, he was sure that "he was meant to paint", and had used the Church as a stepping stone to an education. Had he succeeded, he might have lived with his conscience, but a wife, the depression, and a rapidly-mounting sense of guilt and despair anchor him firmly to the false fronts of Main Street: "having failed he's not a strong or great man, just a guilty one":

> He made a compromise once, with himself, his conscience, his ideals; and now he believes that by some retributive justice he is paying for it. A kind of Nemesis. He pays in Main Streets — this one, the last one, the Main Streets still to come.

As this reference to retributive justice would indicate, Philip's strongest instincts are towards a kind of pagan Nemesis or fatalism. Mrs. Bentley, observing the country people of Philip's charge, senses this same primitive reponse in the "sober work-roughened congregation":

> There was strength in their voices when they sang, like the strength and darkness of the soil. The last hymn was staidly orthodox, but through it there seemed to mount something primitive, something that was less a response to Philip's sermon and scripture reading than to the grim futility of their own lives. Five years in succession now they've been blown out, dried out, hailed out; and it was as if in the face of so blind and uncaring a universe they were trying to assert themselves, to insist upon their own meaning and importance.
> "Which is the source of all religion," Paul discussed it with me afterwards. "Man can't bear to admit his insignificance. If you've ever seen a hailstorm, or watched a crop dry up — his helplessness, the way he's ignored — well, it was just such helplessness in the beginning that set him discovering gods who could control the storms and seasons. Powerful, friendly gods — on his side. . . . So he felt better — gratefully became a reverent and religious creature. That was what you heard this morning — pagans singing Christian hymns . . . *pagan*, you know, originally that's exactly what it meant, *country dweller*."

The primary Old Testament distinction between Israelites and pagans is the monotheism of the chosen people. God's covenant given to Moses states that the

Ammonites and other pagans will be driven from the Promised Land, but that the Israelites must guard themselves carefully from the "images" of the pagans: "for thou shalt have no other gods before me". This association of image or idol-worship with paganism is also suggested in Ross's novel. There are early references to Mrs. Finley, the "small-town Philistine" who would like to mould the town "in her own image". If Philip had a child, Mrs. Bentley tells us, he would mould it "in his own image". Philip is also the product of his own twisted image of his dead father. From a photograph, a trunkful of old books, and the discovery that his father wanted to paint, he has developed himself by emulation: "They say let a man look long and devotedly enough at a statue and in time he will resemble it." Similarly, Philip's concept of the Church is an unhappy child's picture modelled on the image of the Main Street Church: "Right or wrong he made it the measure for all churches." And, as he has moulded his own character on that of his father, so he attempts to mould Steve: "For there's a strange arrogance in his devotion to Steve, an unconscious determination to mould him in his own image...." When Steve is removed from the household, Mrs. Bentley's primary regret is that Philip has never seen through to the real boy, "fond of bed, his stomach, and his own way":

> An idol turned clay can make even an earthly woman desirable ... he's one idol tarnish-proof. Philip will forget the real Steve before long, and behind his cold locked lips mourn another of his own creating. I know him. I know as a creator what he's capable of.

THIS WHOLE COMPLEX of Old Testament idol, image, and paganism, suggests a framework of ironic illusion supported by the names of the characters.[2] In each case there is ironic reversal, Eliot-fashion, in which the novel character can be seen to be acting in a manner similar to, yet opposite from, that of his Biblical counterpart. Philip, deacon and evangelist, did preach "salvation through His Grace" and did convert from idolatry; the apostle Philip is rebuked by Christ because of his request for material proof of the existence of God: "Lord, show us the Father and it sufficeth us." In Ross's novel, Philip the preacher substitutes the image of an earthly father (the photograph) for a heavenly one and, as he has modelled himself upon that image, succumbs to the new paganism, the idolatry of Self.

198

There are also suggestions throughout the text that Mrs. Bentley has been raising up her own images, in particular that of Philip, the sensitive and impressionable artist who must be mothered along in the direction which she best sees fit. She does not come to see how wrong she has been in her wilful attempt to structure her husband's life until after her encounter with the prairie wilderness and Philip's raging attempts to catch the strength of the land on canvas: "Water gets dammed sometimes . . . it seeps away in dry, barren earth. Just as he's seeping away among the false fronts of these little towns." She also realizes that she has attempted to mould her husband's life largely because she has a false image of his real nature: "I've taken a youth and put him on a pedestal and kept him there." With the recognition that the Philip she has known for twelve years is little more than the false front of their single and joint romantic projections, comes the more difficult and sometimes whistling-in-the-dark formulation that Philip's periodic thrashings-out against the hypocrisy of his own life are not as contemptible as she has previously, and somewhat smugly, assumed:

> And if it's finer and stronger to struggle with life than just timidly to submit to it, so, too, when you really come to see and understand them, must the consequences of that struggle be worthier of a man than smug little virtues that have never known trial or soiling. That is right. I know. I must remember.

Mrs. Bentley must remember because her whole life is posited on her husband; although he is her creation, he is also her god and ground of being: "I haven't any roots of my own anymore. I'm a fungus or parasite whose life depends on his." Like Hatty Glenn, for her there is no other way than to keep going on: "Somehow I must believe in them, both of them. Because I need him still. This isn't the end. I have to go on, try to win him again. . . . It's like a finger pointing." But unlike the earlier struggle which borders on the trivial, Mrs. Bentley's struggle is often admirable because there is a strong sense of discipline and the larger good in her sense of direction. There is no doubt that her motives are often self-interested, but it is a self-interest which acknowledges its own presence and which makes some attempt to modify itself.

In the first cycle of the novel, she is threatened by Philip's affection for Steve and in the second by his affection for Judith. As a result, she begins to admit the self-destructive nature of their marriage and to probe her own motives: "For these last twelve years I've kept him in the Church — no one else. The least I can do now is help get him out again." In this conclusion there is some positive choice and her feeling that "there's still no way but going on, pretending not to know" modulates into the discovery that there is one way out of Horizon: "saving a thousand dollars was the only way". Mrs. Bentley's "only way", the bookstore in the city, in contrast to the "no other way" of many of Ross's characters, suggests an intelligence capable of choice. Realizing that the foundations of her own morality have also been modelled on the untried virtue of a smug Main Street, Mrs. Bentley gropes, with lapses, toward some other way.

As in the short stories, nature has a relation to human action; Mrs. Bentley is often impelled towards the way she must follow by the force of the wind. At the beginning of the novel, the wind establishes the emotional landscape of Horizon:

> It's an immense night out there, wheeling and windy. The lights on the street and in the houses are helpless against the black wetness, little unilluminating glints that might be painted on it. The town seems huddled together, cowering on a high, tiny perch, afraid to move lest it topple into the wind. Close to the parsonage is the church, black even against the darkness, towering ominously up through the night and merging with it. There's a soft steady swish of rain on the roof, and a gurgle of eave troughs running over. Above, in the high cold night, the wind goes swinging past, indifferent, liplessly mournful. It frightens me, makes me feel lost, dropped on this litle perch of town and abandoned. I wish Philip would waken.

The wind makes Mrs. Bentley aware that she has been lost and abandoned, dropped, as it were, on this point of Horizon, the place where land and sky meet. In a real sense, Horizon is as much a psychological state as it is a town; it is the place where one is lodged when it is impossible to go either forward or backward, the stationary perspective. The Bentleys are caught in this self-destructive stasis, and it is in the first few chapters of the novel that Mrs. Bentley is forced to recognize her alienation from Philip: "I wish I could reach him, but it's like the wilderness outside of night and sky and prairie, with this one little spot of Horizon hung up lost in its immensity. He's as lost, and alone." But she too is lost on the same horizon: "There's a high, rocking wind ... and I have a queer, helpless sense of being lost miles out in the middle of it, flattened against a little peak of rock." Philip, listening to the wind, slips away from his wife and closes the study door between them: "Not that things between us tonight are much different from any other night ... [but] tonight, because of the wind, we both seem to know." In Philip's next painting of the false-fronted Main Street the wind sets itself against the town and Mrs. Bentley reads there her husband's state of mind: "The false fronts ... are buckled down in desperation for their lives. ... And yet you feel no sympathy ... you wait in impatience for the wind to work its will."

The power of the wind in the painting suggests the destructive force rising in Philip. In the first half of the novel, the Bentleys sat together in a little ravine and watched the railway go by, each knowing it was the way out which repeated Horizons had denied Philip; the second part of the novel would appear to begin at this same ravine where Philip takes stock of himself and determines to shape his own way, to "take things as they come — get what you can out of them". His decision, "if a man's a victim of circumstances he deserves to be," inevitably leads to Judith West. Now aware of Philip's infidelity, Mrs. Bentley despairs in a closed horizon:

> I stopped and looked up Main Street once, the little false fronts pale and blank and ghostly in the corner light, the night encircling it so dense and wet that the hard gray wheelpacked earth, beginning now to glisten with the rain, was like a single ply of solid matter laid across a chasm.

This suggestion of a closed world in which there is only one bridge of solid matter, the road which is also the way of Horizon itself and which ends in darkness, is repeated in Mrs. Bentley's next visit to the ravine. There, cloud and earth join together to form an impenetrable horizon, mirroring her emotional state.

But the novel has already moved to an anticipatory upswing. Mrs. Bentley watching the night train go out is for the first time, like Philip and Judith, and old Lawson of *The Well*, at one with the quickening train wheels: "It was like a setting forth, and with a queer kind of clutch at my throat, as if I were about to enter it, I felt the wilderness ahead of night and rain." At Christmas, she continues this journey to venture over the high prairie snow. From this real horizon, the small town of Horizon is seen in perspective. It is no longer her whole mental horizon, but simply "a rocky, treacherous island" in the snow. When she next visits the ravine with Paul, her perspective is completed. Near the end of the novel, when the wind nails her against the grain elevator, she is still feeling lost and abandoned but there can be no question that she will go on with Philip. Similarly, Philip visits Judith West to tell her that the Bentleys will adopt the coming child and then move to a bookstore in the city. Both decisions pave the way for the final confrontation between husband and wife when the great wind storm blows down most of the false fronts on Main Street.

This novel raises several disturbing critical issues including the death of Judith West, the character of Mrs. Bentley, and the validity of Philip's claim to be an artist.[3] I am inclined to believe that Mrs. Bentley is no more or less culpable than she might be expected to be under her circumstances. Through her own stubbornness and pride of possession, she contributes to her own betrayal, but there is sufficient evidence to indicate that she also suffers toward her own redemption. Judith West's death does seem painfully unnecessary, particularly when juxtaposed to Mrs. Bentley's cruel remarks:

> For me it's easier this way. It's what I've secretly been hoping for all along. I'm glad she's gone — glad — for her sake as well as mine. What was there ahead of her now anyway? If I lost Philip what would there be ahead for me?

Yet, on further consideration, it would appear that there was, in fact, no other way for Judith, either in terms of the deterministic nature of Ross's art or of the novel's mythic structure. Her sacrifice, like that of Steve and El Greco, can be seen as the last sacrifice required by the pagan gods of Main Street. And, as in the short stories involving a betrayal, her death is accomplished through the forces of nature — the soft, spring mud which exhausts her, precipitating the birth of her child.

There is a somewhat similar deterministic situation involved in the melodramatic death of the old farmer Lawson in *The Well*. Betrayed and shot by his young wife, he is stuffed down a well almost despite the efforts of the rather unattractive narrator, Chris Rowe, who appears to be swept along by the currents of destiny. What is most interesting about *As For Me and My House* in comparison with Ross's other work is that a more sophisticated third person is added to the central tragic situation — a Mrs. Bentley whose evolving consciousness is capable of compromise so that the total catastrophe of the stories and the near catastrophe of *The Well* is averted. Chris Rowe is also groping towards a sense of direction, but he is much cruder a character than either of the Bentleys. In fact, the novel itself has the kind of jagged relief which causes the reader to wonder — hopefully — if perhaps *The Well* is not the earlier of the two novels.[4]

Philip, the "non artist" as Warren Tallman calls him, "unable to discover a subject which will release him from his oppressive incapacity to create", does seem to find a subject from the moment he attempts to catch the elusive whiteness of Judith West's face. From this point onward his sketches move from the stasis of despairing Main Streets to the real horizon of galloping stallions, the country schoolhouse, the "strength and fatalism" of the prairie hills. But it is my impression that the real issue here is not whether or not Philip is a successful artist, but rather that he is motivated by some inner sense of direction which is other than the way of Main Street. Like Judith West, and to a lesser extent like Mrs. Bentley, Philip has a dream of an expanding horizon. And, as in the short stories, it is on the process of realizing this dream or of finding the way that Ross is focussing, rather than on the character Philip or on the artist Philip. In this sense, Philip is the abstracted principle and Mrs. Bentley the active process of the Puritan way; the two, as Roy Daniells notes, are part of a larger whole.

THE SIGNIFICANCE of Ross's achievement, and I fully agree with those critics who suggest that *As For Me and My House* is in the mainstream of the English Canadian novel, is that in nature, ethos and hero, Ross had captured all of these qualities which we attempt to invoke when we want to talk about Canadian writing. It is Ross's hard nature given tongue by Mrs. Bentley when she observes that the wilderness frightens us:

> We've all lived in a little town too long.... We shrink from our insignificance. The stillness and solitude — we think a force or presence into it ... for we dare not admit an indifferent wilderness, where we may have no meaning at all ...

which also recurs in Bruce Hutchison's book, *The Unknown Country*,[5] and which is given the status of a literary myth in Northrop Frye's rationale for the "garrison mentality" of Canadian writing.[6]

Yet, in significant difference from the nature which leads to the formulation of Frye's "garrison mentality" or, for that matter, from the mental "pallisade" of William Carlos Williams's *In The American Grain*,[7] Ross does not seem to be suggesting that there is no god in nature if for no other reason than that his people would not allow it. It may very well be the Old Testament vengeful God, the Nemesis of Philip's guilty conscience, or simply the psychological projection of the will to believe. Nonetheless, the people of Ross's prairie appear to keep on waiting and believing that beyond the individual tragedies of such as "Not by Rain Alone", such endurance does have value. And, certainly, in the larger structure of the first novel, there is a kind of grace bestowed: Mrs. Bentley is supported in her struggle to find the way by the Old Testament metaphor of the pointing finger: "It was like a finger pointing again, clear and peremptory, to keep on pretending ignorance just as before." Ross gives an explicit psychological basis for this metaphor; yet, as it springs from the inner recesses of self and is associated with her desire to find the "way", it is not without implications of a transcendent function. Then, too, Philip undergoes a kind of salvation through grace. He does find other-directed subjects for his art and he is given a child which he so desperately wants. Most importantly, it is a child with all of the New Testament implications of "a little child shall lead them."[8]

It would appear that the religious frame of reference, even if only in terms of residual response, is still a very important part of the Canadian novel. It was with considerable surprise that I realized recently that a surprisingly large number of our twentieth century novels refer to specifically moral, often explicitly religious concerns, as is suggested in the following titles: Grove's *Our Daily Bread, Fruits of the Earth*; much of Callaghan, including *Such is my Beloved, They Shall Inherit the Earth, More Joy in Heaven*, and *The Loved and the Lost*; Mitchell's *Who has Seen the Wind*; Klein's *The Second Scroll*; MacLennan's *Each Man's Son* and *The Watch that Ends the Night*; Buckler's *The Mountain and the Valley*; Wiseman's *The Sacrifice*; Watson's *The Double Hook*; Laurence's *A Jest of God*; Wiebe's *Peace Shall Destroy Many*; Horwood's *Tomorrow Will be Sunday* and Kreisel's *The Betrayal*.

Why might this be so? There does not appear to be a comparable movement in the American novel of the last twenty years, although a successful argument might be made for the preceding three decades.[9] There is the obvious fact of the unpopulated land itself: Canada, particularly the prairie, is still largely open space. In the midst of land and sky, as is explicitly suggested at the start of Mitchell's *Who Has Seen the Wind?*, it is difficult not to feel the cosmic setting. Then, too, the country is still basically regional; in the smaller communities religion still remains a strong force. Furthermore, our great wave of immigration was at the turn of the twentieth century rather than in the late eighteenth or nineteenth, as it was in the United States. This turn-of-the-century immigration, particularly of Scotch Presbyterians and European Jews, has greatly strengthened the Old Testament concerns of our literature.

Another possibility may be inferred from the fact that naturalism did not take hold in Canada as it did in the United States. R. E. Watters, in an address to the Third Congress of the International Comparative Literature Association (Utrecht, 1961), gives a convincing rationale for this fact.[10] He further notes that as Canada experienced no wars of emancipation and liberation, Canadian fictional characters do not usually see existing social conditions in Zolaesque terms, nor are they particularly concerned with leaving established communities for a place where they might be more free, as is suggested in the American myth of the journey west. Rather, as the historical fact of the United Empire Loyalists would suggest, and as Frye and Watters both note, the Canadian hero is concerned basically with maintaining his own integrity within a chosen community. I would add to this that the works of Ross would suggest that naturalism cannot flourish where there is even a remnant of divine providence. Religion, even if largely residual or seemingly converted to demonism as it is in *As For Me and My House,* invokes another set of values which, even if psychologically internalized, still supports the individual in his struggle:

> A trim, white, neat-gabled little schoolhouse, just like Partridge Hill. There's a stable at the back, and some buggies in the yard. It stands up lonely and defiant on a landscape like a desert.... The distorted, barren landscape makes you feel the meaning of its persistence there. As Paul put it last Sunday when we drove up, it's *Humanity in Microcosm.* Faith, ideals, reason — all the things that really are humanity — like Paul you feel them there, their stand against the implacable blunderings of Nature....
>
> And it was just a few rough pencil strokes, and he [Philip] had it buried among some notes he'd been making for next Sunday's sermon.

Unlike Huckleberry Finn, the characteristic American hero who determines "to light out for the territory" when civilization becomes too pressing,[11] the characteristic Canadian hero is the one who stays and endures — the farmers of Ross's prairie. If and when there is to be some way as there is for the Bentleys of Horizon, it must be an honourable way and one which is sanctioned by community.[12]

(1971)

NOTES

[1] Margaret Laurence has also noted this motto in her introduction to the New Canadian Library edition of Ross's short stories, *The Lamp at Noon and Other Stories.*

[2] Stephen, a devout Christian, was the first martyr; Paul (formerly Saul) witnessed the stoning of Stephen by the mob and was converted to Christianity; Judith, in the *Apocrypha,* gave her body to save her townspeople and was honoured by them. Mrs. Bentley, unnamed in the novel, would appear to have many of the characteristics of the Rachel of Genesis. She has no children, receives a son through a maidservant and finally does have a son of her own. This Rachel is also associated with the successful theft of her father's household "images" (gods) which she brings to her husband. Added to these references is the suggestion of the "bent twig" implicit in the name "Bentley".

[3] See Roy Daniells's "Introduction" to *As For Me and My House;* Cf. William H. New, "Sinclair Ross's Ambivalent World," *Canadian Literature,* No. 40 (Spring 1969), 26-27; Cf. Donald Stephens, "Wind, Sun and Dust," *Canadian Literature,* No. 23 (Winter 1965), 20-23; Cf. Warren Tallman, "Wolf in the Snow," *Canadian Literature,* No. 5 (Summer 1960), 15.

[4] In author's remarks appended to "No Other Way" in *Nash's* magazine, Ross is quoted as saying that he has written two novels: "failures, which publishers write me are interesting and compelling, but of small commercial possibilities. I am now starting to work on short stories, hoping gradually to build up a better technique. . . ."

[5] Bruce Hutchison, *The Unknown Country*, p. 3: "Who can know our loneliness, on the immensity of prairie, in the dark forest and on the windy sea rock? . . . We flee to little towns for a moment of fellowship and light and speech, we flee into cities or log cabins, out of the darkness and loneliness and the creeping silence."

[6] Northrop Frye, "Conclusions," *Literary History of Canada*, p. 830. "I have long been impressed in Canadian poetry by a tone of deep terror in regard to nature. . . . The human mind has nothing but human and moral values to cling to if it is to preserve its integrity or even its sanity, yet the vast unconsciousness of nature in front of it seems an unanswerable denial of those values."

[7] Cf. Warren Tallman, *Canadian Literature*, No. 6 (Autumn 1960), 43. "The continent itself — the grey wolf whose shadow is underneath the snow — has resisted the culture, the cultivation, the civilization which is indigenous to Europe but alien to North America even though it is dominant in North America." Tallman's thesis in this article would appear to rest on the premises of William Carlos Williams's *In the American Grain*.

[8] Ross, *As For Me and My House*. "In our lives it isn't the church itself that matters but what he feels about it, the shame and sense of guilt he suffers while remaining a part of it. That's why we're adopting Judith's baby. He'll dare not let his son see him as he sees himself: and he's no dissembler."

[9] Cf. Faulkner, Steinbeck, Warren.

[10] R. E. Watters, "A Quest for National Identity: Canadian Literature vis à vis the Literatures of Great Britain and the United States," *Proceedings of the Third Congress of International Comparative Literature Association* (The Hague: Mouton, 1962) pp. 224-241.

[11] *Ibid.*, p. 237.

[12] "Last Friday they had a farewell supper for us in the basement of the church, made speeches, sang *God Be With You Till We Meet Again,* presented us with a handsome silver flower basket. It's the way of a little Main Street town — sometimes a rather nice way."

NOTES ON CONTRIBUTORS

DONALD STEPHENS, a member of the English department at the University of British Columbia, has been an Associate Editor of *Canadian Literature* since 1960. He is the author of *Bliss Carman*, and of essays which have appeared in various Canadian journals. He is editor of *Contemporary Voices: The Short Story in Canada*.

F. W. WATT, a Professor of English at the University of Toronto and a former editor of "Letters in Canada" in the *University of Toronto Quarterly*, is the author of *Steinbeck* and of many critical articles on Canadian writers.

ROY DANIELLS is University Professor of English at the University of British Columbia. He is a poet with two published volumes, *Deeper into the Forest* and *The Chequered Shade*; his other books include *Milton, Mannerism and Baroque* and *Alexander Mackenzie and the North West*, and an edition of Thomas Traherne's *A Serious and Pathetical Contemplation*.

A. T. ELDER is a Professor of English at the University of Calgary and has published essays on Canadian prose writers in a number of journals.

CLARA THOMAS, Professor of English at York University, is author of a number of notable books in the field of Canadian literature, including *Love and Work Enough — The Life of Anna Jameson, Ryerson of Upper Canada*, and, most recently, *Our Nature — Our Voices: a Guidebook to English-Canadian Literature*.

W. B. HOLLIDAY, a member of the Dominion Entomological Service, writes from his personal knowledge of F. P. Grove in his later years.

FRANK BIRBALSINGH, who has contributed critical essays to *Canadian Literature*, *The Journal of Canadian Studies*, and other reviews, has taught English at York University and is now a visiting teacher at the University of Auckland.

STANLEY E. MC MULLIN, who teaches English at the University of Waterloo, wrote the introduction to the New Canadian Library edition of Grove's *A Search for America*.

HELENE ROSENTHAL, a Vancouver writer, has published two books of verse, *Peace is an Unknown Continent* and *A Shape of Fire*.

W. H. NEW is Associate Editor of *Canadian Literature* and Associate Professor of English at the University of British Columbia. He is the author of two books of criticism, *Malcolm Lowry* and *Articulating West*, and has contributed essays on Commonwealth and Canadian writers to many journals in Canada and abroad.

MORTON L. ROSS teaches English at the University of Alberta.

MARGUERITE A. PRIMEAU, a Professor of French at the University of British Columbia, is the author of a novel of Métis life on the prairies, *Le Muskeg*, and has contributed critical articles to *Canadian Literature* and other journals.

RUDY WIEBE'S novels include *Peace Shall Destroy Man, First and Vital Candle,* and *The Blue Mountains of China.* He is editor of *Stories of Western Canada* and teaches at the University of Alberta.

S. E. READ is Professor Emeritus of English at the University of British Columbia and author of *The Contemplative Man's Recreation*.

Among MARGARET LAURENCE'S many books of fiction are *A Bird in the House, The Fire Dwellers, A Jest of God, The Stone Angel, This Side Jordan* (her first published novel) and *The Tomorrow-Tamer*, a collection of short stories. The last two books emerged from her experience of West Africa, while a period in Somaliland produced her fine travel book, *The Prophet's Camel Bell*, and *A Tree for Poverty*, a collection of Somali poetry and prose.

GEORGE BOWERING is a prolific poet and critic. Apart from many articles on Canadian writers, he has published *Alfred Purdy* in the Studies of Canadian Literature series. His books of verse include *Gangs of Kosmos, Geneve, George Vancouver* and *Touch: Selected Poems.* He has published one novel, *Mirror on the Floor*, and teaches at Simon Fraser University.

SUSAN JACKEL'S article on Sinclair Ross was, when it appeared in *Canadian Literature*, her first published work.

SANDRA DJWA, who teaches English at Simon Fraser University, has published critical essays in many Canadian journals. Her book on E. J. Pratt will appear shortly.